The
END
of
BARBARY
TERROR

Also by Frederick C. Leiner

Millions for Defense: The Subscription Warships of 1798

The
END
of
BARBARY
TERROR

~⌣~

*America's 1815 War Against
the Pirates of North Africa*

FREDERICK C. LEINER

OXFORD
UNIVERSITY PRESS

2006

OXFORD

UNIVERSITY PRESS

Oxford University Press, Inc., publishes works that
further Oxford University's objective of excellence
in research, scholarship, and education.

Oxford   New York
Auckland   Cape Town   Dar es Salaam   Hong Kong   Karachi
Kuala Lumpur   Madrid   Melbourne   Mexico City   Nairobi
New Delhi   Shanghai   Taipei   Toronto

With offices in
Argentina   Austria   Brazil   Chile   Czech Republic   France   Greece
Guatemala   Hungary   Italy   Japan   Poland   Portugal   Singapore
South Korea   Switzerland   Thailand   Turkey   Ukraine   Vietnam

Copyright © 2006 by Frederick C. Leiner

Published by Oxford University Press, Inc.
198 Madison Avenue, New York, NY 10016
www.oup.com

Oxford is a registered trademark of Oxford University Press

Library of Congress Cataloging-in-Publication Data
Leiner, Frederick C., 1958–
The end of Barbary terror : America's 1815 war against the pirates of North Africa /
by Frederick C. Leiner.
p. cm.
Includes bibliographical references (p.   ) and index.
ISBN-13: 978-0-19-518994-0
ISBN-10: 0-19-518994-9
1. United States—History—War with Algeria, 1815.
2. Pirates—Africa, North—History—19th century. I. Title.
E365.L45 2006   973.4'7—dc22   2005026644

1 3 5 7 9 8 6 4 2

Printed in the United States of America
on acid-free paper

To my family

In such an enlightened, in such a liberal age, how is it possible the great maritime powers of Europe should submit to pay an annual tribute to the little piratical States of Barbary? Would to Heaven we had a navy able to reform those enemies to mankind, or crush them into non-existence.

—George Washington to the Marquis
de la Fayette, August 15, 1786

And never again will our Jonathan pay
A tribute to potentate, pirate or Dey
Nor any, but that which forever is given:
The tribute to valor and virtue and heaven.

And again if his Deyship should bully and fume,
Or hereafter his claim to this tribute resume,
We'll send him Decatur once more to defy him,
And his motto shall be, if you please, Carpe Diem.

—Dr. C——, "Carpe Diem"

Contents

CONTENTS

Chapter Seven

*The British Bombardment and
an "Occular Demonstration"* 151

Epilogue 177

The
END
of
BARBARY
TERROR

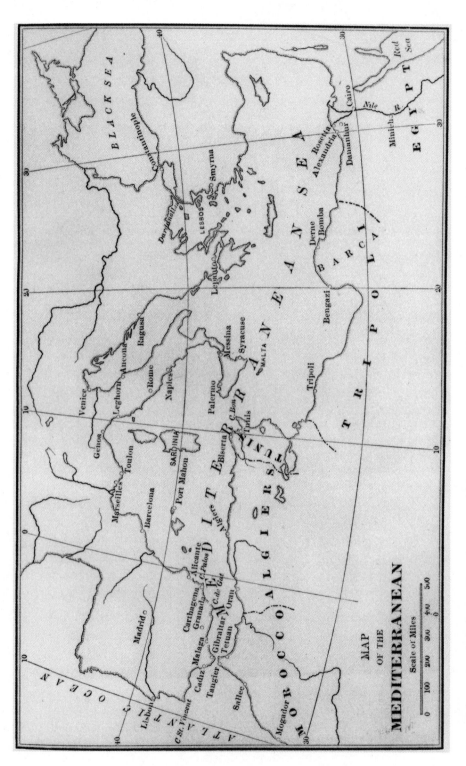

Map of the Mediterranean Sea. From Gardner W. Allen, *Our Navy and the Barbary Corsairs* (1905), author's collection.

Introduction

IN 1762, when the philosopher Jean-Jacques Rousseau famously began *The Social Contract* with the observation that man, who was born free, is everywhere in chains, the "chains" he referred to were the constraints imposed by living in a society with laws and government. His words might also have been taken literally, because almost everywhere in the eighteenth century, men were in chains. Slavery, or something akin to it, was a common feature of Rousseau's world and had existed from time immemorial. The Hebrew Bible, the Christian New Testament, and the Muslim Koran all accepted slavery, albeit with restrictions to ameliorate its hardships. By the time Rousseau was writing, the transatlantic trade in black Africans had been a fixture for more than two hundred years and ultimately would ship ten to twelve million people in chains to the Americas. But slavery was not limited to blacks nor to the New World. In Russia, millions of serfs lived a brutish existence tied to the land and at the sufferance of their manorial lords until Tsar Alexander II freed them in 1861. In the Levant and Istanbul, the burgeoning population needed bread, leading the Tartar rulers of the Crimea to raid the Ukraine, Russia, and Caucuses for hundreds of thousands of white Christians to work as slaves growing wheat in the steppe.

At the time Rousseau wrote, slavery had existed in Islamic North Africa, the so-called Barbary states, for centuries, and was a constant threat to Europe. From dozens of ports in Morocco, Algiers, Tunis, and Tripoli, Islamic corsairs darted out in their row galleys, and later, in their sailing

I

xebecs and feluccas, to seize European ships with their Christian crews and passengers (and cargoes). They boldly landed bands of armed pirates on the coasts of southern Europe and carted off peasant farmers and nobles, fishermen and goat herders, clerics and tradesmen, to slavery in Barbary. The corsairs sometimes seized the entire population of a village; coastal areas of Andalusia, Sicily, Calabria, Tuscany, and the Greek islands were depopulated by "manstealing" over the course of several hundred years.

Barbary slavery differed from slavery elsewhere both in the spirit in which the corsairs operated and the way Barbary societies used slaves. As historian Robert C. Davis notes in *Christian Slaves, Muslim Masters*, "in their traffic in Christians there was also always an element of revenge, almost of *jihad*—for the wrongs of 1492 [when Ferdinand and Isabella finally expelled the Moors from Spain], for the centuries of crusading violence that had preceded them, and for the ongoing religious struggle between Christian and Muslim. . . ." But the Barbary slave trade was driven as much by economics as by religious ideology. The corsairs needed oarsmen for their row galleys, and the captives were even more valuable when traded for ransom. Factoring in losses from the plague, malnourishment, mistreatment, and periodic ransomings, Professor Davis estimates that in the 250 years of peak slave-taking by the Barbary corsairs, from 1530 to 1780, at least one million, and perhaps as many as one and one-quarter million, white Christians were enslaved in Islamic North Africa. Even in the eighteenth century, as the number of slaves the Barbary pirates needed dwindled because sailing ships had replaced galleys, approximately 175,000 white Christians were carried off into slavery.

When the United States secured its independence in 1783, the new republic faced the slave-taking menace in the Mediterranean without the protection that the British navy had afforded to its ships when America was thirteen British colonies. As merchant vessels flying the new Stars and Stripes entered the Mediterranean looking for trading opportunities, the Barbary corsairs presented a constant and galling problem. The governments of Europe either paid tribute to them to prevent their subjects from being enslaved, or were too poor to do so. For the United States, free trade was both a policy and a belief: trade would increase wealth even as it increased freedom. But with no navy and little money, the new republic's merchant ships and crewmen were prime targets for capture and enslavement. The promises of free trade were imperiled.

John Foss, a seaman in the brig *Polly* out of Newburyport, Massachusetts, which sailed from Baltimore bound to Cadiz, Spain, in September

1793, was one of those who became enslaved. Like many who experienced slavery in Algiers, Foss wrote a detailed account of his experience. When the *Polly* was still about 70 miles off the Spanish coast near the end of October 1793, a lookout spotted a brig flying the British flag, but the experienced American seamen recognized by the cut of her sails that she was not a British ship: they supposed her to be a French privateer flying a false flag as a *ruse de guerre*, given the war raging between Britain and France. The strange brig approached, and the *Polly* stopped to wait for her. Since the United States and France were at peace, the master of the *Polly* thought they had nothing to fear. As the distance closed, an officer "dressed in the Christian habit, and . . . the only person we could yet see on her deck" called over the water in English to ask the name of the ship, and where from and whither bound. No one on the *Polly* suspected anything until they spotted the brig's crew, which had been concealed, and

> saw by their dress and long beards that they were Moors, or Algerines. Our feelings at this unwelcome sight, are more easily imagined than described. . . . She then hove too under our lee, when we heard a most terrible shouting, clapping of hands, huzzaing, &c. — And saw a great number of men rise up with their heads above the [gunwale], dressed in the Turkish habit like them we saw on the poop.

The Algerine brig lowered a launch, and about one hundred corsairs, armed with scimitars, pistols, pikes, and knives, rowed across and clambered up the side of the *Polly*. The pirates herded the Americans into the forward part of their own ship, threatening them in several languages. They then went below, and "broke open all the Trunks, and Chests, there were on board, and plundered all our bedding, cloathing, books, . . . and every moveable article." Returning on deck, they stripped every crew member of everything except the shirt and trousers he was wearing, and they conveyed them back to the Algerine brig, which sailed off to Algiers. The men were packed below decks with vermin attacking their bodies and clothes and were given little to eat.

Upon landing, the Americans were taken to the palace of the ruler, the dey of Algiers, through a surging crowd which stunned them "with the shouts, clapping of hands and other exclamations of joy from the inhabitants; thanking God for their great success and victories over so many Christian dogs, and unbelievers. . . ." The dey greeted them with a speech declaring he would never make peace with their country, finishing, "now I have got you, you Christian dogs, you shall eat stones." The next morning, a heavy chain link was hammered around each man's ankle, and Foss called the "dreadful clanking" sound of the iron chain each man had to carry "the most terrible noise I ever heard." The captured men then began their work as slaves, mining rocks in the nearby mountains and hauling them by bodily force down to the port to repair or extend the seawall at the harbor, or working at the port carrying freight on their backs, goaded along by guards with pointed sticks, like cattle prods, with dreadful beatings or death never a distant possibility.

At first, the United States responded to Barbary slavery with powerless outrage. In the early 1790s, the new republic had no navy. Many Americans questioned the need to build one and worried about the risks to civil liberties and the huge expenditures necessary in creating and maintaining a naval establishment. With no effective power to contest Barbary slave-taking, the United States followed traditional European practice and made an enormous payment to Algiers to free its seamen, including John Foss, and promised annual tribute to purchase immunity from Barbary slavery. As the months and years went by, the United States built a navy, even as it dutifully made its yearly payments to Algiers, continuing the practice well into the new century. But when Algiers, the most powerful Barbary state, began once again to carry American seamen off their ships into slavery, the United States, flush with nationalist feeling after the end of the War of 1812, decided it would no longer pay ransom to bring its people home. The United States would speak from the mouths of its cannon; the navy was sent to put an end to Barbary terror.

Chapter One

The Odyssey of the Edwin

IN MARCH 1812, the brig *Edwin* sailed from her home port of Salem, Massachusetts, to New York, and then for Gibraltar and Malta, probably carrying a cargo of food and provisions for the British army garrisons there. The trading voyage of the *Edwin* was tinged with danger. She may have sailed with a British license to carry grain to supply Lord Wellington's army in Spain—a lucrative business that violated American trade laws. Her owners, captain, and crew knew that in departing American waters, she was sailing in the face of an embargo the federal government planned to lay on American shipping, which President Madison presented to Congress on April 1, 1812, but was widely known to be in the offing. The Madison administration pushed for the 1812 embargo to allow thousands of American seamen aboard hundreds of American merchant ships to reach United States ports before the anticipated declaration of war with Britain. The new law did not stop the *Edwin*, which not only wanted to land her cargo at British-owned Mediterranean naval ports, but also expected to return with a load of import goods. To do so, she would have to sail through threats from the British navy, and as she journeyed halfway up the Mediterranean, she would be in waters unsettled by British-French hostilities in the ongoing Napoleonic Wars and the lurking dangers from seagoing corsairs of the semi-independent Barbary coastal states of Algiers, Tunis, and Tripoli. After the *Edwin* sailed, the Essex Fire and Marine Insurance Company of Salem issued an insurance policy on March 31, 1812, for $4,000 on the brig and its "effects." The company charged the named owners, Nathaniel Silsbee and Robert Stone of Salem, an 8 percent (or $320) premium to Gibraltar and back, an additional 1 percent premium if the *Edwin* went to any port "without the Straits [of Gibraltar]," 6 percent more if she ventured as far as Sicily, and a further 4 percent if her master, George Campbell Smith, had the audacity and luck to "go up as high as Smyrna" in present-day Turkey.

The *Edwin* was an unremarkable workhorse of a ship. Built on the Merrimack River at Amesbury, Massachusetts, in 1800, she had been sold and resold five times by the time of her voyage in the spring of 1812. She was a stubby, utilitarian, two-masted vessel with a square rig (the sails hanging perpendicular to the hull), only 71 feet long, slightly more than 21 feet in breadth, and with a depth of hold slightly less than 10 feet. Silsbee and Stone valued the *Edwin* at $7,500 despite the insurance policy for only half that amount. The owners, along with two other Salem merchants, James Devereaux and Dudley Pickman, crammed barrels, casks, and bags of goods valued at more than $14,000 into the hold of the *Edwin*, and they allowed the master, George Campbell Smith, to put aboard his own freight, worth another $4,000. When the *Edwin* departed from New York in March 1812, Smith needed a crew of only nine seamen to man the brig on a transatlantic trading voyage that must have been expected to last at least six months.

After touching at New York and landing some of her cargo at Gibraltar, the *Edwin* sailed on to Malta, reaching Valetta harbor on June 29. Neither British authorities ashore nor Master Smith could have known, in those days when letters were carried by sailing ships and messengers on horseback, that exactly eleven days earlier the United States had formally declared war against Great Britain. Not only was the *Edwin* trading with the enemy, but she was also at risk of seizure as a prize of war. After landing and selling her cargo and using the cash to buy a diverse cargo to take back to Salem—including wine, oils, sulfur, "blue vitrials," opium, linens, and spices—and signing on a New Hampshire man for the return voyage, the *Edwin* left Malta on August 5. Still unaware of the Anglo-American war, the *Edwin* began her return trek under Royal Navy convoy. But she was such a dull sailer that she lost the convoy one evening and was forced to sail on alone.

On August 25, 1812, off the southern coast of Spain, a lookout on the *Edwin* spotted a large ship bearing down on her. The crew was anxious. Five years before, a French privateer had stopped the *Edwin* on the Atlantic and sent over a boarding party to look at the brig and her papers. Adhering to the international law of neutral maritime rights—not always observed by privateers—the Frenchmen were content to ask if they might purchase a spare topmast; they did so and, with that, politely bid the *Edwin* au revoir. What happened in August 1812, however, was the nightmarish drama that all mariners in the Mediterranean feared. The pursuer, a frigate armed with two rows of cannon on her broadside, overhauled the *Edwin*. Although no account exists of the chase and capture of the *Edwin*, the scene was played out hundreds of times in that era, and there is little doubt of the essentials. As the distance closed, the pursuing vessel might have hoisted a green banner with white crescent and stars, the flag of Algiers, or she might have dispensed with identifying herself and fired a single cannon shot across the bow of the *Edwin*, the timeless display of force meant to be answered by force or submission. The unarmed *Edwin* must have heaved to, backing her topsails to stop and submit, as a boat put off from the Algerine frigate loaded with men. Rowed over to the *Edwin*, they would have clambered up her side armed with swords and pistols and, shrieking threatening words in Arabic, taken control of the brig. The crew of the *Edwin*, overwhelmed and unnerved, insulted and spat upon, surrendered. The captors stripped the American seamen of everything of value, even the clothes off their backs.

After a few days' sail, the captured *Edwin* entered the harbor of Algiers. While an Algerine court quickly adjudicated the brig a "good prize," and the *Edwin*'s freight was sold to benefit her new Algerine owners, George Campbell Smith and his crew were trundled ashore and, after being paraded and inspected, became slaves of the dey. Thrust into servitude, Smith did not set an example of stoicism and gallantry. His first letter, dated "Prison in Algiers, Augt. 30th, 1812," informed John Gavino, the United States consul at Gibraltar, that he was "a Slave at work on the Mole" of the harbor, the seaward defenses of Algiers formed by a man-made breakwater. After asking Gavino to send word of the *Edwin*'s capture to one of her owners, Nathaniel Silsbee, Smith pointedly referred to his "good connexions and considerable Property" back in America, and suggested to Gavino that he might try to draft a bill on Gavino for money to effect his ransom, leaving his crew to their own resources. A month later, when Smith wrote a business contact in Malta, Edward Fettyplace, he had become hysterical at the reverse of his fortune. Without mentioning his ten-man crew, he told Fettyplace that he had been put to hard labor at the mole and his situation was "truly distressing, no distinction of persons [being made between him and his men]." He pleaded for help, telling

Fettyplace that he had more than ten thousand dollars in cash at Salem, and he could not survive six months' labor as a captive, ending, "[D]o not let me die as a slave in Algiers."

The Swedish consul at Algiers, Johan Norderling, came to Smith's rescue. By the middle of October 1812, Norderling had arranged for Smith to lodge with him at the Swedish consulate, although Norderling noted that he had to "grease the way a little" with bribes to the requisite officials. As a shipmaster and therefore a gentleman, Smith was allowed some freedom of movement and made exempt from manual labor. The ten crewmen of the *Edwin*, property of the dey, were consigned to grueling work, excavating rock from quarries by hand, carting the rocks into town to build roads and reinforce the harbor walls, and repairing forts around the city. Their food was meager, coarse black bread with a little oil or soup; they were kept at night in a long, low prison-like barracks called the bagnio, and their taskmasters were harsh and unforgiving.

The brig *Edwin* disappeared. The eleven Americans held captive, as well as a twelfth American named James Pollard, a native of Norfolk, Virginia, who was seized a few weeks later while a passenger on a neutral Spanish ship, would change history. They would not be forgotten in America. The United States government would first try to ransom them and then would declare war and dispatch its navy to rescue them. In unleashing the navy, the largest concentration of American power up to that time, to break Algiers's hold on the twelve Americans, the United States decided to put an end to the historic Islamic practice of seizing ships from Christian countries and holding their seamen and passengers as slaves for ransom. The short-lived war would feature dramatic sea battles, ruthless diplomacy, and—behind the scenes and unused—an early weapon of mass destruction.

FROM WEST TO EAST along the coast of North Africa, the four Barbary regencies stretched toward Egypt: Morocco, Algiers, Tunis, and Tripoli. To the Arabs, the region was called *al-Maghreb*, meaning "the west." Nominally subject to the rule of the Ottoman sultan at Constantinople, to whom they paid annual tribute, in practice each Barbary power was governed by its own ruler—an emperor of Morocco, the dey of Algiers, the bey of Tunis, and the bashaw of Tripoli—and was treated by the rest of the world as an autonomous state. In 1815, the city of Algiers, the capital of the regency of Algiers, contained at least sixty thousand people, but perhaps more than a hundred thousand—no one really knew. The city

Terraces d'Alger. Lithograph by Genet from a painting by Bagot. From Adrien Berbrugger, *Algérie historique, pittoresque et monumentale* (1843), Special Collections of The Johns Hopkins University.

rose from the sea, a mass of whitewashed walls, low-roofed and interconnected houses, and mosques with minarets. A warren of narrow and crooked lanes crisscrossed the city. Fortifications ringed the city, and powerful batteries of heavy cannon on the harbor confronted any would-be attacker. The area around Algiers was verdant and beautiful, containing vineyards, citrus groves, orchards, and flower gardens, as well as country estates for the rich and the foreign consuls. Farms produced wheat and barley, and the coastal area contained many fruit and olive trees. The wife of the British consul to Algiers kept a diary for her six-year sojourn in Algiers, which her daughter, Elizabeth Blanckley Broughton, published with her own childhood memories, one of the few European memoirs from Barbary, and the only known recollections of a European woman. Mrs. Blanckley's diary is filled with comments about the physical beauty of Algiers. "This is indeed a land fair to look upon," she noted after seeing wildflowers growing from the side of a mountain, and for a woman who loved her native heath, there could scarcely be a more telling remark than that the fields "have now the appearance of those in England in the month of May, the inclosures being not only covered with leaves, but with blossoms as well."

In contrast to the serene countryside, political life in Algiers was violent, severe, and, at least to European eyes, unpredictable. The dey of Algiers had absolute power over his subjects as individuals but relied on the implicit support of the Turkish military elite for matters of state, and his hold on power was precarious. The dey (Turkish for "uncle") was chosen from among the elite of Turkish soldiers, or janissaries, whose ranks included young men from the fringes of Europe who renounced Christianity and embraced Islam, as well as men Barbary corsairs had stolen away as children, often ethnic Greeks and Armenians, who were trained for military life from their childhood. A dey ruled until a defeat, a badly received treaty, or a lack of money made his janissaries tire of him— creating the groundwork for a brutal coup, where the dey's guards would stab or garrote their leader and install a new dey by a vote of the divan, the council of Turkish soldiers. A dey might rule supreme for years if he was active, successful, and cunning, but always he was surrounded by a praetorian guard of Turkish soldiers. Few deys died of old age. Mrs. Blanckley noted that when the janissaries rose to depose Achmet Pasha on November 7, 1808, he tried to escape by leaping from roof terrace to roof terrace. A janissary shot him, he was thrown off the roof, and after his head was cut off in the street below, it was shown to the new dey, Ali, as proof that the previous regime was done. By the evening, as Mrs. Blanckley reported dryly, "everything was quiet, and the usual order restored." Five months later, it was Ali's turn, and he declined the poison he was offered, stating that he did not want to be an accessory to his own death. Instead, according to Mrs. Blanckley's account, he was led out "like a culprit, to the usual place of execution, where he was strangled. A distinction was, however, made in his case, as he was strangled at once, instead of undergoing the usual refinement of cruelty, in being twice revived by a glass of water, and only effectually executed the third time." Of course, a dey getting wind of such plots could strike first. Mrs. Blanckley laconically began an entry in November 1810, "Five influential men have been strangled, which, for the present, has prevented a revolution" deposing the next dey, who also took the name Ali.

Most of the people of Algiers were Arabs, farmers and shepherds outside the city, who lived in tents. City dwellers, whom Americans and Europeans often indiscriminately called "Moors," some of whom were indeed descended from the Muslims who had crossed into Spain and southwestern France before retreating back to North Africa in previous centuries, performed most of the trade and artisanal jobs. Algiers and its environs had no industry to speak of, and all clothing was either imported or sewn in the interior. In the hills lived the Berbers and Kabyles, fiercely independent tribesmen who were enemies of the Arabs. Only the Turkish janissaries had political power.

Most of the brokers and moneylenders and many of the skilled artisans of Algiers were Jews, who had an ancient and subtle relationship with the ruling Turks. Nominally, Turks, Moors, Arabs, and captive Christian slaves alike despised the Jews, who were subject to being spat upon or stoned in the streets by anyone. The Jews felt their lowly status every day. They were set apart by being forced to dress entirely in black, wear tricorn hats, and live in a ghetto; they were forbidden to carry weapons or ride horses. Yet many of the guilds—silversmiths and goldsmiths, tailors, and jewelers— were composed entirely of Jews, who owned many of the city's shops. Although many of Algiers's seven thousand Jews were poor, the wealthiest Jewish family, the Baccris, were the dey's own financiers and reputedly loaned huge sums to Napoleon. The Jewish merchants' familial and religious contacts in Gibraltar, Marseilles, Livorno, and elsewhere around the Mediterranean gave them credit, information, and insight into the outside world, which enabled them to exert enormous influence over the dey. The Jewish brokers in Algiers acted as facilitators of, and provided advances for, the ransom of slaves through their sophisticated credit and banking relationships in Europe. Yet even the most prominent Jews led a precarious existence. David Baccri was murdered by the dey on February 5, 1811, for no reason apparent to Mrs. Blanckley, and his successor as the leading Jewish figure, Durand, was beheaded that October. There was no "shadow of pretence for the poor man's massacre," according to the British consul's wife, although she supposed he was killed to assuage popular hatred of the Jews. Whenever a dey was killed, the janissaries understood they had license to sack the Jewish population, which led to the Jewish community paying large ransoms to avoid a general pillaging, and forced many Jews to seek refuge in the British consulate.

The Islamic regencies of the Maghreb had long-standing if strained ties to Christian Europe. The ruins of the ancient civilization of Carthage lay near Tunis, and a flourishing Church had produced Saint Augustine. From North Africa had come the Moors who swept through Spain, and when the Islamic expansionist tide receded, Europe grew accustomed to an Islamic presence across the Mediterranean. Though regarded as hostile to

Types des Races Algériennes. Lithograph by Bayot from a painting by Philippoteaux. From Adrien Berbrugger, *Algérie historique, pittoresque at monumentale* (1843), Special Collections of The Johns Hopkins University.

Christians, the Barbary regencies no longer posed a mortal threat. By the turn of the nineteenth century, Algiers, Tunis, Tripoli, and Morocco had become exporters of wheat, fruit, and leather for shoes to European buyers: to the merchants of Alicante, Marseilles, Barcelona, Mahon, and Livorno in times of peace, and to the British army in the Iberian peninsula during the Napoleonic Wars. But historically, the major point of contact between the Barbary regencies and Europe was slavery: corsair ships sailing out of the Maghreb seized European merchant ships and sold their crews and passengers into captivity.

For centuries, the Barbary states had run a lucrative racket of enslaving Christians. Algiers, which Mordecai Noah, later the American consul to Tunis, called "the sink of iniquity and curse of humanity," was the "great depot" of Christian slaves. In the sixteenth and seventeenth centuries, Algiers alone was said to have held thirty thousand captives—in the 1620s, more British subjects lived as slaves in Islamic North Africa than as freemen in the colonies of North America. At the height of the corsairs' activity, their audacity shocked Europe. In 1631, corsairs descended on the village of Baltimore, in Ireland, and seized the entire population, carrying them back to slavery in Algiers. Algerine corsairs raided villages as far away as Cornwall and Devon in England for men, women, and children. Of course, the coastal areas of Tuscany, Sardinia, Sicily, and the Greek isles were closer to the North African ports from which the corsairs sailed, and easier and more constant targets, since they did not have a coast guard or military force sufficient to stop or deter hit-and-run raids.

By 1800, the racket was simple and time-tested. Ships of all the mercantile nations wanted to trade throughout the Mediterranean. Barbary mariners have loosely come down through history as "pirates," but in fact the corsairs were state-owned or state-syndicated, and their practices were not outlawed under the slowly evolving notions of the law of nations. Indeed, under Islamic law, the seizures of ships from Christian countries were an article of faith, part of the jihad against nonbelievers. Armed Barbary ships darted out from a dozen ports to seize European ships and their cargoes, which, upon their return to port, Barbary courts condemned as lawful prizes, with the result that the European seamen and passengers carried back to Algiers, Tunis, or Tripoli, were enslaved.

White slavery on the Barbary coast was essentially a system of regulated commercial kidnapping, the Christians seized from Europe or America in the first instance with the notion of being trading back for cash. In fact, the entire Barbary enterprise was regulated by foreign nations. For generation upon generation, European kingdoms entered into treaties with each of the Barbary regencies, paying an annual bribe called "tribute" as protection money against the seizure of any of their subjects for the duration of the treaty. From time to time, Spain, France, Holland, Denmark, and Britain sent naval squadrons to deter or punish the Barbary corsairs—or at least to try to force upon the Barbary rulers a new treaty reducing the amount of tribute exacted. But for the most part, the European nations were willing to pay cash, or tribute in the form of naval stores, gunpowder, or ships, for the privilege of having their ships and mariners remain unmolested. That paying tribute was a protection racket was widely understood, but paying the Barbary rulers a "license" for trade was less expensive than constantly convoying ships or attacking the Barbary powers in their heavily fortified ports. Besides, wealthier kingdoms recognized that while they could afford to pay off the Barbary powers, other, poorer, European nations could not. With a wink and a nod, the payments by the wealthy kingdoms of northern Europe tacitly encouraged Algiers, Tripoli, and Tunis to seize the ships of the poorer maritime nations of southern Europe, thereby disproportionately raising *their* costs of doing business. Based on that logic, in the 1780s, Benjamin Franklin wrote that the Barbary "Corsaires" might "be privately encouraged by the English to fall upon [American vessels], to prevent our Interference in the Carrying Trade; for I have in London heard it as a Maxim among the Merchants, that, if *there were no Algiers, it would be worth England's while to build one*." The poorer and smaller mercantile states that could not afford regular tribute suffered large losses of seafaring men—the bagnio contained mostly Portuguese, Neapolitans, Sardinians, Sicilians, and Greeks—which helped preserve the mercantile dominance of Britain, Sweden, and Denmark.

After British Admiral Lord Nelson's triumph at the battle of Trafalgar in October 1805, the Royal Navy was able to establish an effective blockade of French-controlled Mediterranean ports, which ranged from Spain through the Adriatic. The British naval ascendancy in the Mediterranean meant that the Barbary corsairs had fewer targets, and the Barbary regencies were forced to promote legitimate trade and to downplay slave taking. While the Barbary regencies were increasingly integrated into Europe by virtue of shipping goods during the Napoleonic Wars, it would be a mistake to think that the taking of Christian slaves was on the wane—particularly by Algiers. Taking and ransoming European slaves remained critical to the economies of Islamic North Africa, a foundation of their society and culture, and literally a life-and-death issue for the ruling dey, whose support among the janissaries required a constant refreshing of the number of slaves held captive. Mrs. Blanckley noted in her diary that the most famous Algerine naval commander, or *raïs*, Hamidou, returned in his frigate from one cruise in September 1807 "with twenty unfortunate Christian slaves, some of them from Augusta in Sicily," and weeks later, another frigate came into port carrying 140 Portuguese captives to be enslaved, along with a few Englishmen who had the bad luck of being passengers on the Portuguese ship. She believed that the greatest achievement of her husband, Henry Stanyford Blanckley, after six years as consul, was negotiating the ransoming and release of 584 Portuguese slaves, many of whom had spent decades in slavery. The dey made clear to her husband, however, that he would not be able to replicate his humanitarian effort with the Sicilians: "[T]he Dey's answer was, 'That the Algerines were [corsairs], and that were he to [make peace], he should lose his head, as he would be obliged to shut up his Marine. That he had already concluded a peace with Portugal at the [British] Consul's insistence, and if they had not a nation to cruise against, it would be his ruin."

Toward the end of the eighteenth century, the Algerine government prohibited privately owned corsairs, after which the captives taken were slaves to the dey, with the result that slave markets and sales of slaves ceased almost entirely. Moreover, if a European consul intervened, as Norderling did for George C. Smith of the *Edwin*, the well-to-do Christian gentlemen among the passengers and the vessel's officers would be kept in a state of parole, able to walk about the city or gardens and live at the consul's residence. The few craftsmen—smiths, coopers, carpenters— might find ready work for their trades, and might earn enough to set up their own establishment. An American named James Leander Cathcart, captured off the *Maria* at age seventeen in 1785, spent eleven years as a slave in Algiers, but through pluck and intelligence rose from being a gardener at the palace to the post of chief Christian secretary to the dey, and he saved his allowances to buy several taverns. After the United States bought the freedom of its captives in Algiers, Cathcart returned home, but he ultimately returned to Barbary as an American consul—surely not the sign of a man devastated by his experience as a slave. While most of the seamen and less well-to-do passengers were put to hard labor and kept in the bagnios, one American commentator termed it "no more than justice to say, that their condition [in Algiers] was not generally worse than that of prisoners of war in many civilized, Christian countries." Travelers who ventured into Barbary noted the relative kindness with which Islamic masters treated some of their slaves: women slaves were almost never physically beaten or lashed, although many disappeared into the seraglio; slaves were not branded, although they did wear ankle rings as a sign of their slave status; and many slaves could earn money and had some freedom of movement within Algiers. On the other hand, they might be granted some freedom of movement because there was no way for them to escape: escape could be only by sea, and on a European ship, and it was almost impossible for an unattended slave to come close to the quays.

In some aspects, Islamic slavery was less severe than slavery in the American South. Seizing on this refrain, some modern historians, notably Robert Allison in *The Crescent Obscured*, have begun to depreciate slavery in Islamic North Africa as not a physical condition but an attitude. According to Allison, Barbary slavery was a "temporary status" for "kinless strangers," with their fate in the hands of their distant families or governments who could ransom them, or their "own choice of Islam." By this hypothesis, Barbary slavery did not mean particularly harsh treatment, and the captives' actual descriptions of bestial labor and draconian punishments are "hyperbolic." In this modern view, slavery in the Barbary world was an "intellectual concept," not wrong because of its harshness but "unnatural" because it deprived captives of their liberty.

To be sure, the nineteenth century was hard and unforgiving everywhere—thousands died in advanced cities such as Philadelphia of yellow fever and smallpox in the summers; bankrupts were put into debtors' prison; orphans worked in poorhouses in abject Dickensian straits; the British navy forcibly "impressed" foreign seamen into their service; most white Americans looked on Negro slavery in the United States phlegmatically. But slavery on the Barbary coast was manifestly not merely an attitude. Most of the Christian slaves put to hard labor in Barbary suffered and toiled, not unlike the ancient Israelites under the pharaoh in Egypt. Most, like the crew of the *Edwin*, worked in the quarries outside of the city breaking, hauling, and carrying rock down to the mole of the harbor to extend and improve the seawall and breakers, or to rebuild and improve the city's extensive seaward-side fortifications, prodded along by overseers who beat them with sticks with a sharpened point. They ate a diet of sour bread, a little oil, and an occasional thin gruel of a vegetable soup. The British consul's family seldom ventured down to the port because they were overcome by the scene of the Christian slaves pressing around them, begging for help, "kissing the hems of our garments, throwing themselves at our feet." The lives of the white slaves limited to menial labor were miserable, and their Islamic masters meant to show them their inferiority. Striking a Turk was a capital offense for a Christian slave, and such offenses were punishable by impaling the criminal, roasting him alive, or hanging him from iron hooks on the city walls. Lesser crimes were punished by hanging the offender upside down and beating his feet and backside, a punishment called a bastinado. Christian slaves with trades or skills could earn a much better existence than the bagnio, but still they were slaves in a hostile, foreign world. There they would remain until they died, adopted Islam (pejoratively termed "turning Turk"), or were ransomed by their family, friends, or government. In the Maghreb, slavery was not necessarily perpetual and unconditional, as it was in the American South, but rather subject to redemption for money or, sometimes, upon profession of the Muslim faith. Yet those very factors made white slavery in the Islamic world seem cynical and galling to the Christian world—it was slavery as systemic kidnapping, where the captives could gain freedom if they abandoned their faith or if their friends could come up with enough cash.

The ruling janissary caste may have been bloodthirsty and the regime based on plunder, but the constant contemporary refrain that equated the name "Algerine" with ferocity and barbarism was overstated. The society built on the Barbary corsairs' slave-taking was opulent. Europeans were not allowed to go out on their roofs after sunset, a time reserved for Algerine women to take their evening promenades to exhibit themselves and their jewelry to their neighbors before their husbands returned from evening prayers at the mosque. Mrs. Blanckley attended the wedding of the daughter of the city's chief judge and was "surrounded by a crowd of the most brilliantly dressed ladies," adorned with dazzling jewels, and she was struck by their politeness, manners, and fair complexions. Similarly, William Shaler, the United States consul in Algiers after 1815, found the Algerines in their daily lives to be courteous and humane. Nothing about them suggested "extraordinary bigotry, fanaticism, or hatred of those who profess a different religion; they profess the Mohammedan creed, and fulfil with the utmost scrupulousness the rites which it ordains, but without affectation, and . . . without hostility to those who adopt different measures to conciliate the Divine favour."

That may have been how the Algerines lived their domestic lives. The Tripolitan ambassador in London had explained to Thomas Jefferson years earlier that the Barbary states' policy toward the Christian world "was founded on the Laws of their Prophet, that it was written in their Koran, that all nations who should not have acknowledged their authority were sinners, that it was their right and duty to make war upon them whenever they could be found, and to make slaves of all they could take as Prisoners, and that every [Muslim] who should be slain in battle was sure to go to Paradise." This duty to war on the infidels was called jihad. The Barbary corsairs' jihad was not based on xenophobia, nihilism, or religious fundamentalism, although the deys varied in their religious fervor and asceticism. Rather, it was the Barbary way of life, a state of perpetual, organized, state-regulated maritime violence and kidnapping, sanctioned by time and the Islamic sense of superiority over Christians. Although their jihad did not have an explicit political goal, as restoring the caliphate (the furthest geographical advance of Islam into southern Europe) is to twenty-first-century militant Islam, slave-taking was jihad, and the tactics employed by the corsairs were a form of terrorism, a method of seaborne violence meant to intimidate the peoples of Europe.

The popular, sensational image of the white Christian slaves in the clutches of Barbary Turks and Arabs was fanned by generations of playwrights and prose writers, even as the menace of the Barbary corsairs literally made them the bogeymen for generations of European, and then American, children. The great Spanish writer Cervantes was captured and imprisoned as a slave in Algiers from 1575 to 1580, during some of which he was chained to the oar of a galley, until his family could ransom him privately. His first play, *Los Tratos de Argel*, which he wrote the year of his release, was based on his experience as a slave, as was the tale of the Captive in *Don Quixote*. More than two hundred years later, the Algerines were still enslaving white Christians, by then including Americans, and writers were still writing of the ordeal. In 1794, Susanna Haswell Rowson, the first American best-selling novelist and an actress and songwriter, wrote a play, *Slaves in Algiers*, which was staged at the Chestnut Street Theatre in Philadelphia. But *Slaves in Algiers* was only one of a huge genre of Barbary captivity narratives and plays. *Narrative of the Captivity of John Vandike, who was taken by the Algerines in 1791* appeared in 1797, as did Royall Tyler's novel *The Algerine Captive*; David Everett's play *Slaves in Barbary* appeared in 1798, as did *A Journal, of the Captivity and Suffering of John Foss*; another, *The History of the Captivity and Suffering of Mrs. Maria Martin*, came out in 1800. Historian Paul Baepler has estimated that between 1798 and 1817, American publishers printed more than a hundred Barbary captivity editions.

Some contemporaries weighed the slavery in Algiers against the domestic American brand. William Eaton, a Connecticut Yankee and the United States consul at Tunis, recognized the hypocrisy of condemning Barbary slavery while slavery existed throughout America:

> [R]emorse seizes my whole soul when I reflect that this is indeed but a copy of the very barbarity which my eyes have seen in my own native country. And yet we boast of liberty and national justice. How frequently, in the southern states of my own country, have I seen weeping mothers leading the guiltless infant to the sales, with as deep anguish as if they led them to the slaughter; and yet felt my bosom tranquil in the view of these aggressions upon defenceless humanity. But when I see the same enormities practiced upon beings whose complexion and blood claim kindred with my own, I curse the perpetrators and weep over the wretched victims of their rapacity. Indeed truth and justice demand from me the confession that the [C]hristian slaves among the barbarians of Africa are treated with more humanity than the African slaves among the professing Christians of civilized America; and yet here sensibility bleeds at every pore for the wretches whom fate has doomed to slavery.

Other Americans looked deeply into white slavery and made the same point. For instance, in his *Short Account of Algiers*, published in 1794, Mathew Carey condemned the seizure of American seamen and their sale into bondage but admitted, "For this practice of buying and selling slaves we are not entitled to charge the Algerines with any exclusive degree of barbarity." In one scene of his 1797 novel *The Algerine Captive*, Royall Tyler invokes a Muslim cleric noting that in the Barbary world, there were no forced conversions, and Christians who accepted Islam became free, but in the Christian world, blacks were baptized into Christianity and then treated as brutes. While Eaton wrote with deeply felt emotion, and Tyler limned the hypocrisy through fiction, Benjamin Franklin used parody. In the last few months of his life, writing as Historicus in March 1790 in the (Philadelphia) *Federal Gazette*, Franklin responded to a speech by a congressman from Georgia who had attacked those calling for the abolition of Negro slavery. Franklin made the connection between black slavery in America and white slavery in Africa. He parodied the arguments against freedom for Negroes in the United States with an imaginary argument against freedom for whites in slavery in Algiers as Sidi Mohammed Ibrahim, a fictitious member of the divan of Algiers a century before:

> If we cease our Cruises against the Christians, how shall we be furnished with the Commodities their Countries produce, and which are so necessary for us? If we forbear to make Slaves of their People, who in this hot Climate are to cultivate our Lands? Who are to perform the common Labours of our City, and in our Families? . . . . If we then cease taking and plundering the Infidel

Ships, making Slaves of the Seamen and Passengers, our Lands will become of no Value for want of Cultivation; the Rents of Houses in the City will sink one half; and the Revenues of Government arising from its Share of Prizes, be totally destroy'd. And for what?

. . .

Are not Spain, Portugal, France, and the Italian states, govern'd by Despots, who hold all their Subjects in Slavery, without Exception? Even England treats its sailors as slaves. . . . Is their Condition then made worse by their falling into our Hands? No; they have only exchanged one Slavery for another, and I may say, a better; for here they are brought into a Land where the Sun of Islam gives forth its Light, and shines in full Splendor, and they have an Opportunity of making themselves acquainted with the true Doctrine, and thereby saving their immortal Souls.

William Eaton despaired that the United States was willing to pay tribute rather than use force. Eaton recognized that Algiers perpetually had the incentive to break the peace when they could seize more American merchant ships. He predicted that the "[r]egencies will fabricate pretexts for accumulating their claims upon us, so long as we shall have a commerce in this sea worth these sacrifices to their avarice for its protection," and no force to protect it. "It is indeed an erroneous calculation," Eaton declaimed, "to seek to save the expense of this kind of protection by stipulating payments to a gang of fearless robbers." It grated on Eaton to "see a lazy Turk reclining at his ease upon an embroidered sopha, with one [C]hristian slave to fan away flies, another to hand his coffee, and a third to hold his pipe; and when I reflect [it is] the sweat of my countrymen contributes to procure him this ease." Worse yet was the accepted notion "that the Turk believes he has a right to demand this contribution, and that we, like Italians, have not fortitude to resist it."

In 1796, without any navy, the United States paid the astronomical sum of $642,000—about one-fifteenth of all federal outlays that year—to ransom 107 American seamen from the bagnio of Algiers, some of whom had been held more than ten years. The United States agreed by treaty to become one of Algiers's tribute-paying customers, paying $21,600 per year in naval stores, "usages" on a biennial basis, and additional "usages," as then Secretary of State James Madison wryly noted in 1808, "for the attainment of any important object," for which he could provide Congress no estimate of cost. One of the additional presents was a new 36-gun frigate for the Algerine navy, called the *Crescent*, which sent the perverse message that America would not build warships to vindicate its rights but would supply a warship to a power that sought to attack those rights. Although sometimes behind, the United States dutifully made its treaty payments each year. With the exception of one year, 1807, when Algerine cruisers seized the schooner *Mary Ann*, the brig *Violet*, and the ship *Eagle* because the American tribute was two years in arrears, Algiers dutifully refrained from capturing American ships and enslaving American seamen. Paying off the Barbary regencies was the inevitable and logical result of being too poor and disorganized a country after the Revolutionary War to afford building and maintaining a navy.

John Adams, as American minister to Britain in the 1780s, and a man almost always able to put his finger on the essence of an issue, put it bluntly in a letter to Thomas Jefferson:

> [I]f our States could be brought to agree in the measure, I should be very willing to resolve upon external war with vigor, and protect our trade and people. The resolution to fight them would raise the spirits and courage of our countrymen immediately, and we might obtain the glory of finally breaking up these nests of banditti. But [C]ongress will never, or at least not for years, take any such resolution, and in the mean time our trade and honor suffers beyond calculation. We ought not to fight them at all, unless we determine to fight them forever.
>
> This thought, I fear, is too rugged for our people to bear. To fight them at the expense of millions, and make peace, after all, by giving more money and larger presents than would now procure perpetual peace, seems not to be economical. . . . Did any nation ever make peace with any one Barbary state without making the presents?

After 1801, however, the United States had a small navy of powerful frigates and speedy smaller ships. It also had a new president, Thomas Jefferson, who shied away from the use of force—except against the Barbary regencies, which he despised. As early as the 1780s, when he served the new republic as a diplomat in Paris, Jefferson schemed about how the Barbary regencies could be confronted by a coalition of navies from the lesser European states. Although the ambassadors he spoke to in Paris were supportive, that plan was nothing more than wishful thinking on a grand scale, especially when it became clear that his own country had neither money nor ships to support such a coalition. While Adams was president, Jefferson fought the creation of the navy in the context of the 1798–1800 maritime Quasi-War against France, and wrote before the election of 1800 that he was for a "naval force only as may protect our coasts and harbors . . . [and opposed to] a navy, which by its own expenses and the eternal wars in which it will implicate us, grind us with public burthens and sink us under them."

Yet from the very first days of his presidency, Jefferson was determined to respond harshly to a Tripolitan threat of war if it did not receive gifts of warships and annual tribute comparable to the 1796 American deal with Algiers. Beginning in 1801, Jefferson ordered successive squadrons of warships to blockade and attack Tripoli. Although there were individual ship battles that resulted in gratifying victories, there were mishaps as well, most notably when the frigate *Philadelphia* ran aground off Tripoli in October 1803, resulting in her capture with all 307 of her officers and men. The annual campaigns of 1801, 1802, 1803, and 1804 stalemated through inept leadership and the inability to mount a direct attack on Tripoli. Finally, in 1805, after William Eaton led an epic trek of Greek mercenaries, rebellious Arabs, and a scattering of U.S. marines from Alexandria to Derna, the United States was able to force a deal without any annual tribute on the bashaw of Tripoli. But, as John Adams had prophesied almost twenty years before, even at the moment of victory, the United States paid $60,000 for the release of the prisoners from the *Philadelphia*, leaving the impression that even at the apex of its power, the United States was willing to negotiate and pay rather than to take the fight to its conclusion. Tripoli, however, was not the major Barbary power. Algiers was.

With the exception of the flurry of the 1807 captures for the lateness of the tribute payments, Algiers was quiet toward the United States for fifteen years—the tribute had indeed bought a certain kind of licensed peace. In April 1812, however, the prince regent of England wrote the dey of Algiers a letter countersigned by the prime minister, Lord Liverpool. The prince regent began with the usual professions of friendship, and then made an extraordinary gambit. He assured the dey that the Royal Navy would protect Algiers from any attack, while at the same time, the British navy, "the terror of all maritime states," would subdue any foe. He asked the dey not to heed the enemies of Britain in their efforts to disturb the harmony existing between Britain and Algiers. The United States consul to Algiers, Tobias Lear, got wind of the letter and reported to Secretary of State Monroe that month that the British had provided the dey with a promise of protection against their mutual enemies. The document not only offered a shield for Algiers, but also served as an open invitation to enlist Algiers against Britain's maritime enemies. The Algerines may have been poorly informed with world events, but they knew enough to understand that the British were providing them carte blanche to strike the Americans, with whom British relations had been unraveling. The fact that the British reputedly refitted the entire Algerine navy in 1812 seemed to corroborate a tacit Anglo-Algiers naval alliance against at the United States.

On July 17, 1812, the dey chose the pretext on which to disturb the relatively tranquil relations that had existed with the United States. On that day, the *Allegheny*, an American merchant ship carrying the annual tribute of naval stores from the United States, arrived at Algiers. The dey demanded the ship's papers and found, first, that the amount of gunpowder the *Allegheny* carried for him—fifty small barrels—was inadequate. Then the dey learned that only four large-diameter rope cables had been shipped, not the twenty-seven he had demanded, and he took great umbrage at that failure. Finally, he complained that the *Allegheny* had stopped at Gibraltar to land cargo, and that she also freighted personal cargo not meant for him, which, he asserted, showed the Americans' disrespect for his person. The dey ordered Consul Lear, the former private secretary to President Washington, to depart eight days later on the *Allegheny* with his family and every American resident in Algiers, but only after Lear paid $27,000, all the money the dey claimed was due and owing. If Lear did not pay, the dey promised to confiscate the *Allegheny*, put Lear in chains, and treat all the Americans as slaves. This was not an idle threat. In front of Lear's own eyes, on March 25, 1808, the dey had ordered the Danish consul seized and carried through the streets to the bagnio, where, in Lear's words, "he was loaded with an enormous Chain."

Lear protested but ultimately had to obey, borrowing the money from Jacob Baccri with a 25 percent commission added. Lear and his suite duly departed. But forcing Lear and the handful of other Americans to go away meant that the dey had no Americans within his power. That is why, the next month, the dey declared open season on American merchant ships. But the Algerines had fundamentally miscalculated: there was only one American merchant ship left in the Mediterranean that fell into the clutches of the dey's corsairs. Ironically, the only prize Algiers gained in the maritime war they began against the United States was an otherwise insignificant little brig called the *Edwin*.

THE *EDWIN* AND HER CAPTIVE CREW were not forgotten, even through the din of the war with Britain. American newspapers reported what had occurred to the *Edwin* as soon as word filtered back to the United States. Under the headline "Distressing Capture," *Niles' Weekly Register*, a Baltimore publication with a national readership, noted in January 1813 that the Algerines had seized the brig and the crew had been put to "hard labor as slaves." Observing how the American public had become agitated by the news, editor Hezekiah Niles advocated "*any* exertion of force or negociation to bring back our tars to their fire-sides and little ones. *They must be released*—the *American* will not sit down contented, while *eight* or *ten* of his fellow-citizens are slaves to the *Dey* of Algiers."

From Gibraltar, Tobias Lear tried to ameliorate the captives' situation. In November 1812, he asked Johan Norderling, the Swedish consul, to provide support for George Campbell Smith, and to advance each of the seamen from the *Edwin* a monthly stipend of $6, at least until he received directions from Washington. With that sum per month, he hoped the seamen could "live as well as their situation will admit," but if any were to become sick, he asked Norderling to intervene to supply whatever might be necessary. Before departing for America, Lear sent ten sets of winter clothes for the American captives, at a cost of $123, and in the peculiarly obsequious style of the day, he ended his letter to Monroe with the hope that President Madison would approve of his initiative on behalf of the captives. Then Lear, too, was gone, escaping back to America before the British naval blockade shut in America's ports.

It is unclear how letters written from the bagnio of Algiers made it through the British blockade of the American coast, but some letters did arrive. In March 1813, George C. Smith wrote that he was "very comfortably situated" with Norderling, and was fulsome in his thanks for the "ample provision and supplies." He assured Lear that his men were as comfortable as their situation as slaves would allow and remained in good health. Less than three weeks earlier, however, the first mate of the *Edwin*, Francis Garcia, wrote Nathaniel Silsbee and James Devereaux (whose names he misspelled), two of the Salem merchants who owned or had cargo on the brig. Garcia noted first that the crew had "but Little to Subsist upon," and he asked for an advance upon their wages in the form of thirty Spanish dollars so that they could use "a bed for to Rest our much fatigued Lim[b]s." He was grateful for the $6 allowance that Lear had arranged, but it was a "Small pitance which hardly Su[f]fice[s] for our Vi[c]tuals." He noted that George C. Smith lived almost as a free man at Norderling's residence, but all Garcia could say for the rest of them was that they still had their health. Garcia begged Silsbee and Devereaux to press the government to ransom them, but said that "if we are to be the Victims for the good [of] our Country we freely lay down our Lives."

Yet two months later, Johan Norderling wrote Richard Hackley, the United States consul at Cadiz, Spain, that not only had he arranged for Smith to live with him at the Swedish consulate, but Garcia boarded with the British vice consul, one of the *Edwin*'s boys had been placed in the household of the Algerine minister of marine, and he hoped to get Pollard into the French consul's hands. As for the others, while they were still in the bagnio, he at least had arranged for the Americans to have a room for themselves, "free from vermin, filth and corruption," and had them take their meals with a tavern keeper. The Algerines knew that Norderling was aiding the Americans and allowed all the measures to keep the Americans reasonably well nourished and safe. Their reason was not humanistic, of course; as Norderling wrote, the dey "puts an immense value on them." In other words, the dey valued them because he thought he could get value for them. Precisely because the Algerines had been unable to capture more Americans, they were a scarce commodity, and the dey was not averse to allowing the Americans to support his stock in trade. Two months later, Norderling wrote that he had not been able to get James Pollard out of the bagnio, but he and two other foreign consuls had applied for his release to live with them. Norderling wrote enigmatically that while Pollard had been spared from the worst of the backbreaking labor Algiers had to offer its slaves, his "going to and coming up from the Marine with the other slaves, is still a great hardship, for a man accustomed to more ease and better company." Norderling promised to use his influence to prevent any of the captives from being ill treated. Out of pure altruism, the American merchants in Cadiz and Gibraltar privately subscribed $2,000 for the relief of the *Edwin* captives, and Norderling promised to distribute the funds with Smith's and Pollard's help, but quietly and slowly, both so that the "slave drivers" would not coerce the money from the seamen and also because seamen were notoriously profligate with money and undoubtedly would waste or fight over any windfall. But Norderling cautioned Hackley to be secretive about his letters and the money because, he warned, Algiers had "among the Jews, and other people too, its Spies everywhere," and he and the slaves would be in danger if he was known as the source of news about them. By the spring of 1814, word filtered back to America that the *Edwin* captives were allowed to write their friends, and that they were "supplied with many of the comforts and conveniences of life, through the liberality of their fellow citizens."

The War of 1812 with Britain had begun nearly two years previously, and required most of the Madison administration's attention. An early American attempt to seize Canada ended in a complete fiasco with the surrender of an American army at Detroit, but the U.S. Navy's ships won some battles against the Royal Navy, and swarms of American privateers took to the sea to harass and capture British trade. Britain's naval supremacy made it impossible for the United States to do anything in the Mediterranean; after the first six months of the war, the United States found it difficult to get even single warships through the British blockade of its own coast. But the embargo laid on before the war, and the return of hundreds of American ships from all over the world in the spring and summer of 1812, suggested to the administration that no other ships besides the *Edwin* had been captured, and thus that Algiers held less than a dozen Americans. Indeed, however calamitous the War of 1812 might prove for the United States in relation to Britain, it removed from the Mediterranean the very ships that Algiers wanted to capture to establish a powerful negotiating position with which to insist on new terms for peace. The administration in Washington therefore hoped that a comparatively small sum might ransom the Americans from Algiers. Given both the popular desire to free the captives from Barbary slavery and the lack of any military alternative, President Madison and Secretary of State Monroe decided that it was best to swallow their distaste for paying any more in bribes and make a quiet effort to pay off Algiers and get the Americans back. The man the Madison administration chose to make the quiet overture to Algiers was an unlikely envoy without diplomatic experience named Mordecai Manuel Noah.

Mordecai Noah was born in Philadelphia in 1785. Noah's father, Manuel, an immigrant from Mannheim, Germany, was declared a bankrupt that same year (with all the moral opprobrium and shame then associated with bankruptcy) and deserted his family six years later, ultimately to return to Europe. Noah's mother, born Zipporah Phillips, was made of sterner stuff. She was the daughter of a prominent Jewish family in Manhattan, whose father served as the lay cantor, or *hassan*, at Shearith Israel Congregation, the oldest synagogue in New York. Mordecai Noah had an itinerant grammar school education in Charleston, New York, and Philadelphia. His early adult years are obscure; he peddled goods in the northern reaches of New York State and into Canada. But somehow he remade himself into a newspaperman able to turn a memorable line, a vigorous pamphleteer for Jefferson's Republican party, and a playwright. In 1808, while in his early twenties, Noah campaigned for Simon Snyder, a Republican and the first self-made man elected governor of Pennsylvania, who rewarded Noah with the position of major in the state militia, thereby entitling Noah to use a military title, although he had no experience with military matters. The next year, 1809, his first play, *The Fortress of Sorrento*, was published, although in the opinion of his modern biographer, Jonathan Sarna, it was a "thin melodrama" that never made it to the New York stage; the same year, Noah wrote *Shakspeare* [*sic*] *Illustrated*, an attempt to prove that the Bard of Avon was a plagiarist, or at least overrated.

By 1810, Noah had settled on attaining a diplomatic appointment from the administration in Washington as a method of gaining wealth, developing connections that would help him later, and seeing the world. He saw himself as a man on the rise as well as a representative of American Jews. Noah began courting the support of possible influential patrons, and he duly received backing from prominent Jews scattered around the country and from men of letters such as Joel Barlow, who had served as consul in Algiers. Although other Jews had held diplomatic positions before—President Jefferson had appointed Solomon Nones the United States consul general to Portugal—Noah openly and aggressively relied on his Jewish identity to gain personal advantage. He reminded then Secretary of State Robert Smith that American Jews, who overwhelmingly supported the Republicans, would appreciate and reward any favors bestowed upon him, their self-appointed representative. He saw in his own future appointment to a position of trust and responsibility a statement by the United States of the nature of the new republic. He wrote Smith that if he was made consul, the appointment would "prove to foreign Powers that our Government is not regulated in the appointment of their officers by religious distinction" and, more dubiously, that the appointment would be a signal to "the Hebrew Nation to em[m]igrate to this country with their capitals." Whether Smith wanted to have more of the "Hebrew Nation" immigrating to the United States, with or without their capital, is unclear.

In June 1811, President Madison appointed Noah as United States consul in Riga, and the Senate promptly confirmed his appointment. Although Noah accepted the post, he never reported there or even tried to get to the Baltic. Instead, he journeyed to Charleston, where he wrote satirical articles for local newspapers, fought a duel over his biting political writing (he withstood his antagonist's fire and then wounded his opponent in turn, thereby establishing that he was a gentleman by Charleston standards), and wrote a successful play, *Paul and Alexis, or the Orphans of the Rhone*. But what he wanted was to be United States consul to a Barbary state so as to develop connections and to gain wealth by private commercial dealings, and by letter dated November 27, 1811, he requested that he be "transferred" there. His persistence paid off. President Madison agreed to meet with him at the White House, where Noah pleaded his cause, and in March 1813, his appointment as consul to Tunis was published. But before he was to assume that post, the government gave him the clandestine job as unofficial agent of the United States in releasing the captives held in Algiers.

Few Jews lived in America in the early 1800s, perhaps four thousand or so, largely in Charleston, Philadelphia, and New York. Although a number of Jews served in the Continental Army during the Revolution, most Americans had little contact with any living Jews and knew them only from the Bible and by reputation from medieval Europe. To leading political figures, when they thought and wrote about the Jews, they saw them more as artifacts, a tribe of ancient Israel, than actual contemporaries. George Washington, in responding to a congratulatory address from Touro Synagogue in Newport, Rhode Island, in 1791, provided the classic American formula for religious toleration, that the government "gives to bigotry no sanction, to persecution no assistance." Less known is Washington's final, more quaint paragraph, in which he expressed the hope that the "children of the Stock of Abraham" would be accepted by other Americans "so that every one shall sit in safety under his own vine and fig tree, and there shall be none to make him afraid." The sentiments are liberal, the imagery purely biblical. John Adams, who would have known few Jews in Boston before the Revolution because there were only a handful, met and respected Dutch Jews he met as the American minister in Amsterdam seeking financial help for the desperate, rebelling colonies. In 1809, as an ex-president, Adams mused that the "Hebrews have done more to civilize men than any other nation." The Jews, Adams recognized, had introduced and nurtured "the doctrine of a supreme, intelligent, wise, almighty sovereign of the universe, which I believe to be the great essential principle of all morality, and consequently of all civilization." James Madison, who knew no Jews in the Piedmont of Virginia, met several Jews in Philadelphia in the 1780s when, living beyond his means, he borrowed money from Chaim Salomon, whom he termed "the little Jew" or the "Jew broker," and who surprised Madison by refusing to accept any interest for the loans that he had made.

Madison's personal financial dealings with Salomon hinted at the larger issue. All of the leaders of the early republic understood that freedom of religion meant toleration of the Jews, and publicly expressed support for their civil liberties. But from the Middle Ages had come a conception of the Jews as strange and exotic and physically repellent, overlaid with imagery of the Jew as moneylender, complete with tricks, sharp practices, and greed—the Shylock figure. Yet Madison and Monroe knew that the leading Jewish brokers of Algiers, the Baccri family, had been instrumental in ransoming the American captives of Algiers in 1796, when they advanced the astronomical sum of $200,000 in hard currency and personally guaranteed the balance of the United States's payment to Algiers, a remarkable statement in support of the United States at a time when no one in Algiers had seen a penny of the promised American money. Madison and Monroe also knew that Jewish brokers and merchants throughout the Mediterranean provided critical contacts with Europe for the Barbary regencies. In short, Madison and Monroe knew, as Joel Barlow, the poet and writer who served as consul to Algiers in the late 1790s remarked, that the Jews were the most influential group in Algiers.

President Madison did not know Mordecai Noah when he presented himself for a Barbary consul post, young and untested, but Noah was a Jew. Most of the Americans whom Madison and his predecessors had named to foreign posts were enterprising, self-reliant men, some who had prospered as merchants overseas, others who had careers as soldiers or merchant shipmasters, men who were used to the stresses of command and foreign ways. Noah might call himself "Major," but that was farcical. He fit the contemporary stereotype of a Jew, with a thin face, unruly wiry hair, a hawkish, large nose, and sideburns. The only basis to think that a twenty-seven-year-old, self-promoting journalist, playwright, and political

activist such as Noah, a man devoid of any diplomatic experience, was suitable for the sensitive and byzantine task of ransoming American Christian slaves being held by Algiers was that he was Jewish. Indeed, Noah appealed precisely on that point, noting in his 1811 letter that as U.S. consul

Mordecai Noah, the Madison administration's behind-the-scenes agent to ransom the American slaves in Algiers. Aquatint by Gimbrede from a portrait by J. R. Smith. Frontispiece to Noah's *Travels in England, France, Spain, and the Barbary States* (1819), author's collection.

to a Barbary state, he would be backed by the "wealth and influence of forty thousand residents"—in other words, his fellow Jews living under Barbary rule. Whether a man as insightful and intelligent as James Madison believed any of Noah's posturing is hard to determine. Nevertheless, appointing Jews as intermediaries to Muslim countries had a long history in Europe, and began in the United States with President Washington's appointment of Colonel David Franks to negotiate a treaty with Morocco in 1795. Noah was not the first American Jew to be used as an interlocutor with the Islamic world, and presidents would continue to appoint American Jews to the Ottoman Empire well into the twentieth century, when Woodrow Wilson appointed Henry Morgenthau to Turkey. The idea of sending an American agent to ransom the captives "unofficially" called for private communications with chosen messengers, what today would be called "back channels," the very type of thing at which Jews, with their web of influence and contacts, were supposed to be adept.

Secretary of State Monroe's diplomatic instructions to Noah read as follows:

> On your way to Tunis, perhaps at Malaga, or Marseilles, you may probably devise means for the liberation of our unfortunate countrymen at Algiers, whose situation has excited the warmest sympathy of their friends, and indeed of the people generally of this country. Should you find a suitable channel, through which you can negotiate their immediate release, you are authorised to go as far as three thousand dollars a man; but a less sum may probably effect the object. Whatever may be the result of the attempt, you will, for obvious reasons, not let it be understood to proceed from this government, but rather from the friends of the parties themselves.

Being on his way to Tunis was much easier said than done in the midst of war with Britain, whose fleet blockaded both the coast of the United States and Napoleonic Europe as well. On May 28, 1813, Noah sailed from Charleston aboard the schooner *Joel Barlow*, a vessel coincidentally named for one of his sponsors, bound for Bordeaux. Thirty-five days out, close to the coast of France, a British frigate called the *Briton* stopped and captured the *Joel Barlow*. Although the British officers treated Noah courteously, he was not allowed to proceed on his mission. Instead, he was transferred to a battleship that sailed to England, where Noah arrived as a penniless diplomat from a country at war with his host. Noah spent nine weeks touring Britain, enjoying himself immensely. Finally, the British provided him with a passport, and in October 1813, he arrived at the Spanish port of Cadiz, just west of Gibraltar.

Monroe's instructions had left Noah great discretion as to how he might accomplish the mission of ransoming the American captives. The stated parameters were that there was to be no official involvement of or reference to the United States government as the source of the funds, and that there was a per capita limit on how much the government was willing to pay in the unseemly business of buying off the professional kidnappers of its citizens. Unstated, but a vital reason for Madison's choice of Noah, was the expectation that he might insinuate himself into a Jewish mercantile community in some Mediterranean port and then use unofficial, Jewish connections across the Mediterranean to quietly liberate the American captives. The whole operation was meant to be quiet, almost clandestine. Backroom efforts, however, were not Noah's style.

In early October 1813, Noah presented himself to the United States consul at Cadiz, Richard Hackley, the man who had been in contact with Johan Norderling in Algiers after Lear had sailed home to America the previous December. After identifying himself and his putatively secret mission, Noah asked Hackley for his ideas, or to recommend a suitable agent to send directly into Algiers. Hackley replied the next day, convinced, as he put it, that the release of the Americans held in bondage "will be attended with much difficulty, if effected at all; yet, under the instructions you bear from our government, I am of opinion that the attempt should be made." In lieu of a personal effort by Noah, Hackley suggested a merchant named Richard R. Keene. Noah had already met Keene in Cadiz and was impressed by his intelligence and the respect with which he was treated by the resident American merchants. Keene was a colorful and shady character, always involved in mysterious doings. He had married Eleonora Martin, the daughter of Luther Martin, the brilliant but unstable Federalist lawyer who was anathema to the Republicans, after reputedly seducing her while reading law under her father's tutelage. Keene, too, was a Federalist, rumored to be complicit in the Aaron Burr conspiracy and in smuggling goods through the embargo that the Jefferson administration had laid on U.S. shipping in December 1807. Keene also had tried to establish an Irish Catholic colony in Mexico, an innately suspicious project to the Madison administration, and to that end Keene had written to the king of Spain and ultimately renounced his American citizenship. Noah, without actually inquiring as to why Keene had turned Spaniard, presumed that he "intended to cover some commercial views." Hackley thought that Keene's Spanish citizenship and mercantile interests would act as a cover that no American would have in

Algiers, and would guarantee his personal safety; had an American such as Noah traveled to Algiers personally, even (or especially) in a private capacity, there was a real risk that the dey would throw him into slavery. In Washington, however, Keene was thought to be an out-and-out political enemy, and probably a traitor. In short, he may have seemed to be a man of parts to a young naif such as Mordecai Noah, but he was certainly not the man that the Madison administration would want in any role, much less running such a delicate mission. Yet within a few days of his acquaintance, Keene offered his services to Noah, and Noah, ignorant of the personal baggage his new friend carried, signed Keene up to be his go-between with the dey of Algiers.

In November 1813, Noah drew up a formal agreement with "Don Ricardo R. Keene." It provided that Keene would receive $1,000 in advance for his costs and expenses, which promised to be significant because he first had to seek passage to Algiers, sustain himself there, and if he was able to speak to the people who might influence the dey, or perhaps the dey himself, he would have to provide the substantial gifts that seemed to be the coin of the regency's realm. But Keene would receive nothing further if he was unable to ransom any of the seamen, and Noah forbade him from paying more than the stipulated $3,000 per man. On the other hand, if Keene was successful in freeing the *Edwin* captives, then Noah (acting for the United States) promised to reward him with $3,000 and any of the unspent ransom money that Noah figured the United States had at least informally allotted to the effort.

Keene was well connected and energetic. He scurried around Cadiz seeking the help of other governments. Despite the Anglo-American war then raging, the humanitarian problem of Barbary slavery was so compelling, and the distaste for Algiers was so overwhelming, that Sir Henry Wellesley, the British ambassador to Spain and the brother of Lord Wellington, wrote a letter to the British consul at Algiers, Hugh MacDonald (who had replaced Henry Blanckley in April 1812), which he handed to Keene for personal delivery. At least with Wellesley, the fiction was maintained that Keene was traveling at "the solicitation of the American merchants residing at Cadiz." Wellesley, "solely dictated by motives of humanity," asked MacDonald to afford Keene any assistance he might require. A Spanish government minister provided a note for Keene to deliver to Don Pedro Ortiz de Zugarte, the Spanish consul general in Algiers, asking Ortiz to "make all possible exertions" in helping Keene obtain the liberation of the twelve Americans.

Noah and Keene traveled from Cadiz to the British colony of Gibraltar via Tangiers in a British transport. Passage to Algiers could be had only from Gibraltar, and Noah found that the disturbed state of Spanish affairs made it impossible for him to establish credit in Cadiz for his bills of exchange for the release of the American seamen. The Jews of Gibraltar warmly received Noah, who prayed at the local synagogue and revealed to them that he was the accredited representative of the United States to Tunis, and a major in the Pennsylvania militia to boot. The most prominent Gibraltarian Jew, a merchant named Aaron Cardoza, to whom Noah disclosed his confidential mission of ransoming the captives in Algiers, told Noah to approach the dey through the Baccri family. Cardoza had business, personal, and religious ties to the Baccris, and wrote Noah a special letter of introduction to them. Here was a glimmer of the very thing that Madison and Monroe had hoped for. Cardoza's letter might have been a powerful instrument for Noah, the young representative of the young republic, but also a Jew, had he gone to Algiers, asking for help from the powerful Baccris. But Noah handed it to Keene, who sailed off to Algiers, out of Noah's control, an agent of an agent for the United States.

Noah dispatched "Don Raynal" with his set of instructions dated January 14, 1814. Noah directed Keene to proceed to Algiers without delay to negotiate for the release of the Americans in slavery, the eleven from the *Edwin*, Pollard, and any others—though Noah had no reason to believe that there were any others, since Pollard had been taken off the Spanish ship. Noah carried over Monroe's injunction, ordering Keene to "carefully abstain from letting it appear that the United States are acquainted with your object, or authorise your proceedings. On the contrary, let it be distinctly understood, that the relief proposed, proceeds direct from the friends of the parties." Noah provided that Keene could draw bills of exchange on Horatio Sprague, an American merchant at Gibraltar, to ransom the Americans, but advised Keene to beware of usurious rates of interest that Algerine moneylenders might charge. Noting the "warm sympathy" Americans felt for the plight of the captives, and the "anxious desire" of the United States government to obtain their release, Noah reinforced the need for Keene to display both perseverance and circumspection to ensure success.

Keene arrived in Algiers in February 1814. It was immediately apparent that word of the "confidential" mission was everywhere. Noah need not have told anyone the true nature of his mission or his official status. He might have posed as a "friend" of George Campbell Smith or James

Pollard, or even the merchant partner of one of the owners of the *Edwin*; no one would have questioned too closely where the money came from or the source of his authority. Noah had been entirely too free with sharing his confidences, having rather blithely mentioned his delicate mission to Hackley, Keene, Sprague, Cardoza, and who knows who else. Noah must have not heard of the adage of Benjamin Franklin, a former diplomat himself, that "three people can keep a secret if two of them are dead." The dey of Algiers himself seemed to have heard about Keene as an American ransom agent despite his Spanish mercantile "cover." No sooner had Keene landed at Algiers, purporting to be the bearer of dispatches to Don Pedro Ortiz de Zugarte, the Spanish consul, and been transported to his residence, than Ortiz informed him that the dey already had demanded to know the "precise and specific objects" of Keene's visit. The idea that American merchants resident in Cadiz might lead a consortium on behalf of the family and friends of the captives seeking their release was certainly plausible—they had shown their generosity already, by providing $2,000 for the relief of the captives—and echoed the way that wealthy European families had sought the private release of slaves in Barbary captivity with their personal funds. This was the legend that Keene and Ortiz agreed to communicate, with the fillip that the Spanish regent had allowed his good offices to be used. But that myth was punctured even before Keene landed, and as the Algiers government suspected the involvement of the American government, negotiations took on an entirely different cast, and the price for release surely skyrocketed.

Through his minions, the dey delivered a brief message to Ortiz and Keene: "Tell the consul, and the agent of his government, and of the American merchants in Cadiz, that my policy and my views are to increase, not to diminish the number of my American slaves; and that not for a million dollars would I release them." Keene approached the Swedish consul, Norderling, for help. Norderling, chagrined that he had not been informed of Noah's mission or consulted as to how to accomplish the ransoming, had an audience with the dey. He raised the issue of the going price for the Americans, but the dey's answer was that "not for two millions of dollars would he sell his American slaves."

Keene was about to return to Cadiz in defeat when circumstances unexpectedly changed. A seaman from Baltimore named Charles Walker, impressed by the Royal Navy in Lisbon from an American vessel, deserted from the British frigate *Curacao* while at the Algerine port of Bona, and arrived at Algiers. He had "turned Turk," converting to Islam as soon as he made it ashore, and sought sanctuary in a mosque, knowing that Algerine sensibilities would shrink from turning over to the Royal Navy a follower of the true faith. The dey allowed Walker to flee into the hinterland, despite British fulminations. The moral opprobrium to Barbary slavery figured so large for Hugh MacDonald, the British consul, that he promised Keene that he would use his best efforts to deliver Walker over to Keene, an American, war or no war, Muslim or no Muslim. But MacDonald could not pry him from the dey. MacDonald then threatened the dey that he would advise the British captain to impress two Algerines into the Royal Navy. The dey feared the power of the British navy but was adamant in not relinquishing Walker. MacDonald changed his demand to two of the Christian Americans as compensation for the loss of Walker. The dey agreed and released into the British consul's hands two of the *Edwin* seamen, eighteen-year-old William Turner, a native of Salem, and John Clark of New York, described by Noah as "a bungling carpenter." The dey ritually referred to them as "Englishmen," and although he turned them over to MacDonald, the British consul, the dey pressured MacDonald for money for them, which he only would have done from the Americans. When MacDonald paid $6,000, Keene promptly signed bills of exchange for $6,000 from the credit Noah allotted him.

Making the situation still odder, four French-speaking sailors off the British frigate *Franchise* arrived in Algiers claiming to be native Louisianans (and therefore American). MacDonald, realizing that they were sure to be severely punished, probably hanged for desertion, if he returned them to the Royal Navy, and that they would likely be consigned to the bagnio as slaves if he turned them over to Algiers, offered them to Keene. Keene realized that MacDonald would not have done so if he were not convinced that they were Americans. As Noah later pointed out, the four sailors did not speak much English, but they had been impressed from an American ship, called themselves American, and when they came to Algiers did not seek protection from the French consul, although France was then at peace with Algiers. Although this situation was unexpected, Keene decided to stretch his instructions to cover them, reasoning that "[t]o rescue from actual slavery, and to snatch from impending slavery, . . . admit only of a distinction, without the slightest essential difference." He wrote out additional bills of exchange in the amount of $6,000 for the four Louisianans. The four men were kept in close confinement until Keene was ready to return to Gibraltar aboard a small Spanish vessel, *La Fortuna*, which Keene had chartered to convey the freed captives.

Despite numerous efforts to begin a negotiation about the remaining captives, the Algerines showed no interest in talking to the American agent. Keene had Cardoza's letter of introduction to the Baccris and called on Jacob Baccri, the head of the family. Keene found him polite and helpful. Baccri indicated that the dey wanted to conclude a new treaty with the United States and that he "set the highest value upon the American citizens then in his power." For the privilege of passing the Straits of Gibraltar, Baccri told Keene, the dey would insist on a flat fee of $2 million, as well as everything in arrears under the 1796 treaty, information that Keene accepted as being from someone in the know without a motive to deceive. Keene suggested that the terms were more onerous to the United States than any other nation paying protection, and Baccri agreed, but launched into a long statement of what the dey had told him:

> [T]he United States are considered by this cabinet to be rich, and always disposed to adopt that alternative which is the least costly. Their captive citizens here, they must release; and, above all, they must establish a security against further captivity, and against the spoliation of their commerce, in the Mediterranean and the neighbouring seas. Now, the treaty which is indispensable to secure to them these important objects, must either be purchased, or extorted, by means of a naval armament. The question then arises, under the known policy of the American government, which of these two expedients, purchase, or naval equipments, will cost the least money, or be of the cheapest attainment? The American navy, only about equal now to that of the Dey, will undoubtedly be annihilated by the English, in the present war; so, that being without any naval force at all, on the return of peace with England, on which return only, they would be in a situation to attack Algiers, they would have to incur expenses in preparing an adequate force to make that attack, to an amount much greater than that of the Dey's requisitions. Consequently, then, as he makes those requisitions the *cheaper* alternative, he conceives that there will be no difficulty in their being submitted to.

In a nutshell, that was an insightful analysis of the Americans' strategic problem. The dey in one swoop of logic showed an understanding of power and risk. The Americans were far away, and temporarily preoccupied by Britain. Expecting the United States Navy to have been destroyed in the Anglo-American war, and yet knowing how critical Mediterranean trade would be to the young republic emerging from such a war, the dey recognized that, from the Americans' perspective, the cheaper and quicker alternative was to pay more in tribute, not to rebuild a shattered navy with a depleted treasury. The United States was a nation that often made strategic choices based on a balance of cost compared to benefit, and the dey of Algiers knew it.

In such circumstances, Keene clearly could not make headway about releasing the other Americans from the *Edwin:* the dey needed them as bait to make the United States negotiate with him a new treaty with higher tribute. Keene reported that, because of the intervention of Johan Norderling, the dey had exempted Pollard, Smith, and Garcia from all physical labor, and they were treated as prisoners on parole, able to walk around the city unattended and draw upon funds subscribed by the American merchants at Cadiz to provide ample food and drink, and even for amusements. The residue of the crew were "continually subject to rigorous labour, and to the coarsest and most scanty rations," but contributions from the American merchants sufficed to supply them with enough food and clothing. Keene embarked on *La Fortuna* with the six men he had ransomed, well satisfied with what he had been able to accomplish, and returned to Gibraltar.

Keene wrote a long report to Noah dated May 22, 1814, and arrived at Cadiz a few days later. Noah was relieved to hear from Keene after four long months without word. Noah thought that Keene, who had devoted himself to the "secret" mission for six months of his life, had done well at great personal risk. The total costs of Keene's mission, including Keene's compensation for ransoming the Americans, came to $15,852. Noah arranged to ship the six men home to America, and passed through Keene's payment and his own costs and expenses in Spain in a bill to the United States government totaling $25,910. Not only did he think the amount reasonable, but he was also aware that Lear, the U.S. consul kicked out of Algiers in July 1812, had disbursed a half million dollars over five years for presents and tribute without complaint from Washington.

Noah thought that, under the circumstances, his mission had succeeded. When the Madison administration learned what had happened, months later, the cabinet was aghast and unforgiving. Secretary of State Monroe and Attorney General Richard Rush were stunned that Noah had not embarked on the negotiations personally, an effort that was supposed to be private, quiet, and relying on Jewish contacts. No one in Washington had said anything about an agent, and Monroe could not imagine employing Keene under any circumstances, much less how Noah could have guaranteed him money, success or failure. Instead of backroom, indirect diplomacy, Noah had all but blown a bugle announcing the involvement of the United States. Rush observed that "[s]ecrets are prone to escape through much smaller openings" than requesting support from the European ambassadors; he was certain that the dey knew all about Keene and his mission long before he landed in Algiers. The Madison administration questioned Noah's judgment and believed their future consul to Tunis was not to be trusted in a sensitive diplomatic post. The government decided not to honor the bills of exchange Noah drafted on the ground that Noah had not acted in conformity with his instructions.

All this would play out in the future. In the meantime, Clark and Turner, the two freed men of the *Edwin* crew, and the four Louisianans made their way home; the others from the *Edwin* and Pollard remained behind in captivity in Algiers. The effort to ransom them with bribe money had been a humanitarian effort during war with Britain that prevented any stronger effort but, ironically, had succeeded only because of British diplomatic help. Perhaps unavoidably, it had been amateurishly conceived and executed, but through luck, it had succeeded in part.

Having attempted ransom, however distasteful it was to American leaders, and having found it largely unsuccessful, the United States government had only one other way to free the captives, and that was force.

Chapter Two

At War with Algiers

As 1814 TURNED INTO 1815, a new secretary of the navy was en route to Washington. Benjamin W. Crowninshield, age forty-two, came from a wealthy and famous shipowning family in Salem, Massachusetts. Lantern-jawed, with short, wavy hair and the newly fashionable sideburns framing a high forehead, Crowninshield gave an appearance of stolidity and calm. In an era when an unwritten requirement for secretaries of the navy was personal experience with shipping, as a merchant, ship captain, or admiralty lawyer, Benjamin Crowninshield had the credentials for the post. He had gone to sea as a cabin boy and rose to master of Salem ships to the East Indies by the time he turned twenty. Along with four of his brothers, Benjamin came ashore to work with his father as a merchant in the family countinghouse, Geo. Crowninshield & Sons. The Crowninshield firm owned wharves and a fleet of merchant ships. By 1809, when the father and sons split the business into three, Geo. Crowninshield & Sons owned a dozen oceangoing ships rated between 250 and 500 tons, and were the leading American merchants in the pepper trade with the East Indies. Benjamin Crowninshield is said to have been the "solid brains of the firm." Unlike most wealthy families in New England, the Crowninshields were strong and vocal supporters of Jefferson and the nascent Republican party, including the embargo policy on American overseas trade, established in December 1807, even though it ultimately ruined the family firm.

Benjamin Crowninshield's older brother, Jacob Crowninshield, who was elected to Congress in 1802, played a leading role as a New England defender of the Jefferson administration. In 1805, Jefferson nominated him to be secretary of the navy, but Jacob never wanted or accepted the post, retaining his seat in the House even though the Senate confirmed him. When Jacob died in 1808 at age thirty-eight, Benjamin Crowninshield slowly assumed his brother's role in public life. In 1811, he became president of the Merchants Bank of Salem, formed in opposition to the Federalist monopoly of capital, and in 1811 and 1812, Salem voters elected Benjamin Crowninshield first to the Massachusetts state house and then to the state senate. During the War of 1812, the Crowninshields converted their merchant ships into privateers and renewed their fortunes in the prize game: one of the dozens of privateers in which they had an interest or owned outright, their ship *America*, took twenty-six prizes on four cruises during the war, reputedly yielding $1 million in sales.

The outgoing secretary of the navy, William Jones of Philadelphia, had performed capably since coming into the administration in 1813, but the never-ending demands of running the wartime navy—and, temporarily, the Treasury, when George Washington Campbell fell ill—had worn him out and threatened to cast him into the poorhouse. Jones informed President Madison that he had to resign. Madison first approached Commodore John Rodgers to replace Jones, a tribute to Rodgers's administrative abilities and judgment about ships and strategy, but Rodgers did not wish to resign his commission, and Attorney General Rush advised the president that a serving officer could not sit in the cabinet. Madison then decided on Crowninshield, presumably as much because he was a New Englander for a cabinet then without anyone from the area as because of his understanding about ships and the men who sailed them. On December 15, 1814, Madison wrote Crowninshield in Salem that he had chosen him as a "desirable Successor" to Jones and that his name had already been submitted to the Senate. Rather fantastically, as with Jefferson's nomination of Jacob Crowninshield ten years before, Madison had not sounded out Crowninshield in advance. He hoped, nevertheless, that it would not be "inconsistent" with Crowninshield's "views" to accept the post, and asked Crowninshield to come to Washington as soon as the Senate confirmed him.

Overwhelmed at receiving such a letter from the president, modest about his talents, and reluctant to leave five young children at home with his wife, who was expecting their sixth child, Crowninshield first hesitated, then declined the job, and finally wrote Madison on December 28, 1814, that he accepted. Given the difficulties of winter travel over land in the early nineteenth century, Benjamin W. Crowninshield assumed office as secretary of the navy only on January 16, 1815, just as the War of 1812 was coming to a close.

Crowninshield was unassuming, friendly toward the naval officers who immediately surrounded him, and a little awed by his sudden ascendancy. His wife, Mary Boardman Crowninshield, unpretentious and saucy, wanted to know what the women in Washington wore (he obliged with the details) and was wide-eyed at the Madisons' invitation to Crowninshield to visit them at Montpelier (he declined the invitation). Crowninshield understood that a man with his family name, status, and wealth had an obligation to serve, but he enjoyed the friendships he made in Washington more than shaking hands with his innumerable visitors seeking patronage. Crowninshield remained devoted to his family, especially to his wife. Coincidentally, Crowninshield's sister had married Nathaniel Silsbee, the wealthy Salem merchant who owned the *Edwin*, which meant that the incoming secretary of the navy probably had as good an understanding of what had happened to the *Edwin* and her crew as anyone in Washington.

Benjamin W. Crowninshield, secretary of the navy. Crowninshield chose Decatur to command the lead naval squadron to the Mediterranean. Portrait by U. D. Tenney. From the Naval Historical Center, Washington, D.C.

ON FEBRUARY 22, 1815, Stephen Decatur, a commodore in the United States Navy, arrived at New London, Connecticut, a passenger aboard the British frigate *Narcissus*. Decatur was in pain, battered by a severe bruising on his chest, perhaps broken ribs, that he had received from a huge wooden splinter that had cast him a glancing blow a month before, when he had surrendered his ship, the 52-gun frigate *President*, after a fierce battle with the British blockading squadron off New York. But he was more sorely tried by concerns about his honor. Newspaper accounts preceding him from Bermuda, where he and his captured crew had been taken, suggested that he had surrendered to a single British warship after a less than stout defense. Decatur carried with him from Bermuda his own report to the secretary of the navy, and he knew the press reports were false, but he was worried that he had lost his luster with the American public, which had embraced him as their hero since he had burst on the national scene in 1804.

He had become a hero as a mere lieutenant when he led the expedition that burned the captured frigate *Philadelphia* on the night of February 16, 1804, in the harbor of Tripoli, under the massed guns of the fortresses protecting the port, without losing a man. The hapless *Philadelphia*, a ship once commanded by his own father and built by public subscription in his hometown, had been run on the rocks outside of Tripoli by Captain William Bainbridge. When word of Decatur's exploit in burning the ship reached Washington, President Jefferson promoted the twenty-five-year-old to captain, the highest rank in the navy, effective from the date of her destruction. Several months later, Decatur led small boat attacks against Tripolitan gunboats, engaging in fierce hand-to-hand combat in which his brother, James, was killed, and his own life was saved by a sailor, Reuben James, who deliberately took a saber slashing meant to kill his commander. These exploits off North Africa made Decatur a household name, and inspired ballads and poems written in his honor.

Earlier in the War of 1812, in October 1812, he had commanded the frigate *United States* when she dueled the English frigate *Macedonian* at long range in a heavy swell off the Azores and battered down her masts, leading the British warship to surrender. Under a prize crew, the *Macedonian* was able to sail back to America, where she was bought into the U.S. Navy, giving Decatur a tidy fortune in prize money. But the rest of the war had been frustrating for him, blockaded with his squadron in New London, Connecticut, by a powerful Royal Navy squadron under the command of Nelson's former flag captain, Sir Thomas Hardy, the man who had kissed the dying Nelson at Trafalgar in October 1805. The British controlled Long Island Sound and the approaches to New York. Toward the end of 1814, the navy sent him to New York to supervise the defenses of the city against an expected assault, and then to command the most powerful ship in the U.S. Navy, the *President*.

Decatur had tried to break through the British navy blockade, taking advantage of a northwesterly winter storm in January 1815 that had blown the blockading ships out to who knew where. Uncharacteristically, he had been victimized by repeated bad luck. The *President* had run aground on a sandbar off Sandy Hook, incorrectly marked by three navy gunboats, with the result that the ship thumped heavily on the bar for almost two hours, twisting and hogging her keel, and ruining her vaunted speed. Decatur set his course not south, the direct path to the open Atlantic, but east by north, to sail close by the Long Island shore to bypass where he expected the British to be, but he had unwittingly sailed right into the British squadron. At 6:00 a.m. on January 15, 1815, the *President* was spotted. The rest of the day was one long stern chase, dispiriting because the *President*'s sailing had been slowed by the damage to her keel. Decatur tried valiantly to get away. He ordered the watch aloft to wet the sails to better catch the breeze; pumps brought frigid North Atlantic winter salt water all the way up 120 feet to the royals, the highest sails on the masts, which the topmen tossed by the bucket on the sails. Decatur ordered his lieutenants to lighten the ship. The crew cut away anchors and tossed over the side the ship's boats, spare spars, cannonballs, and barrels of food; they also pumped overboard tons of drinking water. But the pursuing British ships narrowed the gap. By 1:00 p.m., one of the pursuers, the 40-gun *Endymion*, had closed enough to try the range with her bow guns, and by five o'clock, she had, in Decatur's words, "obtained a position on our starboard quarter, within half point blank shot on which neither our stern nor quarter guns could bear." The *Endymion* began to rake the *President*, and the situation grew intolerable; exposed to the full force of enemy fire, Decatur's officers and sailors on the spardeck began to be struck down, and the rigging and sails became riddled. Decatur attempted to board the *Endymion*, thinking that he would take her over and then blow up the *President*, a fantastic idea, but pure Decatur in boldness and reminiscent of John Paul Jones's swapping of his own sinking *Bon Homme Richard* for the *Serapis* in the Revolutionary War. But he could not get close enough.

The ships came abreast, however, and the *President* finally went one-on-one with the *Endymion*. A dozen American salvoes shattered the *Endymion*. The British frigate ceased firing and rapidly dropped astern, her masts and rigging crippled temporarily. Decatur could not linger. The other British ships were almost within gunshot. The *President* struggled along until 11:00 p.m., when another British frigate opened fire off the *President*'s port bow, and another was only two cable lengths (1,200 feet) astern. Decatur reported that, with one-fifth of his crew down, "my ship crippled, and more than a four-fold force opposed to me, without a chance of escape left, I deemed it my duty to surrender." Decatur offered his sword to the commander of the British squadron. Three of his lieutenants had been killed in action, and overall, twenty-four men had been killed and another fifty-five wounded, including Decatur himself. The British admiral politely declined to accept Decatur's proffered sword, and he and his crew were conveyed to Bermuda as prisoners of war. They were treated well and soon learned that the War of 1812 had ended with the treaty signed at Ghent on Christmas Eve, six weeks before. But there were the newspaper accounts in Bermuda that brazenly stated that the *President* had surrendered after a ship-to-ship action, and suggested that he had not done his utmost to defend his ship. Decatur was stung by such criticisms and wondered how much credence the Madison administration and the people of the United States would give to these stories. He knew that as a commander who had surrendered his ship, a court of inquiry would convene upon his return to examine his conduct. On February 8, Decatur took passage on the *Narcissus* to return to America.

As Decatur landed on a wharf from a boat from the British ship, a crowd of New Londoners greeted him. They did not taunt or jostle him. They lifted Decatur into a carriage and, with a mass of younger men grabbing the harness straps, began to pull the carriage into town. Up and down the streets they went, and by the hundreds the people of New London came out of their houses and shops and cheered him with thunderous clapping, hats flying, handkerchiefs waving, and cries of "Huzza!" The men pulling his carriage stopped at Brown's Hotel, where Decatur attempted to address the multitude, but whether the "acclamations were so loud and incessant, that he could not be heard" or whether he was so moved that he

could not speak, the commodore fell silent. Some saw tears in his eyes. Somehow, the showing of his fallibility, with the loss of his ship and his own wounding, had made him even more of a hero to a broad swath of the American people. That night, Decatur, with other American naval and army officers, as well as more than forty British naval officers

Stephen Decatur, the "pride and boast of our infant navy," who returned to the Mediterranean in 1815 in command of a ten-ship squadron. Engraving by A. B. Durant from James Herring's copy of a portrait by Thomas Sully. From the Naval Historical Center, Washington, D.C.

who had lately served in the blockading squadron in New York Bay and the Long Island Sound, watched fireworks together and attended an elegant ball, given to celebrate the peace and the birthday of George Washington, one of the new republic's holidays. Four days later, on February 26, Decatur arrived at New York, where he convalesced at a boardinghouse off the Battery frequented by naval officers.

An account written immediately after Decatur's return from Bermuda "unhestitatingly pronounce[d]" him the "pride and boast of our infant navy." Decatur was a handsome man, only thirty-six years old in 1815, with a high forehead, a rounded face with a longish, aquiline nose, and the Romantic-era style of a deliberately unruly mop of light brown hair. He was rather quiet in company, and disinclined to letter writing except for official purposes. He professed that he was conscious of the deficiencies in his education, in that he was no student and had left grammar school in Philadelphia (the Academy of the University of Pennsylvania) as a teenager. But Decatur was intelligent and committed to his profession, one of the few naval officers not to take leave to sail a merchant ship during the low point of the navy in the years after the 1807 *Chesapeake-Leopard* incident in which a British warship stopped an American frigate on the high seas, demanded the return of British subjects said to be aboard, and, when refused, fired into the unprepared U.S. ship, killing three and wounding eighteen to impress four allegedly British seamen into the Royal Navy. Contemporaries were always struck by Decatur's deportment, described by an early writer as "manly and unassuming," and by his engaging and unaffected manner.

Although the social gap between officers and men aboard warships in that day was enormous, Decatur treated the men aboard his ships with respect, confiding his plans to them and even once reportedly referring to them as "comrades." He rarely ordered the cat-o'-nine-tails to whip a disrespectful or disobeying sailor. His preferred disciplinary remedy was to cut a miscreant's daily allowance of whiskey. He achieved a unique status among his sailors, many of whom followed him around from ship to ship, as well as with younger officers, to whom his style and courage were inspirational. But there was something enigmatic about Decatur, too. While a proud man, and fond of wearing the ribbon of the Order of the Cincinnati when he donned his formal navy blue uniform with gold lace and cocked hat, he often came on deck in plain clothes and an old hat.

ON FEBRUARY 15, 1815, President Madison was resident at Octagon House in Washington because the President's House, already popularly called the "White House," was no longer white and no longer habitable, having been burned and sacked by British invaders six months before. On that day, Madison received from the American diplomats at Ghent the treaty signed on Christmas Eve, 1814, to end the War of 1812. The president sent it to the Post Office and Patent Building, where Congress convened in one of the few government buildings to escape the fires set by the British soldiers who had taken the capital; the Capitol lay in shambles. With the treaty of Ghent, the United States ended a needless, blundering war, almost completely mismanaged by the administration, a war that ended with Washington sacked, the Treasury insolvent, and no material or territorial gain. That same day, February 15, 1815, Representative Thomas Newton of Virginia, a Republican from Norfolk, offered a resolution on the floor of the House requesting the president to provide his view on relations between the United States and the Barbary powers. The House approved the resolution without debate and appointed a delegation to lay it personally before Madison.

Eight days later, on February 23, 1815, this least military-minded of American presidents, the slight, scholarly Madison, a man who displayed his republican virtue by dressing in modest black, sent another message to Congress. In two scant paragraphs, the president noted the Algerine attacks on American merchant ships in the Mediterranean, the last of which involved the *Edwin* thirty months before, and reminded Congress that some Americans—precisely ten men—were "still detained in captivity, notwithstanding the attempts which have been made to ransom them, and are treated with the rigor usual on the coast of Barbary." The War of 1812 had made it impossible to deal forcefully with Algiers, but Madison thought that with the war over, the United States faced opportunity and risk: an opportunity to use the navy to free the slave-hostages and force the dey of Algiers into a new treaty banning the taking of seamen into slavery as bargaining chips; and the risk that with the prospect of renewed trade with the Mediterranean with peace, American merchant ships in increasing numbers would fall "within the range of the Algerine cruisers." A free country on the cusp of heady nationalism, having withstood British invasions at Baltimore and New Orleans within the last six months, had no other choice but to resort to force. Washington, D.C., might be blackened and smoldering, and the Treasury might have recourse to print paper money to cover an unprecedented national debt—the country was insolvent—but President Madison asked Congress to declare war against the dey and the regency of Algiers.

Madison's decision to go to war against Algiers was notable for many reasons. For one thing, Madison was never very interested in military or naval matters. Twenty years earlier, the most support he could muster for a navy in the *Federalist Papers* was a civil libertarian one, that the "batteries most capable of repelling foreign enterprises on our safety are happily as such as can never be turned by a perfidious government on our liberties." Ten years before, as secretary of state under Jefferson, he had been a principal champion of economic coercion, embargoing American shipping in port as a way to bring the anti-American policies of Britain and France into line—a policy that proved a complete failure. As president before the War of 1812, he never even referred to the navy in his annual messages to Congress. But despite what the country and Madison administration had presumed, the War of 1812 showed that the conquering of Canada was not a "mere matter of marching" by the militia. The navy, that Federalist holdover barely tolerated by Jefferson and largely ignored by Madison, had unexpectedly emerged from the war with glory. Against tremendous odds against the renowned British fleet, the United States Navy had become the symbol of American will and national pride. Although many of the ships with which the navy had started the war had been sunk or captured, new ships were launched, and by the close of the War of 1812, the navy was in high popular and political regard. With the peace concluded with England, the highly professional navy had ships ready for sea and officers ready to win new glory.

Yet a decision to go to war is not made because a country has the tools for it. The Barbary regencies were a problem that had festered from the beginning of the American republic; indeed, they had been a problem for the European world for centuries. Americans of every persuasion found paying tribute an abhorrent practice, particularly with the contempt, fear, and racial and religious superiority they felt for the strange Islamic peoples on the African shore. There was no international system in place to deal with sordid protection practices such as the tribute system, no international organization or world court to which the cause might be pleaded. There was just a simple choice: pay annual tribute to buy a certain form of protection that passed as peace, or break the system with force.

That force could only be American. Despite Jefferson's attempt in the mid-1780s, it was difficult for Americans to think of a multinational naval effort. At least since Washington's Farewell Address, in which the departing president urged his country to stay clear of entangling alliances, American foreign policy was philosophically set against military commitments overseas. One of the original and enduring principles of American foreign policy was unilateralism, and the United States took seriously the need to defend its own interests by methods of its own choosing. Even if Americans had been predisposed, however, the countries with the largest fleets were simply not possible allies. Britain had the most powerful navy in the world, but the United States had agreed to a cold peace with Britain just days before, after a war marked with mutual recriminations about atrocities that would culminate on April 6, 1815, more than three months *after* the treaty of Ghent, with British troops firing into American prisoners of war held at Dartmoor, killing six and wounding sixty. France's navy had been crushed by years of British victories and blockade, and the restored Bourbon king was too busy reinstalling the ancien régime to be worried over a nuisance such as the Barbary pirates. Spain and Naples were impoverished and desolated by war, and their returning absolutist monarchs were busy settling scores internally. Besides, over the centuries, there had been many costly expeditions to the North African coast, and after all the bombardments and explosions, the deys, beys, and bashaws were still on their thrones, still taking Christian slaves. Far easier and cheaper, the European thinking seemed to run, to regularize the Islamic maritime nuisance than to eradicate it.

Madison's conception was strikingly different. Perhaps the cardinal principle of American foreign policy was free trade. The United States had just fought a war against Britain based on "free trade and sailors' rights." Americans were an entrepreneurial people, and shipping and trading goods to overseas markets had been one of the spectacular aspects of the republic's economic growth ever since the Revolution. Not only had the United States grown prosperous on the seas, but the revenues of the federal government (shaky as they were following the War of 1812) were largely dependent in peacetime on the customs duties levied against imports. Besides the hapless men from the *Edwin* and Pollard, there were no Americans known to be held as slaves, but with peace, American mariners would be putting out in their ships to reestablish Mediterranean markets and bring back goods. Madison had no time to appeal to the various European capitals seeking allies for a naval venture against Algiers, with the inescapable slowness in the days of windborne communications—six months was the expectation to get an answer to a routine letter—and the Americans likely would have had to wait a year for responses to dribble back to Washington to any American suggestion of a joint force, with the inevitable delays for diplomatic deliberations and consultations and counterproposals. By that time, even assuming European nations would be willing, there was no telling how many merchant ships would have been captured by the Algerine corsairs and their seamen thrown into slavery, every one of them an expensive commodity to ransom. If the United States did not go to war against Algiers immediately in 1815, Algiers would create a foreign debacle for the United States; the longer Madison waited, the more intractable the problem.

Accompanying Madison's message advocating war was a report from the State Department. According to the latest accounts he had received from Morocco, Tunis, and Tripoli, Secretary of State Monroe wrote, U.S. relations with those states remained more or less peaceful. In reviewing events in Algiers, however, Monroe cast a different light, reminding Congress that Algiers had ordered Tobias Lear, together with all other Americans then residing in Algiers, to depart, and forced Lear to pay for his own personal freedom with a huge loan. Then Monroe recounted the seizure of the *Edwin* (without naming her) and the plucking of the hapless Pollard off the Spanish vessel, and stated that the "unfortunate persons thus captured, are yet held in captivity." Without naming Noah as the American agent, Monroe noted that two of the American seamen had been ransomed but denigrated the chance that diplomatic efforts might secure the release of any more, observing that the dey held them "as a means by which he calculates to extort from the United States a degrading treaty" providing for additional annual tribute payments as a bribe against taking more slaves. The House journal ominously noted that, after the introduction of Monroe's report, the public galleries were "cleared, and the doors of the House closed, and so remained until near five o'clock, when the House adjourned." It later emerged that, in secret session, Madison's recommendation for

President James Madison, who recognized the need to use force against Algiers, even as the United States had just finished fighting the British in the War of 1812. Portrait attributed to Maurin. From the collection of the National Portrait Gallery, Smithsonian Institution.

war was read aloud, and a proposed resolution asking the president to provide the dey's ostensible reasons for Algiers's actions was voted down.

The next day, Friday, February 24, 1815, the House sent its war authorization, "[a] bill for the protection of the commerce of the United States against the Algerine cruisers," to a select committee of seven. Newton of Virginia, who had started the war ball rolling by introducing his resolution, was named to the committee, as were three other Republicans. Despite the Federalist party's minority status, William Gaston, a Federalist from New Bern, North Carolina, was made chairman of the select committee, clearly because he had introduced the bill in the House of Representatives, but also perhaps an indication that, with the War of 1812 over, the "Era of Good Feelings" in national politics had begun. Gaston was ably seconded by John Forsyth, a Republican of Georgia, in his second term in Congress at age thirty-four, in a career that would lead him to become governor of Georgia, U.S. senator, and secretary of state. Gaston and Forsyth needed only four days to prepare and present the select committee's report, which added detail to what Secretary of State Monroe already had reported.

The select committee report recounted the story of United States relations with Algiers since July 1812, when the dey had extorted money from Consul Lear and then forced all Americans to depart. The select committee referred to Noah elliptically, as an "agent (whose connexion with the Government was not disclosed)" who was sent to Algiers to try to ransom the crew of the *Edwin*, and noted that the attempt failed because the dey wanted more, not fewer, slaves. The fact that he had been able to free two seamen, the select committee observed, was not to be mistaken for a change of Algiers's attitude. Of the ten left in captivity, the report noted that Smith and Pollard were neither confined nor forced to work at hard labor, "but the rest of the captives are subjected to the well known horrors of Algerine slavery." Only the lack of opportunity had prevented any more captures, the committee opined, because American ships had been shut out of the Mediterranean for nearly three years. In sum, the select committee viewed Algiers as waging war against the United States.

Charles Goldsborough, a Federalist from the Eastern Shore of Maryland and, coincidentally, kinsman to a man of the same name who had served as chief clerk of the Navy Department, moved to amend the bill with language that would require a demand made upon the dey to deliver up all detained Americans before opening fire or commencing hostilities, but his temporizing amendment was rejected decisively. Similarly voted down were proposals to require any maritime prizes taken by U.S. war-ships to be brought into an American port, and therefore an American court, for adjudication (an almost insurmountable obstacle given the distance involved, as everyone surely understood), and limiting hostilities to maritime warfare, whatever that might mean. The House read the war authorization bill for a third time as required, approved the bill by a 94–32 vote, and sent it to the Senate.

In the late afternoon of March 1, 1815, Congressmen Forsyth and Gaston walked the still-confidential bill around the Post Office Building to the Senate's makeshift chamber. The Senate went into secret session and twice read the bill. The next day, March 2, 1815, after desultory debate over reducing the size of the army, expanding the jurisdiction of the federal courts, and compensating slaveowners for British "depradations" in taking away slaves from their coastal Virginia and Georgia plantations in the war just ended, the Senate went back into secret session to consider war. With no recorded debate, the question was called, and the Senate passed the bill by a vote of 27–2. On March 3, 1815, Madison signed the bill into law. The act authorized the administration to man, equip, and employ the naval force as the president judged necessary to protect trade and seamen in the Atlantic, the Mediterranean, "and adjoining seas." Not only were U.S. warships, and any privateers for which the president would provide an appropriate commission, authorized to take Algerine ships as prizes of war, but also Madison was left unfettered in his ability to order "all such other acts of precaution or hostility, as the state of war will justify, and may, in his opinion, require."

With Congress solidly supporting military action, Madison led the United States into a foreign war. America had tangled with the Barbary pirates a decade earlier but had been unable to beat Tripoli decisively. In 1815, the United States sought a showdown against Algiers, the strongest Barbary power. America's war aim was simple: to break a system of state-sponsored maritime terrorism, to end the Islamic North African practice of enslaving Americans or forcing the United States to pay tribute to meanly buy peace.

Chapter Three

Fitting Out the Squadrons

SUSAN DECATUR was no blowsy sailor's wife. Slim, fashionable, and vivacious, a coquette in her earlier days as a belle in Tidewater, Virginia, she was a drawing-room sophisticate, a woman who hosted James and Dolley Madison in the Decaturs' rented townhouse west of the White House in the muddy, primitive national capital. At her parties, Susan Decatur played the harp and sang, and engaged in polite conversation with foreign ambassadors and famous statesmen. She was well educated and well read—her library contained books in Italian and French—and she had a particular interest in religion. Born Susan Wheeler, the daughter of Luke Wheeler, a merchant and mayor of Norfolk, she had married her sailor husband in Norfolk in March 1806 after a whirlwind courtship. They had met only four months earlier, in November 1805, when Susan, part of an afternoon boating party, came aboard the frigate *Congress*, the ship in which Decatur returned from the Mediterranean after two years' service. Though Decatur was ashore, Miss Wheeler happened upon a miniature portrait of the twenty-six-year-old captain in his cabin. They met the next night when her father, the mayor, hosted Decatur and the Tunisian ambassador at a dinner and ball in their honor. The attraction of Stephen Decatur and Susan Wheeler was overwhelming. Three years older than Stephen, Susan previously had fought off the advances of the notoriously lecherous Aaron Burr, then the vice president of the United States; and she had declined a marriage offer in 1803, when a French midshipman, Jérôme Bonaparte, the brother of Napoleon, whose frigate was anchored on Hampton Roads, had become smitten and impulsively asked for her hand.

In 1815, although married nine years, the Decaturs had no children. As the years passed, Susan Decatur found the loneliness of her husband's long absences at sea, and the fear that he would be killed or maimed or lost at sea, more and more oppressive. In October 1812, on the same day he reported to the Navy Department that he had captured the British frigate *Macedonian*, Decatur wrote a lighthearted, whimsical note to his wife. Glossing over the death and destruction wrought by the fearsome display of American gunnery—the British ship lost thirty-six killed and another thirty-six severely wounded—Decatur charmingly observed that he had captured the *Macedonian*, by which he had "gained a small sprig of laurel, which I shall hasten to lay at your feet. I tried burning [the frigate *Philadelphia*, in 1804] on a former occasion, which might do for a very young man; but now that I have a precious little wife, I wish to have something more substantial to offer, in case she should become weary of love and glory. . . . Do not be anxious about me, my beloved. I shall soon press you to my heart."

In the days of wooden warships, combat typically was at close range, close enough not merely for cannonballs and grapeshot to mow down officers and sailors indiscriminately but for musketballs fired from enemy marksmen to pick off conspicuous officers as they walked the quarterdeck imperturbably under fire. For the captain's wife, it was a nerve-wracking occupation. Captain James Lawrence, who had been Decatur's second in command in burning the *Philadelphia*, was killed in June 1813 in command of the *Chesapeake* in a battle that ended with 146 American casualties of the 395 aboard. Master Commandant William Henry Allen, who served for five years as Decatur's first lieutenant aboard the *United States*, fell

Susan Decatur, who feared her husband would be killed in battle and asked the navy to keep him at home. Portrait attributed to Gilbert Stuart. Courtesy of a private lender to Decatur House, a National Trust Historic Site.

mortally wounded in August 1813. Trying to get to sea in the *President* in January 1815, Decatur had been knocked down and wounded by a huge splinter, while one-fifth of the crew was killed or wounded. Susan was staying at the home of her husband's parents in Frankford, Pennsylvania, on the outskirts of Philadelphia, when she heard the news that he had returned, hurt but alive, to New London. To her, Providence had sent a warning, one that she could not disregard.

On February 25, 1815, three days after Stephen Decatur's return to New London, probably the very day Susan received news from him, she took the remarkable step of writing Secretary of the Navy Crowninshield a private letter, which read:

Dear Sir,

It is reported that the Government have it in contemplation to fit out a Squadron for the Mediterranean; and as I presume the whole of our naval force will not be requir'd for that purpose, I have to request the favor of you, that Commodore Decatur may not be included in the number—as he has already a very arduous tour of duty in that quarter; I know that he has no wish to go there again unless it shou'd be deem'd indispensably necessary—and as for myself, I have been so horrifi'd and perturb'd during the last two or three years, that I really long for a little rest. I am still so anxious about my husband's safety, that I have not yet been able to enjoy the glad tidings of Peace [with England]. I trust, however, that a very few days more, will restore him to me.

I have the honor to remain, Dear Sir,
Yours respectfully,
Susan Decatur

The national interest comes first, of course; but what should a gentleman who was secretary of the navy to do? Crowninshield thought the matter through, balancing the private anxieties of a wife with the public good. He responded by private letter to Susan Decatur, and wrote another private letter to Stephen Decatur, then recuperating at a New York boardinghouse. Neither was copied in navy records. To the commodore, Crowninshield wrote on March 14, 1815, that a fleet was being prepared to send against Algiers, and "I need hardly inform you it is [the administration's] intention & wish to give you an honorable command in it." Crowninshield envisioned the fleet sailing in two separate squadrons, the first with two or three frigates and a parcel of smaller ships, and the second with the navy's first ships-of-the-line and "our other Frigates as fast as they can be manned & prepared for Sea." Then the secretary of the navy did something extraordinary: he let Decatur choose his command. He offered the first squadron, with the frigate *Guerriere*, "to sail immediately," or one of the 74-gun ships-of-the-line if he wished to go with the second squadron, or command of the Boston Navy Yard, if he wanted to stay home. "[I]n short my dear sir," Crowninshield wrote, "*your wishes are to be consulted*, any service, or any station, that is at the disposal of this Department, rely on it, you can command." Commodore William Bainbridge would command the second squadron, but only because, as Crowninshield informed Decatur with President Madison's express approval, Bainbridge had superintended the construction of the navy's first ship-of-the-line, the *Independence*, which would be ready to sail with the second squadron, and since he was senior to Decatur, he would have to be in overall command if they sailed together. Crowninshield asked for a frank response.

On March 20, 1815, Stephen Decatur responded privately, which allowed him not only to resolve issues raised by Susan, but also to pour out the considerations weighing on him in a way that an official letter to the secretary would not have allowed. Decatur appreciated the expression of goodwill tendered by Crowninshield and the confidence of the president, he stated, as well as the "polite" answer Crowninshield had written to his wife. Were the navy to think that he had had prior knowledge of and approved of Susan's letter, he wrote Crowninshield, he would feel humiliated. Although Decatur understood how worried his wife was, "I cannot permit her to interfere with [*sic*] in any way with my official duties." Should he want "any indulgence," he, not Susan, would apply for the favor—which is exactly what Decatur did.

First, stung by articles in the Bermuda newspapers as to the supposedly weak resistance the *President* had put up in the January battle, reports that he feared had tarnished his reputation despite the confidence in him that the administration had expressed, "it would be particularly gratifying to me at this moment to receive an active & conspicuous employment, in Europe it would be seen that my statement had been satisfactory to my Government." Nevertheless, Decatur continued, he would prefer "remaining on shore to taking a situation as second [in command] in the Fleet," because he had held independent commands for nearly eight years and skeptics might think that the government had indeed lost faith in him if he went in a subordinate role. Decatur laid down his cards: he asked for command of the frigate *Guerriere* and "the first Squadron bound to the Mediterranean with permission [that] on the arrival of Com: Bainbridge in that Sea to . . . return home." Decatur saw no "objection to such an arrangement, as the Government intend[ed] to send out the first division immediately some one must command," and if he returned in a sloop of war when Bainbridge arrived, "the force left will [still] be so vastly superior to that of the enemy that they will not dare to shew themselves." More routinely, as another favor, Decatur asked that his "followers"— men who enlisted in the navy but sought to serve only under a chosen captain—from the *President* returning with the peace from Bermuda "as may be disposed to accompany me" be allowed to ship out in the *Guerriere*.

Suggesting that Decatur had made a deal with his wife, he added to Crowninshield that he actually would prefer *not* to command the whole fleet for any length of time because staying "in those Seas beyond the summer Months would not be desirable." Indeed, as a final favor, Decatur requested that after his return he would be appointed to "some situation on shore, one in the middle States anywhere between Washington & New York (should a vacancy occur)," a request he attributed rather unconvincingly to his health.

The favors Decatur requested were uncommon for an officer writing the secretary, but since he was the favorite of Madison and Crowninshield, they agreed to all his "indulgences." Yet it is simply inaccurate for David Long, the modern biographer of Bainbridge, to state that Decatur accepted "none of the three" choices Crowninshield had offered, "mixing them up to his own advantage." Decatur chose, in the words of Crowninshield's offer, "to have the *Guerriere* to sail immediately." By definition, given his own seniority on the navy list of captains, that choice meant that Decatur would have the command of the first squadron as commodore— as Crowninshield certainly understood in making the offer. The extraordinary favor that Decatur sought, and received, was to be relieved from command and allowed to return home when Bainbridge arrived.

On March 24, 1815, about as quickly as Secretary Crowninshield could have received and read Decatur's letter, he wrote an official response. His order was simple and direct: Decatur was to take command of the *Guerriere* when she arrived in New York from Philadelphia and "superintend the whole armament and equipment of the Squadron destined for the Mediterranean." Crowninshield listed the ships in the squadron and enjoined Decatur to "have the whole put in perfect readiness for further Orders, to Sail at an hours notice." Three days later, Crowninshield wrote again, explicitly giving Decatur command of the first squadron in operations against Algiers, and again impressing upon him the need for haste. "[A]s the Algerine Cruisers may pass the Straits [of Gibraltar, into the Atlantic Ocean] and capture some of our merchantmen," Crowninshield noted, "it is of importance to expedite the sailing of the Squadron without delay, and as the terms of Peace may be greatly enhanced and made more difficult after they shall have captured more of our Ships & Men, the Fleet should be put out to operate against them as early as possible."

The choice of Decatur was a surprise to some of his fellow officers. Although a popular hero and undoubtedly a brave man, Decatur had surrendered the *President* just two months before, and normally there would be a court of inquiry pending to examine his conduct in the loss of the most powerful ship in the navy. Officers under scrutiny of a court of inquiry typically do not receive commands before the court even convenes; sometimes they do not receive commands even if a court vindicates their conduct. Decatur himself twice urged Crowninshield to convene the court of inquiry. Crowninshield, a courteous man who regarded Decatur as a national hero, informed him that he would do so once all the surviving officers of the *President* returned and were able to testify. But he told Decatur that the result was a foregone conclusion and that he had a "full conviction of the bravery and skill with which that Ship has been defended, and a confidence in the result [of the court] proving honorable to your high character as an Officer." The pending court proceedings did not delay Crowninshield for one moment. Indeed, for a matter of such importance as the command of a United States Navy squadron with 2,500 men going to war in the Mediterranean, Crowninshield must have sought and received the advice of the president. The administration would have been perfectly content to have Decatur sail with his squadron before the court transmitted its findings and opinions to Washington, although as it turned out, the court had time to complete its inquiry, and ultimately extolled Decatur's defense of the *President*.

Nonetheless, the administration's appointment of Decatur to command the lead squadron was not universally applauded within the navy. The command of a ten-ship squadron, the largest concentration of American naval force to that date, would bring recognition in itself, and every officer recognized that the first squadron undoubtedly would see fighting. Combat meant possible victory, fame, and glory, and with a successful capture would come large sums of prize money. Decatur already had achieved glory and wealth; the naval officer corps grumbled that it was time for another captain to have his moment. Some hint of the rumbling appears in a letter Alexander J. Dallas, the secretary of the Treasury, sent to Crowninshield, his cabinet colleague, before the navy secretary selected

Decatur. "You are not aware," Dallas noted, of "the popular and professional frustration on the question of the Commander of the Mediterranean Squadron. Commodore Rogers [*sic*] says he is willing to take the command, if the President thinks it best for the service. Such an arrangement would reconcile all the jarring opinions. The Commodore will see you in a few days; and you can decide." Even the secretary's wife, Mary Boardman Crowninshield, chimed in about the jostling for the appointment. She reported to her husband that, in Salem, rumor had it that Rodgers "would prefer going out in this expedition" to his new appointment to the Board of Navy Commissioners, but that opinion "hoped that Bainbridge will not have the command—some think Decatur the most fit for it—this is what I pick up here and there." It is possible, of course, that many officers had complained to John Rodgers (the "jarring opinions" Dallas reported), who was both senior to Decatur and fully capable of serving afloat, and thus that Rodgers had stepped forward, disinterestedly and discreetly, to resolve this bitterness among the brotherhood of captains. Yet given the type of man Rodgers was, a man who yearned for glory of command in battle but always seemed to miss success, it is far more likely that he decided that he wanted the command for his own glory, and played the Washington insider game to try to topple Decatur.

But not only was Stephen Decatur Crowninshield's choice, he was also the obvious man. Although Decatur was only thirty-six years old in March 1815, he was a senior captain, his rank dating from February 1804. Only five captains on the navy list were senior to him: Alexander Murray, John Rodgers, James Barron, William Bainbridge, and Hugh Campbell. But not all five were available or active officers. Of these men, the most senior, Alexander Murray, was a Revolutionary War veteran, relegated since 1808 to safe duty commanding the Philadelphia Navy Yard. When he had last served in the Mediterranean a dozen years before, William Eaton, the United States consul at Tunis, had sneered that the United States "might as well send out Quaker meeting houses to float about the sea, as frigates with Murray in command." Murray was sixty years old in 1815, nearly deaf, and described by Commodore Rodgers as "an amiable old gentleman . . . [whose] pretensions . . . as a navy officer are of a very limited description."

The next captain in seniority, John Rodgers himself, was only forty-two, vigorous, blustery, a good judge of men, and a thoroughgoing seaman, but President Madison had just chosen him in February 1815 as the president of the newly created administrative Board of Navy Commissioners. No one could have possibly opted for the third most senior captain, James Barron, the pariah of the navy, who had been court-martialed in 1807 for surrendering the frigate *Chesapeake* to the British frigate *Leopard* after she had fired into her and taken away four sailors as alleged deserters from the Royal Navy. As punishment, Barron had been barred from the service for five years, and he missed the entire War of 1812 after being stranded in Copenhagen at its outbreak; in the spring of 1815, Barron was still overseas, a forgotten and humiliated man.

The fourth most senior captain, William Bainbridge, was to bring out the second squadron, more powerful than the first, and would succeed Decatur in overall command. As additional balm for his pride, Bainbridge would have as his flagship the *Independence*, the first ship-of-the-line built by the U.S. Navy. The last of the five captains more senior to Decatur, Hugh Campbell, was another Revolutionary War veteran, tellingly known as "Old Cork" in the service. Campbell was shorebound as a result of a festering leg injury. Commodore Rodgers devastatingly described him as "a good old gentleman, but . . . an enemy to everything that is likely to call the reflections of his mind into operation."

Of course, there were captains junior to Decatur who were worthy of the command, but the best ones were unavailable: Isaac Hull, the captain of the *Constitution* when she sank the British frigate *Guerriere* in August 1812, was another just-appointed navy commissioner, as was David Porter, who had commanded the *Essex* on her odyssey in the Pacific Ocean in 1812–14; Charles Stewart was just coming home in the *Constitution* after simultaneously whipping two smaller British warships, the *Cyane* and the *Levant*, in February 1815. To have a superannuated captain, or a capable but more junior one, instead of Decatur would have excited comment, and even perhaps raised questions in Congress; to have given Rodgers the job would have caused organizational instability to the navy and raised the issue of why the newly appointed president of the Board of Navy Commissioners was the only fit officer for the command. Yet it is doubtful that Crowninshield or Madison went through such an analysis. Stephen Decatur was a national idol; he was in his prime; he would be returning after a decade to the seas where he had gained glory; he was their man.

What is surprising, however, is that Crowninshield kept William Bainbridge in the dark about what his and Decatur's roles would be. On April 8, 1815, by which time Decatur's appointment to the lead squadron was two weeks old and Decatur was scrambling to ready his ships "to Sail at an hours notice," Bainbridge wrote his old lieutenant, Commodore David Porter, a confidential letter. Bainbridge complained that Crownin-shield had treated him unfairly "in keeping me in utter *Ignorance*." Bainbridge depreciated the newspaper reports that Crowninshield had named Decatur to the Mediterranean squadron, though he informed Porter the idea was "rather mortifying to my feelings." The first Bainbridge heard from the secretary was on May 31, 1815, ten days after Decatur's squadron had sailed from New York. In the course of a letter in which Crowninshield mentioned ship movements and personnel transfers, the navy secretary stated that the sloop of war *Erie* would remain at Boston "as part of the Squadron destined for your Command in the Mediterranean." "From that," Bainbridge wrote Porter, he gathered for the first time that the depart-ment planned to have two squadrons sail to the Mediterranean. He felt insulted, and he petulantly (but only momentarily) asserted that he would command neither. On June 16, two weeks after suggesting that Bainbridge would have a squadron—after Decatur's squadron passed the Straits of Gibraltar—Crowninshield wrote Bainbridge that he would be sent his orders in a day or two, but that he assumed that Bainbridge had placed his ships "in readiness to sail."

Why Crowninshield treated Bainbridge, one of the most senior offic-ers in the navy, with such casual rudeness is hard to understand. Bainbridge was a notoriously harsh disciplinarian with the men aboard his ships. He regarded his sailors as social misfits and brutes and called them "damned rascals." He was, not surprisingly, unpopular with the men of the lower deck. But to officers and gentlemen, he was avuncular and considerate. A beefy, muscular, broad-faced man with strong features, Bainbridge had personal magnetism. No one questioned his seamanship or his sense of professionalism, but disgrace and defeat wracked his career. He had sur-rendered his first command as a naval officer to a French warship in the 1798 Quasi-War. In 1801, during the first Barbary campaign, the dey of Algiers ignominiously forced Bainbridge to convey hundreds of janissaries and a menagerie of exotic animals—camels, tigers, lions, antelopes—to the sultan at Constantinople in the *George Washington* after Bainbridge mistakenly anchored his ship within the range of the cannon at the dey's palace. Two years later, when he returned to the Barbary coast command-ing the frigate *Philadelphia*, he ran her onto uncharted rocks off Tripoli while chasing a small ship, and was forced to surrender his vessel with all 307 souls aboard into eighteen months of captivity. Bainbridge thus bore the unpleasant distinction of being both the first and the second U.S. Navy captain to surrender a ship to an enemy. Decatur served on the 1805 court of inquiry that absolved Bainbridge of fault, but Bainbridge was known as an unlucky officer. In the War of 1812, Bainbridge finally met with success and acclaim, sinking the British frigate *Java* off the coast of Brazil while in command of the *Constitution*.

Clearly, Bainbridge yearned to return to the Mediterranean to add a new chapter to his history. But in early 1815, Crowninshield wrote him the most routine letters regarding discipline and supplies, saying nothing to him about the vital issue of the Mediterranean command. Crowninshield's neglectful treatment of Bainbridge was out of character. Nothing in their official correspondence hints at an explanation, and their official relationship had begun only two months earlier, in January 1815, when Crowninshield was sworn in. Perhaps the answer turns on an earlier relationship. For several years prior to 1815, Bainbridge was the senior naval officer at Boston, and Crowninshield was a leading merchant, shipowner, and banker in Salem. The Crowninshield family, like all mercantile families, had been hurt by the embargo and nonimportation policies of the Jefferson and Madison administrations, which Bainbridge had helped enforce in Boston. In short, the two may have had business dealings then that did not sit well with the future navy secretary.

Commodore William Bainbridge, the hard-luck sailor who found himself overshadowed by Decatur in 1815. Portrait by John Wesley Jarvis. From the Naval Historical Center, Washington, D.C.

Crowninshield's seeming disdain for Bainbridge, whatever its cause, has been largely laid at Decatur's feet. David Long, Bainbridge's biographer, wrote that the navy "owed" Bainbridge the Mediterranean command but "despite his seniority, Stephen Decatur elbowed him aside." Bainbridge "on the basis of seniority" had "the better claim," according to this view, and Decatur and Crowninshield knew how desperately Bainbridge wanted to revenge the indignities meted out to him. Other revisionist historians of the navy, such as Leonard Guttridge and Jay D. Smith, portray Decatur as a ruthless man out to restore the luster of his glory tarnished by the loss of the *President*, who manipulated

Crowninshield, confiscated ships, men, and matériel to sail first, and acted indifferently toward, if not specifically to embarrass, Bainbridge.

There is a kernel of truth in all this. Decatur was mortified at having surrendered his ship, even though no contemporary American ever questioned his courage or his efforts, and he wanted a chance to redeem himself at least in his own eyes. Decatur also knew that Bainbridge longed to have another command against the Barbary corsairs. As a lieutenant, Decatur had served under Bainbridge and had gotten along with him well, but in 1815, he seems to have considered Bainbridge both overbearing as an officer and ponderous as a man. Washington Irving, the famous man of letters who considered both Decatur and Bainbridge his friends, and who in 1815 was the editor of the *Analectic Magazine*, which published articles on the navy and profiles of its leading figures, privately advised Decatur to "whip the cream off the enterprise"—to strike quickly, garnering most of the fame and fortune in this new war before Bainbridge would arrive with the balance of the fleet. These revisionist historians have seen Irving's comment as prescient or as an underhanded or unprincipled motivation for Decatur, who was neither prescient nor dependent on Irving's advice.

These criticisms are baseless. First, it was Crowninshield who offered Decatur "any service, or any station, that is at the disposal of this Department." Decatur hardly can be faulted for taking the secretary up on his offer and choosing the lead squadron. Seizing the mantle of command in such circumstances is hardly wrongful or ruthless. Indeed, what kind of naval leader would Decatur have been if, at the onset of a new war, instead of an active sea command, he had chosen, say, to superintend the Boston Navy Yard? Second, strict seniority, much less regard for the bypassed officer's feelings, is scarcely the desideratum in choosing commanders. Crowninshield and Madison saw Decatur as the navy's greatest fighting captain and wanted him leading the vanguard of American power. In modern times, when President Franklin Roosevelt chose George C. Marshall to be the U.S. Army chief of staff in April 1939, a decision historian Eric Larrabee called among the "finest and most consequential choices of FDR's presidency," he selected Marshall over thirty-four senior generals. Seniority per se gave no more entitlement to Bainbridge in 1815 than it did to General Hugh Drum in 1939. Third, Bainbridge was not racing Decatur to get to sea first. He did not do so—he could not have done so—precisely because Crowninshield kept him in the dark so long about the first squadron. Decatur, urged on by Crowninshield, worked hard to get his squadron to sea and to arrive off North Africa. His sense of urgency was to get to the Straits to bottle up any Algerine warships from emerging into the Atlantic, to attack any Algerine cruisers at hand, and to begin the summer offensive campaign before Bainbridge arrived with the balance of the fleet.

In light of the historians' criticisms, it is ironic to note that it was Bainbridge who tried to grease the command choice through political influence. Weighing in with Crowninshield on Bainbridge's behalf was Henry Dearborn, a Revolutionary War veteran (he had commanded the First New Hampshire Regiment at Yorktown) and the senior general of the army in the War of 1812 who previously had served Jefferson as secretary of war, and thus was the long-serving cabinet colleague of then Secretary of State Madison. Dearborn had known Bainbridge for eight years, while Bainbridge was the senior naval officer at Boston and Dearborn the port's collector of customs. Dearborn sent Crowninshield not one but two letters in his nearly illegible scrawl in the space of two days. In his April 10, 1815, letter, Dearborn hoped that, "for the honor of the government the Navy Dept. the Navy & Com. Bainbridge" there would be not be such an enormity of an "injustice" as an appointment of Decatur over Bainbridge. Bainbridge was the senior officer, and Dearborn believed that he was the superior one, with a keen sense of duty and nautical skill "not surpassed by any man," an officer who had "faithfully & honorably served his country by flood & fire" who now "deserved the confidence of the country." In his second letter, Dearborn assured Crowninshield that he had not discussed the earlier letter with Bainbridge, a letter, he said, that came from the "feelings of my heart." Dearborn explained that Bainbridge wished nothing more than to have the 74-gun *Independence* "carry him before Algiers," which he hoped the navy secretary would order. There is no record that Crowninshield responded to Dearborn.

The navy wanted Decatur's squadron to get to the Straits as quickly as possible, to bottle up any Algerine warships from getting into the broad swaths of the Atlantic. If the squadron found any Algerine cruisers, Decatur was to attack, sink, or capture them, and his ships were to begin the summer offensive campaign before Bainbridge arrived with the balance of the fleet. Dated April 15, 1815, the Navy Department's orders to Decatur consist of a five-page folio signed by Secretary Crowninshield but almost certainly drafted with the professional advice of the new Board of Navy Commissioners. The orders authorized Decatur to "subdue, seize and make Prize of all Vessels, goods & effects belonging to the Dey or Subjects of Algiers," even as Decatur was to "endeavor to capture or destroy" any

Algerine cruisers that he encountered. On the squadron's arrival, Decatur was to establish a blockade of Algiers to "prohibit all intercourse by ingress or egress, of all Vessels, of any nation whatever." Significantly, because Crowninshield and the navy commissioners "considered that the Squadron at present under your command is not sufficiently Strong to attempt offensive operations against the Town and Batteries of Algiers," Decatur was given discretion to conduct operations "to produce the most effect on the Enemy" or to protect American merchant shipping by instituting convoys, the premise being that a direct assault on Algiers would have to "await an augmentation of force," that is, Bainbridge's squadron.

In addition, the Department's orders covered various contingencies. The United States consul at Barcelona, Richard McCall, whom Decatur would take out with the squadron, was made the navy agent for the fleet, with £10,000 lodged in London to pay bills of exchange McCall would issue for critical expenditures. The department gave Decatur an additional $20,000 in coin for expenses. Decatur was allowed to open a naval hospital at Cagliari in Sardinia, and a doctor was sent out with the squadron to staff it. As a general rendezvous, the department suggested Majorca Bay because from there, the squadron could sail back to Algiers whether the wind came from the west or east. The State Department would send Decatur a commission to negotiate as a diplomat, and with those instructions would come a diplomat named William Shaler, who would act as co-commissioner with Decatur (and later with Bainbridge). Given his dual naval and diplomatic authority, Decatur was in a uniquely responsible position in American history. In Crowninshield's words, he might "either fight and subdue them, or make an honorable peace if you can." Crowninshield did not forget his private promise to Decatur: without mentioning Bainbridge by name, the orders authorized Decatur to "shift your Flag and return in a Sloop to New York or Philadelphia" if a superior officer succeeded him in command. And for the third time, Crowninshield ordered Decatur to sail "without any delay, so soon as the orders for the commissioners shall arrive."

The man that the State Department selected as Decatur's co-commissioner to negotiate a peace treaty with Algiers was William Shaler. Shaler, age forty-two, was a native of Bridgeport, Connecticut. Orphaned as a teenager, he learned about business in a New York countinghouse and then went to sea. He may have been the most traveled man in America. In the 1790s, as the supercargo on merchant ships, Shaler sailed to the West Indies and then to France, becoming an early enthusiastic supporter of the French Revolution and learning many of the principal languages in Europe. From there, he went to Montevideo, Mauritius, Copenhagen, the Pacific coast of South America, Hamburg, and Macao. Later, as a ship-master, Shaler sailed to Canton, the northwest coast of America (the mouth of the Columbia River in what is now Oregon), and then to Europe. He kept an account of his travels from Canton to the California coast—his ship, the *Lelia Bird*, was the first American trading vessel to call at what is now the port of Los Angeles—which was published as *Journal of a Voyage Between China and the Northwestern Coast of America*, the first extensive account of California. His voyages tested his self-reliance, and he was not found wanting. At Mauritius, a French privateer captured his ship and he was stranded for fifteen months, and in March 1803, he returned cannon fire from a Spanish battery guarding the tiny mission port of San Diego, California, with the single 3-pounder cannon his ship carried. Few Americans could boast a greater experience overseas. He was a handsome man, with a lantern jaw and a determined look that suggested that he was prepared to ram his head through any wall.

William Shaler, who called Algiers "that Den of banditti." Portrait by unidentified artist. From the collection of The New-York Historical Society.

The Madison administration brought Shaler into diplomatic service in 1810 as United States consul at Havana, a crucial listening post in the center of Spanish colonial rule in the Americas. After the United States seized West Florida in 1810, Shaler installed himself on the southwestern frontier, based at Natchitoches, Louisiana, where he promoted the Gutiérrez-Magee raid into Texas and supported efforts by Mexicans and Americans to "filibuster" the Spanish colonial government there. He was sent to Ghent in 1814 as a "confidential agent" to assist the American peace delegation. What the government wanted him to do there is unclear. He may have had an undercover mission, as he later cryptically wrote that Napoleon's abdication in April 1814 rendered it "out of [his] power to render any useful service during the negotiation." Instead, he acted as a secretary to the mission, copying out dispatches. When the ministers decided that they would not disclose to him the contents of what Shaler expected was a critical British memorandum, an insult Shaler termed "an oblique reflection on my integrity," he decided that his presence was not important to the mission, and that since "their decision reflected no honor on me and placed me in so equivocal and painful a situation," he requested permission to return to the United States. He left Ghent at the end of November 1814, brought dispatches to Paris, and arrived back in Washington in March 1815, imagining that Albert Gallatin or John Quincy Adams used their private letters to damage his standing in Washington. But Shaler had returned to the United States at an opportune moment. The news of the Christmas Eve peace with Britain, as well as the climactic battle of New Orleans, had "thrown the nation into a delirium of joy." Far from being marginalized, Shaler found his reception by Secretary of State Monroe "flattering beyond my most sanguine expectation." After a series of meetings, Monroe told him that President Madison had decided to appoint Shaler to negotiate a new treaty with Algiers—a place Shaler called "that Den of banditti"—and then become the consul there. On April 8, 1815, Shaler met with Tobias Lear. He received copies of Lear's letters and reports from 1812 and presumably heard from the ex-consul about the realities of dealing with the dey and the people with whom he would have to negotiate. The next day, April 9, 1815, Madison and

Monroe signed and sealed his commission, a one-sentence document providing Shaler, Decatur, and Bainbridge with authority to "negotiate and conclude a settlement of the subsisting differences and a lasting Peace and friendship between the United States and the Regency of Algiers."

Secretary of State James Monroe, who wrote that an "honorable and lasting peace is the great object of this expedition." Portrait by John Vanderlyn. From the collection of the National Portrait Gallery, Smithsonian Institution.

Monroe's diplomatic instructions to the Decatur-Shaler-Bainbridge co-commissioners, dated April 10, 1815, arrived with the commission. Monroe recounted that Congress had declared war and that the "largest Squadron that ever sailed from this Country, is now ordered against Algiers." The secretary of the navy had provided instructions to the commander for the conduct of the war; Monroe's letter was meant to "prescribe the conditions of the peace."

"An honorable and lasting peace is the great object of this expedition," Monroe noted. Although an early peace would be "agreeable," Monroe made clear that "none must be made, unless it be honorable." He had little "hope of obtaining such a peace, by other means, than the dread, or success of our arms." Indeed, Monroe posited that "[i]f a just punishment should be inflicted on those people, for the insult, and injuries we have received from them, the peace might be more durable than if it should be concluded at the first approach of our Squadron," although he quickly added that peace should not be delayed merely to inflict greater destruction. Monroe was unsure "[w]hether it will be better to proceed directly with the Squadron in front of the town, before an attempt is made to negotiate, or to remain at some distance," and left that decision to the negotiators, whom he knew would gain better intelligence of Algiers's force and fortifications. He urged Shaler and Decatur to follow diplomatic practice in dealing with the Barbary powers and suggested "hoist[ing] the flag of a neutral friendly power to invite negotiation with a view to peace, before proceeding to extremities. The Consul of that nation then comes on board in an Algerine boat, and he is made the organ of a Message to the Dey."

Monroe suggested that the Swedish consul at Algiers, Johan Norderling, would be the preferred go-between; presuming that the U.S. negotiators would reach out to the dey through a neutral consul, the president had enclosed a letter to the dey. When the negotiations began, the Americans were to be guided by the following principles: first, "no tribute will be paid, [second], no biennial presents made; the United States must hold the high ground with that power." Third, with the conclusion of negotiations, the United States expected to "stand on the footing of the powers of Europe, who are most respected there," like England. Fourth, the freeing of the *Edwin* crew and Pollard, "so unjustly captured will be a necessary consequence of peace." But Monroe forbade the commissioners from paying a penny for the captives' liberation because a ransom would create the moral hazard of seeming to reward the dey for declaring war and seizing innocent citizens. "It is the object of the United States," Monroe made clear, "to put an end to these odious practices, as to themselves, so far as circumstances will admit, and in which they cannot fail to succeed, if the undertaking is favored by the powers who are supposed to have a common interest in it." If the dey would not agree to renounce taking slaves by treaty—or as Monroe phrased it, if insistence would be "a formidable obstacle to a peace"—then the negotiators could agree for the cessation of the practice by an "informal understanding that it is not the mere question of the sum demanded, that prevents a provision for it in the Treaty, but the recognition of the principle." Monroe closed by asserting that, with the United States concluding peace with Britain, the dey had to realize that "he has much to dread from the continued hostility of the United States. From the formidable force ready to assail him, he must anticipate the most serious disasters," and Monroe expressed confidence that the commissioners "will readily succeed in accomplishing the important objects of the expedition."

The chief clerk of the State Department sent Shaler his commission, the diplomatic instructions, letters President Madison had signed for Shaler to convey to the foreign ministers of Sicily, Sardinia, and the other Barbary states, and his own best wishes on April 26. Shaler wanted to send a note to the sultan in Constantinople, but a State Department clerk informed him that the United States had no diplomatic representative there; the department did not think it safe to transmit a letter through a foreign ambassador and decided to withhold it. Shaler pressed the point with Secretary Monroe himself, reiterating that it was important that the American squadron be "known" at the Ottoman Porte, particularly if the war bogged down. Shaler suggested that if naval operations went slowly, he might "pound up" to Constantinople himself in the small ship that was to bring Decatur home, with a letter similar to those Monroe dispatched to Tunis, Morocco, and Tripoli.

Ultimately, Decatur sailed to the Mediterranean with ten ships carrying approximately 2,500 men and 240 cannon: the frigates *Guerriere*, *Macedonian*, and *Constellation;* the sloop of war *Ontario;* the brigs *Epervier*, *Flambeau*, *Spark*, and *Firefly;* and the schooners *Torch* and *Spitfire*. Strangely enough, although the United States had ended a long war scarcely two months before, most of the collected ships were new or untested in battle.

Decatur's flagship was the *Guerriere*. Launched in Philadelphia in June 1814, the *Guerriere* was named for the British frigate (captured from the

French navy) sunk by the *Constitution* in August 1812. Like many American-built frigates, the *Guerriere* was large (1,500 tons) and heavily armed, mounting thirty 24-pounder cannon on the gundeck and twenty 42-pounder carronades, short-range "smashers," topside. She had never been to sea, due to the British wartime blockade, but would soon gain renown as a speedy sailer. Crowninshield ordered the *Guerriere* to New York on March 15, 1815, but gave leave to Commodore Rodgers, her commander, to sail her to New York or to delegate his first lieutenant to do so in his stead, "as your wishes and convenience may dictate." Crowninshield wanted Rodgers to begin his duties as president of the Board of Navy Commissioners, to which the Senate had confirmed him two weeks before, to deal with the massive paperwork required in administering the navy and to advise the civilian secretary, and at the same time not to interfere with Decatur in readying the squadron assembling at New York. Rodgers seems to have gotten the hint; he sailed the *Guerriere* twenty miles down the Delaware to New Castle, Delaware, to catch the stage to Wilmington and then to his administrative post in Washington, handing the frigate over to a lieutenant to bring to New York.

In conformity to one of Decatur's requests, Secretary Crowninshield assigned a newly minted master commandant, William Lewis, to command the *Guerriere*. Lewis, a graduate of the College of William and Mary, was a thoughtful officer given to introspection. He had joined the navy as a midshipman in 1802 at age twenty-one, after trying his hand at medicine and law. Over the course of the next five years, Lewis served aboard six ships in the Mediterranean. He saw little combat, but his intelligence and knowledge of foreign languages made him an ideal courier of naval and diplomatic dispatches. For part of 1807, Lewis resided in the U.S. consulate in Algiers with the consul, Tobias Lear, and Lear's family. Upon his return to Washington, his childhood friends, Isaac Coles and Burwell Bassett, who served as secretaries to President Jefferson, confided to Lewis that the president was considering him to be consul at Tunis. That appointment was not made, but Jefferson sent Lewis to Paris and London in 1807 with diplomatic dispatches for the U.S. ministers. Upon his return, Lewis was assigned as a lieutenant on the frigate *Chesapeake* and then on the *United States*, both commanded by Decatur. After more than three years as a Decatur lieutenant, Lewis thought that the likelihood of war, which had seemed so imminent in the aftermath of the *Chesapeake-Leopard* incident off Cape Henry in Virginia in the summer of 1807, had faded, and with it his chances of further promotion. He determined that he needed

to make at least a modest fortune so that he might better press his romance with Frances Whittle, his sweetheart in Norfolk. In the spring of
1811, Lewis took leave from the navy and sailed as master of a Philadelphia merchant ship voyaging to China. When the War of 1812 broke out,
Lewis was in Macao. Much to his chagrin, he missed the entire war, although he avoided capture as he slowly circumnavigated the globe.

He arrived back in the United States in March 1815, after an odyssey of
almost four years, and found that he had not been forgotten; friends in the
United States Senate had insisted that the navy include Lewis on the list
of promotions to master commandant, an appointment dated March 3,
1815. Lewis reported in person to Secretary Crowninshield at the Navy
Department. The interview "sorely mortified" Lewis, as Crowninshield
asked questions to ferret out how energetically Lewis had tried to return
to the United States to fight the British, although Lewis recognized that a
man as courteous as Crowninshield did not intend to hurt his feelings.
Ultimately, Crowninshield allowed Lewis one month of leave and told
him that he would try to find a command for him. Decatur asked if Lewis
would like to command the *Guerriere*. He accepted the offer on the spot.
Lewis hurried to Norfolk, renewed his romance with Frances Whittle,
married her on April 19, and learned the next day that Decatur had convinced Crowninshield and the navy commissioners that Lewis should be
his captain. After just three days of marriage, Lewis hurried to New York
by steamboat, sailing packet, and stagecoach to assume command. Decatur
never specified his rationale for choosing Lewis, but the reasons probably
were the obvious ones. Lewis had served under Decatur before and was
known and trusted. He was smart and a good seaman, knew foreign languages and North African waters, and had actual experience on the ground
in Algiers.

Besides the *Guerriere*, Decatur's squadron contained two other frigates, the *Macedonian* and the *Constellation*. Unlike the *Guerriere*, a new,
American-built warship that commemorated a sunk British warship, the
Macedonian was the real McCoy, a British-built 38-gun frigate. Launched
at the Woolwich Naval Dockyard in 1810, at the height of the Royal Navy's
struggle against Napoleonic Europe, the *Macedonian* was a plain, basic
model of the type of frigate the British navy turned out by the score, a
boxy seagoing gun platform. In October 1812, Decatur, then commanding the frigate *United States*, had encountered the *Macedonian* off the Azores
and methodically dismasted her from long range, leading to her surrender. The *Macedonian* sailed back to the United States as a prize, and was

repaired and bought into the U.S. Navy, although for the rest of the war, the British navy blockaded her in New London. Crowninshield waffled about the squadron to which he should assign the *Macedonian*. Decatur requested Crowninshield to adhere to the plan the navy secretary had laid out in his March 14 letter—to have her sail with Decatur's lead squadron—and Crowninshield obliged "upon the express condition that the Squadron will not be delayed a day after the arrival of the Commissioner," William Shaler, because the campaign season was "far advanced already, and much injury may be done to our commerce before [Decatur's] arrival at the destination."

Leaking badly, the *Macedonian* came into New York under her stolid captain, Jacob Jones. Jones had entered the navy in 1799 as a midshipman at the incredibly advanced age of thirty-one, after trying his hand at medicine and law in Delaware. He was a quiet, formal man, respected by his contemporaries and able to avoid the feuds and rivalries rife in the naval officer corps. Like Decatur and Bainbridge, Jones had a personal stake in fighting on the Barbary coast; as one of Bainbridge's lieutenants in the *Philadelphia*, he had been taken prisoner and held captive in Tripoli for sixteen months in 1803–5. Jones was a minor hero of the War of 1812 for a Pyrrhic victory he won in the sloop of war *Wasp* in a bloody ship-to-ship battle over the British sloop of war *Frolic*—short-lived as a victory, for a British battleship soon appeared and captured both vessels.

The final frigate, the *Constellation*, was one of the first frigates completed for the U.S. Navy in the 1790s. With her sharp lines, the *Constellation* was a speedster, but notoriously "crank"; in 1812, at considerable cost—$120,000, one-third of the cost of a new ship—she had been rebuilt to alter her lines. During the War of 1812, the *Constellation* was blockaded in the Elizabeth River at Norfolk, but for all that, sailors, always a superstitious lot, thought that she was a lucky ship. Even before the Congress declared war against Algiers, Secretary Crowninshield ordered the *Constellation* readied for sea, and then to New York, under Captain Charles Gordon, one of the star-crossed officers of the early navy. Family ties had pushed him high early, and protected him after a court-martial ended with his reprimand. Through marriage, Gordon was a nephew of both Joseph Hooper Nicholson, formerly a powerful congressman, and Albert Gallatin, Treasury secretary to Jefferson and Madison and one of the peace negotiators at Ghent. In Commodore Rodgers's estimation, Gordon was a "good seaman and qualified for command at sea; but his opinions are too flexible to qualify him [for a seat as a navy commissioner]." He was a competent seaman, but undistinguished in the war just ended, and as Commodore Barron's flag captain aboard the *Chesapeake* in June 1807, when she had been fired upon by, and surrendered to, the British frigate *Leopard*, his reputation had been stained forever. Gordon was responsible for the ship, and though he manfully admitted at his court-martial that the *Chesapeake* was unprepared, and was thus found guilty, the court-martial panel (which included Decatur) sentenced him to the mildest of punishments, a private reprimand. In the spring of 1815, Gordon was a sick man, a semi-invalid from a grievous dueling wound that he had suffered in 1810 after challenging a newspaper editor who had disparaged his conduct in the *Chesapeake* incident. The wound to Gordon's lower abdomen never healed properly and continued to drain. Gordon had a special sleeping couch made for him, which he took aboard the *Constellation*. In pain much of the time, he still yearned for combat glory to redeem himself. William Lewis, like many of his brother officers, thought Gordon was a difficult man, morose and always finding fault.

In addition to the three frigates, the squadron included the sloop of war *Ontario*. "Sloops of war" were in fact not sloops at all. Sloops are one-masted vessels, rigged fore and aft—in other words, with large triangular sails set along the line of the hull. Sloops of war were three-masted, square-rigged ships, with sails set perpendicular to the hull. Smaller than frigates, they drew less water and carried lighter and fewer cannon. The *Ontario*, rated at 18 guns, had been built at Baltimore in 1813 but had never been able to slip past the British blockade of the Chesapeake Bay to get to sea. Crowninshield ordered her commander, Master Commandant Jesse Duncan Elliott, to ready her for sea, and then one week later he explained, "Ships comprising the Squadron destined for the Mediterranean by this time are at New York, and nearly ready to proceed, you will, therefore, make all the despatch possible to join them." Even if Elliott could not completely man the ship in Baltimore, he was to use all his "exertions to join the Squadron in time." He did.

Jesse Duncan Elliott was the dark knight of the U.S. Navy officer corps. He, too, served on the *Chesapeake* in her 1807 disgrace (as a midshipman) but alone among the officers he testified in support of Commodore Barron and, later, against Charles Gordon, crimping his relations with his brother officers, including several who were Decatur protégés. Elliot's contemporaries were divided as to whether Elliott was a young man of great moral courage, bucking all the officers with their fingers to the wind—the wind blew most decidedly against Barron—or just obtuse and mule-headed.

While Elliott had shown great spirit and boldness by seizing two British ships on Lake Erie during the winter of 1812–13, his conduct at the pivotal battle of Lake Erie in September 1813 may never be understood. As the second-ranking American officer, Elliott in his ship, the brig *Niagara*, did not stand in to assist Oliver Hazard Perry, the squadron commander, for three hours as Perry's ship, the *Lawrence*, was shot to pieces. Whether the wind dying away prevented him from coming up or whether some perceived slight from Perry or some character defect kept him mysteriously aloof will never be known for sure; recent historians have gone so far as to question Elliott's mental stability. Although Perry himself did not initially criticize Elliott, the growing animosity between the two and their circles of friends wracked the navy for thirty years. Decatur and Perry were close friends, and although the Perry-Elliott animosity had not boiled over by 1815, it is unclear what Decatur thought of Elliott at this time.

The brig *Epervier*, like the *Macedonian*, was a capture from the Royal Navy, and confusingly, like the *Guerriere*, she had been named for an earlier French warship. This *Epervier*, rated for 16 guns, had been built in Rochester, England, in 1811–12 and had been taken in combat off Cape Canaveral, Florida, in April 1814 by the sloop of war *Peacock*. The commander of the *Epervier* was twenty-nine-year-old Master Commandant John Downes, who had been first lieutenant of the frigate *Essex* during her famous cruise into the Pacific in the War of 1812—"an Officer of uncommon merit," in the words of William Jones, former secretary of the navy. A large, friendly man, Downes was a rarity in the navy in that he came from a working-class family; his father was a navy steward who seems later to have found employment as a boatman in Boston harbor. Downes lacked the sophistication and the polish of many of his genteel brother officers; indeed, he was often profane and crude. These traits led to occasional embarrassing moments, but, along with his undeniable ability as a seaman, they made him popular with his men.

The balance of the ships in Decatur's squadron were smaller vessels, brigs and schooners, which had been purchased for the navy in late 1814 and collected at New York to form a flying squadron slated to cruise as a pack to the West Indies and destroy British trade. Three were brigs, the *Firefly*, *Spark*, and *Flambeau*, and two were schooners, the *Spitfire* and *Torch*. Brigs carried two masts and were square-rigged; schooners had two masts as well but carried their sails fore and aft, which allowed them to sail on an angle closer to the direction of the wind but limited their size. All five of these ships were small, between 260 and 330 tons, and yet all were built to cross the Atlantic, packed with cannon, shot, powder, and enough food and water to sustain one-hundred-man crews. They were commanded by young, vigorous lieutenants out to make their mark, although the commander of the *Spitfire* was Alexander J. Dallas Jr. (the son of the secretary of the Treasury), about whom there were some doubts. The *Spitfire* and *Torch*, formerly privateers, were Baltimore-built pilot-boat schooners, and the *Firefly* and the *Flambeau* had been built in Baltimore as well; Baltimore was then at its apex in designing fast ships with sleek, sharp-built hulls and towering amounts of sail area. The one non-Baltimore brig, the *Spark*, had been built at Sag Harbor on Long Island in a mere forty days, although she was built for a Baltimore owner and perhaps to a Baltimore design as well. Observing these schooners and brigs at anchor from the quarterdeck of the *Guerriere*, Master Commandant William Lewis wrote, "Our small craft look very well. They are all *clippers*. Only listen to their names; Firefly, Spark, Torch, Flambeau, Spitfire. If we don't burn these Algerines with so many combustibles it will be odd."

As his squadron assembled at New York, Decatur began to consider what he would do when he arrived off Algiers. On entering the waters off North Africa, or perhaps even earlier, outside of the Straits of Gibraltar, Decatur first would have to neutralize—sink, burn, capture, or blockade—the warships of Algiers. Accounts published in the popular press listed the naval force of Algiers as five frigates, three corvettes, and eleven smaller vessels, including six coastal gunboats, an estimate consistent with what Consul Tobias Lear reported when he was kicked out of Algiers in July 1812. Popular opinion, fed by centuries of lurid tales of Islamic terror, held that the Algerines were brave fighters in hand-to-hand melees but did not have the understanding of naval tactics or the discipline for withstanding the strain of ship-to-ship battles. As Lear departed from Algiers, he gave Monroe an intelligence report on the Algerine navy. The crews of the Algerine ships, he observed, were the "lowest and most miserable order of people," a combination of Arab tribesmen and unlucky men taken off the streets when a press gang happened by. Each ship contained only a few good seamen. As to their prowess at war, in truth "[t]hey know nothing of regular combat," and if they were unable to grapple onto and board an enemy, a ship with half the firepower of an Algerine but with a trained crew would beat them handily. "It is on boarding that they depend entirely," he reported, for they relied on their large, ferocious-looking crews to overawe their enemies.

As part of their doctrine of relying on mass hand-to-hand fighting, the heaviest cannon the Algerine ships mounted were 18-pounder cannon, although the larger American frigates carried 24-pounders. Though numerically inferior, the U.S. frigates were more powerful ships. Decatur's squadron had three other advantages as well. First, when the Americans arrived on the scene, they would have the benefit (if managed well) of being concentrated in one squadron, while the Algerine warships likely would be scattered around the western Mediterranean, with some ships cruising, some in port, and others under repair. Second, in those days before satellites and radar, the American squadron would have the benefit of surprise: the Algerines had no ability to know the U.S. warships were at sea or when they would arrive until they were spotted at Gibraltar, Alicante, or Algeciras, or by chance by a ship that would hail the news to a passing Algerine vessel. Finally, the United States Navy had just concluded a three-year war with Britain, the greatest naval power in the world. The Americans had fought well and won many battles. The navy's officers and sailors regarded themselves—and their countrymen regarded them—as the pride of the new republic.

If Decatur might look with some confidence on the tactical problems in dealing with the Algerine fleet, the strategic problems presented a far murkier picture. Assuming the American squadron swept through the Mediterranean and arrived off Algiers, what next? Merely taking or burning a few warships did not necessarily mean breaking the will of the dey of Algiers or his circle of advisers, or forcing them to negotiate a favorable treaty. How could Decatur force the issue further? In modern terms, how could the Americans apply force from their offshore squadron against Algiers?

The most obvious strategy, and the one Crowninshield specifically ordered Decatur to begin with, was to blockade the ports of Algiers. Decatur, of course, was personally familiar with blockading and with being blockaded. Even with just ten ships, Decatur had sufficient numbers to prevent any ships entering or leaving Algiers, but he noticed that his orders referred specifically to a blockade of Algiers, not Bona (now called Annaba) or Oran, two smaller ports within the regency of Algiers, which therefore would be "open," as Decatur phrased it, "for trade & tribute." Decatur knew his force would be "ample for the Blockade of these places which would very much increase the pressure on the Enemy." He requested that his orders be amended, and Crowninshield did so immediately.

Blockades, if successful, worked by slowly strangling the coastal nation. In the last few years of the Napoleonic Wars, the Barbary regencies had become more integrated into the European economies, sending their neutral merchant ships across the Mediterranean to supply Wellington's army in Spain and the Royal Navy base at Malta with grain, cattle, fruits, and other products. Although Algiers was still not much of a mercantile state and could rely on its own subsistence agriculture and roads to bring products to local markets, it might be damaged by a cordon of warships interdicting all seaborne trade. Yet earlier blockades of Tripoli, in the years 1801 to 1805, had been intermittent and, ultimately, ineffective because Tripoli was not dependent on seaborne trade. In 1815, Decatur might need more direct and lethal weapons against Algiers.

Within one week of receiving command of the squadron, Decatur reached out for such a weapon: he wrote Secretary Crowninshield that he wanted to bring mortar vessels, known as "bombs," to the Mediterranean. The ugly, squat mortar placed on the forecastle of an anchored bomb vessel was a formidable and terrifying weapon, capable of blasting a 196-pound explosive shell four thousand yards in a thirty-second, high-arcing flight. Decatur thought "2 small [bombs] could be built & prepared for Sea in six weeks at the utmost & could follow the squadron out. There are Sea Mortars mounted on the forts at this place which I presume could be procured for this purpose." Bomb vessels first had been deployed in the French navy in the 1680s to bombard Algiers, and their use in 1683 destroyed much of the city, forcing the dey to free 1,600 Christian slaves and sign a peace treaty that lasted a century. Whether Crowninshield or Decatur knew this history is unclear. The U.S. Navy's use of bomb vessels had been uneven. Bomb ketches borrowed from Naples in the 1805 campaign had fired mostly duds into Tripoli. More recently, the British navy had used bomb vessels in the War of 1812 against the United States, including five that bombarded Fort McHenry (what Francis Scott Key called "the bombs bursting in air") on the evening of September 13–14, 1814, but they had not been able to crack the defenders' will.

Secretary Crowninshield received Decatur's request for bomb vessels and, new to the Navy Department though he was, Crowninshield's response showed a keen understanding of the ways of Washington. He wrote Decatur that there was no provision in law allowing the department to build bomb vessels, but Decatur could select any ships that "may answer the purpose and have them repaired and placed in a situation for that special Service." The mortars "can be had from the Forts on application to the Commanding Officer." Ultimately, Decatur could not find any ship that could be "prepared as a Bomb vessel without costing the Government infinitely more money than it would be to build, & then they would not be properly qualified for the purpose." Instead, he counted on countries friendly to the United States loaning him vessels suitable for temporary conversion into bomb vessels when he arrived in the Mediterranean. Interestingly, seven weeks later, when Bainbridge prepared to sail with the second squadron from Boston with much of the available naval force of the United States, including the 74-gun *Independence*, he expressed his regret that "five or six bomb vessels have not been prepared and ordered out, as they would be the most efficient means of annoyance against the town of Algiers."

Neither Decatur's lead squadron nor Bainbridge's ships, which transited later, carried an expeditionary force to storm the city. One of the lessons of the 1805 campaign against Tripoli was that a negotiated settlement became possible only after a motley force of United States marines, Greek mercenaries, and insurgent Arab horsemen had captured Derne, the second city of Tripoli (commemorated in the Marine Corps's anthem with the line "to the shores of Tripoli"), and threatened the stability of the bey. The Marine Corps in 1815 contained fewer than two thousand men, counting the last drummer and fifer in the band, and they were scattered among all the naval yards and stations and all the warships in service (including the ships in Decatur's and Bainbridge's squadrons). The navy had no proper troop transports to convey them and no logistical means to sustain a sizeable land force overseas. There was no plan to mobilize and bring the marines to bear against Algiers.

However, in a rare display of interservice cooperation, the army agreed to provide Decatur and Bainbridge with artillerymen and cannon. The War Department ordered Major S. B. Archer with his artillery company to New York, where Decatur assigned them to berth aboard the *Macedonian*. An unknown scrivener in the frigate's log inventoried the soldiers as if they were bosun's gear, laconically noting, "Received on board, one Major, one Captain, and 45 Artillery Men, with sundry stores belonging to the said establishment." Crowninshield similarly ordered Bainbridge to accommodate another artillery officer, Major Alexander C. Fanning, with his artillerymen and ordnance stores, to ship out with the second squadron. A young midshipman on the *Guerriere*, Joseph B. Nones, saw the ten brass cannon the army brought aboard. He knew that the administration meant business when one of the artillery lieutenants turned out to be Lieutenant James Monroe, nephew of the secretary of state; every officer who sought distinction or advancement wanted to be aboard the ships of Decatur's or Bainbridge's squadrons so that they could see combat. Shaler took young Monroe under his wing, writing the secretary of state about the "regular plan of study that will embrace all his leisure time," particularly mathematics, essential knowledge for an artillery officer. Once Archer's and Fanning's batteries were reunited, the army could have guns on the ground in North Africa, a powerful nucleus for a small force of sailors and marines stripped from the ships of the combined squadrons who might cooperate with any local rebel troops.

Finally, a secret weapon was passed to Decatur's squadron right before it sailed. On May 9, 1815, a man named W. D. Robinson sent a three-page memorandum to Shaler suggesting the use of poison gas against Algiers. Robinson informed Shaler of experiments conducted by Thomas Lord Cochrane, a British captain, in the Mediterranean, using sulfur gas against sheep and oxen grazing several hundred yards from where he released the gas: "as soon as the smoke spread over them, they drop'd down in a state of *stupefaction*, and many of them *immediately died*." This should not have been so surprising, since sulfur was already in use as a rat poison in confined spaces. Knowing what sulfur did to rodents, Robinson suggested the navy "try the principle in smoking barbarians."

The previous year, Lord Cochrane had proposed a poison gas attack on the French fleet at Toulon, and Robinson reported that Cochrane also "contemplated to use sulphur on a large Scale for the purpose of *neutralising* the batteries of New York and the other cities on our Atlantic Coast," although the British government had rejected his plans. Robinson instructed how the poison gas could be delivered. Two or three expendable small ships would be loaded with layers of sulfur between layers of dried wood; the vessels would be towed or sailed as close into the bay of Algiers as possible and then set afire (in the contemporary language, turning the ships into "infernals" or "fireships"). The fireships would "wait until the wind or tide enable[d] them to float directly into the harbour, . . . the match [to set them afire] to be applied at the proper moment." If the infernals approached within a few hundred yards of the quays or batteries, "the effect will be inevitable." According to Robinson, two sulfur infernals "would decide the fate of Algiers in a few hours." He cautioned, however, "to use due precautions" and not to begin a poison gas attack without a "*steady wind* blowing directly into the harbour." Robinson stated that he had learned of the British experiments, plans, and methods directly from

Alexander Cochrane-Johnstone, the British captain's uncle, a man of legendary corruption and venality as ex-governor of Dominica, member of Parliament, and stock market swindler.

The poison gas concept was no crackpot scheme. Cochrane conceived of using sulfur gas after visiting the sulfur mines in Sicily in 1811. The highest reaches of the British government considered the weapon after Cochrane wrote directly to the prince regent urging the use of sulfur vessels to attack any of the ports of the Napoleonic empire. The duke of York chaired a committee that ultimately refused to authorize the weapons, not on moral grounds but because a number of the members of the committee detested Cochrane. Significantly, Admiral Lord Keith thought enough of the scheme to suggest the attack on Toulon with poison gas to the commander of the British fleet in the Mediterranean, Sir Edward Pellew, who turned the invitation down. Forty years later, when Cochrane raised the idea again to use against the Russians during the Crimean War, no less a scientific authority than Michael Faraday, the English scientist who discovered the principles of electromagnetic induction and rotation, and who acted as a scientific advisor to the Royal Navy, wrote that Cochrane's scheme would emit sulfuric acid gas, which, being heavier than air, would form a low-lying cloud and move along the surface of the water, expanding laterally to form a low, broad stream. He opined that 400 tons of sulfur mixing with sufficient air would create 20,000 tons "of a very bad mixture, and one, which, if a man were immersed in it for a short time, would cause death."

What Decatur thought about poison gas is unclear. Decatur may have had practical objections to using sulfur gas, as did Admiral Lord Keith when Cochrane raised the idea—that the wind might turn the weapon upon those who unleashed it—or he may have had moral objections, as did Lord Wellington in 1814 when asked by the British cabinet. There was also the issue of the Americans held captive in Algiers who might perish in an indiscriminate poison gas attack as easily as their captors. Yet he may have had no scruples about using poison gas; his letters simply do not mention it.

Consequently, once Decatur arrived off Algiers and cleared the seas of Algerine warships, his squadron would lay a blockade of Algiers, Oran, and Bona. And if stopping the "trade & tribute" flowing into the regency did not bring the dey to heel, Decatur could hire bomb ketches to bombard Algiers. Fighting Algiers on the ground was inherently risky and probably would have to await the added weight of Bainbridge's squadron. And perhaps Decatur could contemplate unleashing poison gas.

But first the squadron had to get to sea. Decatur left most of the details to William Lewis, the newly married, newly promoted, newly appointed commander of the *Guerriere*. Lewis had left his bride and hurried to New York, arriving on April 29, sending letters to his beloved Fanny from every stop. Decatur was all hospitality on Lewis's arrival, staying up to the early morning hours to talk about old times. The next day, Lewis dined with commodore and Susan Decatur, who remembered Fanny from her own days as a Norfolk belle, and sympathetically lamented that Fanny, too, had married a sailor. But Lewis's life was all business thereafter, from sunrise to late at night. Decatur stayed ashore with his wife, coming aboard only once as Lewis wrestled with the countless details and paperwork of getting a ten-ship squadron ready for sea and war.

The last ship to rendezvous at New York was the *Macedonian*, which first "came too" at 6:00 p.m. on April 20 in eight fathoms, or forty-eight feet, of water off the Battery. Two days later, the *Macedonian* sailed up the East River to the Brooklyn Navy Yard. On her first night at the yard, the *Macedonian* swung afoul of the *Epervier* and carried away her flying-jib boom. The next morning, Sunday, April 23, and for two weeks after, forty or fifty men came aboard to caulk and patch the *Macedonian*'s leaky seams while her own crew reset her rigging and put the ship in a seaworthy condition. By the end of April, the *Macedonian* began the enormous effort to ship all the food, water, and stores that the ship and her four hundred men (and forty-five artillery supernumeraries) would need for a campaign more than three thousand miles away. She took aboard 18½ cords of firewood. The men aboard consumed about 300 gallons of water each day, which needed to be continually replaced while in port. Just as important as the water were the nine puncheons and eleven casks holding more than 2,000 gallons of Kentucky bourbon (the United States Navy had abandoned the Royal Navy's practice of doling out rum, a foreign beverage, for the all-American liquor). To feed more than four hundred men for at least three months, the *Macedonian*'s log lists 79 barrels of bread (she sailed with a total of 47,425 pounds of ship's biscuit), 13 barrels of flour, 6 tierces of beans, 12½ tierces of rice, 6½ tierces of cheese, 2 puncheons of molasses, and 9 finkins of butter, all brought aboard on a single day, May 1. The *Macedonian* carried 114 barrels of salted beef and 100 barrels of salted pork, as well as chocolate, tea, 30 barrels of sugar, and an unbelievable 23 kegs of tobacco. Every day in port, the ship was alive with activity. Gangs went ashore on Staten Island "to water," to fill wooden casks with thousands of gallons of fresh water that, weeks later, would be fouled with green algae but would be the sole, and severely rationed, supply of drinking water. Men swayed the yards aloft, tested and bent new sails, stored powder and small arms. The entire frigate was repainted, and the crew received new sets of clothes, making a natty appearance in navy blue "round jackets," off-white cloth and duck trousers, and scarlet vests.

The log of the schooner *Torch* also survives, and of course that ship went through similar evolutions to get ready for sea and war. Her crew was almost entirely new. Of her one hundred men, eighty came from the *John Adams*, ten marines came aboard from the Navy Yard, there were two new midshipmen and a lieutenant aboard, and a Midshipman Peterson returned from a recruiting rendezvous in Manhattan on May 1 with three prime seamen and a landsman. Yet they all knew the drill. The *Torch* log reflects days spent remasting the schooner, setting up the rigging, stowing all the food and other stores brought aboard, and, of course, in that timeless naval ritual, "all hands employed in scraping & painting." The log entry for April 18, 1815 is typical: "[A]ll hands employed scrubbing Ship. [L]oosed and dried all Sails. Tarred down the lower rigging. Set up the Fore and Main top mast[s] and topgallant rigging." For the ten carronades that the *Torch* mounted, five on each side, the sailors loaded two hundred 18-pound roundshot and more than a half ton of powder in the magazine; for hand-to-hand combat, the *Torch* received fifty muskets with bayonets, seventy-five cutlasses, and forty pistols. Because the *Torch* was small and light, she also carried eighteen oars, "sweeps," for movement in calms. For the hundred souls aboard, 675 gallons of Kentucky sour mash was shipped, which came to a very stiff tumbler of whiskey for each man each day.

Secretary Crowninshield bombarded Decatur with last-minute changes and developments. On April 17, he sent Decatur some sort of intelligence estimate or, as he phrased it cryptically in his cover letter, "sundry communications relative to Algiers, which we considered as authentic in respect to the source from which they are derived." Quite likely Crowninshield sent Decatur information (erroneous, as it turned out) that Algerine warships had passed into the Atlantic, for by early May, William Lewis joked to Fanny, in the style of Gilbert and Sullivan's *Pirates of Penzance*, that "we have heard the Algerines are in the Atlantic, [although] it is not probable they have found their way to Sandy Hook yet." In a more serious mood, he again referred to the news that "their fleet has passed the Straits of

Gibraltar. If we can be lucky enough to arrive there before they return, we shall catch them all. But I fear some more of our unprotected merchantmen may fall a prey before then." On April 20, the secretary sent to Decatur by express a map of the harbor and city of Algiers. Over the next few days, he sent the artillery company. On April 29, Crowninshield slammed the brakes on the squadron, prohibiting Decatur from sailing until he heard from Washington.

The administration had just learned that Napoleon Bonaparte, supposedly safe in exile on the island of Elba, had landed at Cannes in March 1815 and had begun what became a triumphant march to Paris and a brief resumption of the empire. Before the squadron sailed, Crowninshield informed Decatur that he wanted to discuss matters with President Madison, given the developments in Europe, but he ordered Decatur not to share the reason for the delay with anyone. Decatur wrote Crowninshield on May 7 that the day after he and Shaler had received instructions from the State Department, the squadron had lifted anchor from its position off the Battery and dropped down to Staten Island, where they had anchored "in perfect readiness for Sea." He hoped, he wrote, that the government would not detain them long, because "injury may be done to our commerce by the Algerines, who it is stated are now at Sea, & without the Straights [through Gibraltar, into the Atlantic]." Such were the fears for Britain that Monroe mused in a letter to the treasury secretary, Dallas, that "altho' the temptation [for Britain] is great, that the object is too inconsiderable compared with the consequences for her to attempt the seizure of our squadron." As secretary of state, he realized that if the squadron succeeded against Algiers, "the measure will raise us in the estimation of the powers of the Continent . . . [and] of England, tho' at the expense of other feelings, & will raise us in our own estimation."

Decatur moved his gear aboard the *Guerriere*, which stayed at anchor day after day in lower New York Bay. Bainbridge, forming up the second squadron at Boston, sent orders to the *Firefly* to sail to Boston, but Decatur, "[f]eeling Satisfied that Commodore Bainbridge could not have been Apprised of the Situation," countermanded them to keep the *Firefly* with him. Yet he also informed the secretary that he had received, and obeyed, Crowninshield's orders to return men to the *Independence* and *Congress*, both ships in Bainbridge's squadron, whom he had "borrowed" to make up for the difficulties in shipping sailors at New York. Then again, there were orders that Bainbridge had sent directly to a Lieutenant Spencer in Decatur's squadron instead of to Decatur as the senior officer at New

York, which to Decatur so sharply deviated from the "established usage of the Service" that they appeared to reflect Bainbridge's belief that he "has the command of this [Decatur's] Squadron at this moment." Decatur countermanded those Bainbridge orders as well. There was unquestionably rancor developing between Decatur and Bainbridge, and although Decatur copied his letter to Bainbridge, he also asked Crowninshield to lay it before his "Brother Officers" on the Board of Navy Commissioners so that his own conduct would be understood.

The officers of the squadron surmised that the tension between the two commodores was the reason that the squadron did not put to sea. William Lewis wrote his father-in-law on May 7 that "from something I have heard today, I doubt whether we shall sail till Bainbridge is ready. In that case, Decatur will not go & of course I shall have to seek another place [another post]." Six days later, Lewis wrote Fanny, "Heaven only knows when we shall sail," and two days after that he wrote again to Fanny's father that "when we shall start is a profound secret." The rumor sweeping the squadron, which Lewis was "half inclined to believe," was that the administration had decided that Bainbridge was to command a single fleet, that Decatur was superseded and "will not go, and that we shall go to Boston." If that were to happen, Lewis would leave the navy and find a merchant ship to command on a trading voyage to the Northwest Coast and China. The public could not understand why there was a delay, either. Even Mary Crowninshield wrote to ask and tease her secretary husband, "[I]s the fleet never a going [?] I could have fitted out a dozen."

If there were escalating tensions between the two commodores, there was little public dissension about going to war. Although the United States had just emerged from an indecisive war with Britain with a near-empty Treasury and many of its cities and towns burned and devastated, the mood of the country, if contemporary newspapers were a fair proxy, was decidedly in favor of war. *Niles' Weekly Register* editorialized that the war against Algiers, a place it called "a notorious nest of *pirates* and *manstealers*," was "among the most popular that one people ever declared against another." *Niles'* canvassed the entire country and found only one newspaper, the *Connecticut Mirror*, that opposed the war—that arch-Federalist bastion denouncing the Madison administration for going to war when the country's finances were in dire straits, accusing the Madison administration of "fight[ing] for fun," hoping that a "brilliant war" would help in the 1816 elections. *Niles'* understood that "if we were to sit down and 'count the cost of war,'" the value of the trade in jeopardy to Algerine corsairs would not equal even half the expenditures. But the Algiers war was not an accounting exercise; it was about the honor of the country, which reviled at paying for the freedom of its countrymen. Indeed, *Niles'* was convinced that the war was about the liberty of humanity, that it was up to the young republic to set an example for the Old World, to "relieve Christendom of its shackles." A successful result would give "additional influence in the councils of Europe, and tend to a good understanding with all nations, on the broad principle of reciprocal justice," since even the cynical European governments would be forced to admire the energy of the United States.

In mid-May, convinced that the imminent resumption of a coalition war against Napoleon neither threatened a U.S. naval force in the Mediterranean nor forced keeping the navy in home waters, Crowninshield finally allowed Decatur to depart.

Chapter Four

Mediterranean Triumph

AT TWO O'CLOCK ON MAY 20, 1815, the *Guerriere* signaled for the ships of the squadron to up anchor and make sail. The keeper of the log of the schooner *Torch* noted that the day had begun with gales and rain squalls, but by the afternoon, Peter M. Potter, the captain's clerk who kept a diary aboard the *Spitfire*, noted that it was "remarkably fine with a favorable wind." At three-thirty, the *Torch* weighed her anchor "together with the Fleet & stood to Sea." The squadron set out in a preassigned formation, the flagship in the lead and the other ships behind in two parallel columns, the frigate *Macedonian* leading the left column and the frigate *Constellation* leading the right. As the *Guerriere* cleared the Narrows, Decatur dashed off a last note to Crowninshield, which he handed to the pilot to send to Washington, that he "had passed the Bar with a fair wind" and was destined for the Mediterranean "with all possible dispatch."

A few days out, when the squadron had reached the far edge of the Gulf Stream, a gale whipped down. The captains sent down on deck the yards high on their ships' masts to reduce weight aloft, and reefed the few sails needed for headway. The gale began to blow at 4:00 a.m. on May 24, with what seasoned mariners called "thick weather" and "heavy seas," laconic language for hurricane conditions of monstrous waves and cross seas, thunder and lightning, and torrents of rain. When he woke that morning, Peter Potter, the captain's clerk on the *Spitfire*, found that "[b]oots, clothes, water kettles & plates were flying as doctor [Samuel] Johnson would say in heterogeneous proximity. The schooner [was] pitching and rolling in

Decatur's squadron sailing from New York, May 20, 1815. Painting by Irwin John Bevan. Courtesy of and © The Mariners' Museum, Newport News, Virginia.

such a manner as to preclude all possibility of standing." By noon, the ships had stripped down to storm canvas and were "hove to," sails furled and everything tied down, trying to ride out the waves. Most of the bigger ships were able to labor over the roiling sea, but the smaller ships were knocked about and scattered. Potter was awed by the massive seas breaking over the *Spitfire*'s bow, almost burying the ship in the waves.

The brig *Firefly* had the worst of it because of her smaller size and weight, falling farther and farther away from the rest of the ships. Her carpenter's mate, Samuel Holbrook, then just twenty-two years old, recalled in his memoirs, written more than forty years later, that the "brig labored very much, and was continually under water." By evening, both her foremast and mainmast, as well as her bowsprit, became sprung (cracked), and at first light, the crew braved the waves and weather and fished (strengthened) the masts by coiling heavy lines many times around the bases of each pole to secure them. Holbrook was in charge of the work. He had gone below at daylight to change out of his saturated clothes when a bosun's mate, the petty officer in charge of the deck, ran down to tell him that the foremast had sprung. Holbrook returned on deck to find that it had broken in two places. The rigging, taut in the cool weather of New York Bay, had become slack in the warmth of the Gulf's water and gave little support for the masts. With the topmasts still aloft, the weight threatened to topple the mast. If the foremast went over in the towering seas, it would have so destabilized the *Firefly* that she would have turned over on her beam ends and broached to, taking the ship and her hundred men to the bottom in seconds. Reporting on the state of the foremast to the quarterdeck, the first lieutenant, David Geisinger, told Holbrook to "do the best you can with it." While Holbrook and the four men in his carpenter's crew knocked out the mast wedges, the bosun's mates cleared away the wooden mast fishes (timbers lashed to the mast, like a huge splint) that were designed to support the mast. Other men began to pass thick cordage around and around to wold the mast like some enormous tourniquet, to lash it into place and prevent it from breaking completely.

Holbrook then asked the gunner to haul four large gun tackles up around the foremast, which the crew tightened with jiggers, a combination of pulleys in a double and single block that exerted multiple mechanical power. The brig wallowed and rose in the troughs and tops of waves, making it almost impossible to hold on. The fishes were then replaced, and Holbrook, recognizing that he had to take on the most hazardous part of the repair, placed himself in a bowline and had his crew haul him up with a pulley so that he could hammer the heads of the tackles into the mast. The sea thumped him again and again against the mast, pounding him as he swayed back and forth at crazy angles, but during the half hour he was up there, he had time to grab hold and hammer sixteen spikes through the tackles and into the masts.

Having secured the foremast, Holbrook descended to find that the mainmast had broken. The *Firefly*'s crew lowered the main boom on deck and, as with the foremast, ranged two large tackles on each side of the mainmast, fished it firmly, set up shrouds on each side, and spiked and wolded the mast. Holbrook observed that, without being "egotistical," had he not taken charge of securing the masts, "they would have gone over as sure as the world."

The *Firefly* was trailing the rest of the squadron. She began firing signal guns at 9:30 a.m. on the twenty-fifth, though with the heavy squalls and the pounding waves, no one heard her distress signals. The *Firefly* hove to again, and Lieutenant Commandant George Washington Rodgers, the commander—Commodore John Rodgers's younger brother—quickly surveyed the damage. Finding his masts were "so much disabled as to prevent our making sail to come up to the Squadron, or of keeping in company with [it had he been able to do so, he] thought it most prudent to make for the nearest port in the United States." He managed to bring his damaged ship into New York, hoping that after two weeks of repairs, Secretary Crowninshield would order him back to the Mediterranean. The subsequent court of inquiry under the ever-ready naval jurist Commodore Alexander Murray found that Rodgers's efforts to save the ship were "prudent and judicious" and that there was "no cause for censure." Rodgers did not forget Holbrook's services. Six days after the *Firefly* arrived back in New York, the time needed for an express letter to make its way to Washington and back, a warrant came rating Holbrook as carpenter. Rodgers mustered the crew and presented the warrant to Holbrook on the quarterdeck of the *Firefly*, with his thanks for saving the brig. By the time the *Firefly* was repaired and ready to sail again, Decatur's squadron had been out for more than a month, and the *Firefly* joined the second squadron under Commodore Bainbridge.

After the two-day brush with the storm, the rest of Decatur's squadron had a rapid and tranquil cruise across the Atlantic. Passing ships reported that the Algerine fleet was out. On the afternoon of June 11, the *Spitfire*, then nearing Europe and the squadron's rendezvous point at Gibraltar, but sailing alone as a result of the gale two weeks before, came within hailing distance of an Irish vessel, whose captain reported that the Algerine navy was cruising between Cape Trafalgar and Gibraltar, dead ahead of the U.S. schooner. On June 12, the *Guerriere* hailed a passing Portuguese ship and learned that the Algerines had been seen off Cape Trafalgar two days earlier. They were also told the rumor—false, as it turned out—that the Algerine ships had captured several American merchant vessels. When the American squadron approached the great Spanish port of Cadiz the next day, the *Guerriere* hoisted out a boat, and Decatur sent Lewis ashore, given his fluency in Spanish, to learn where the Algerine warships might be. The squadron lay off the port, backing and filling their sails. There was just enough time for Lewis to write Fanny a note that the squadron expected to fall in with the Algerine ships at any moment, that they were in a great hurry, but that she occupied all his thoughts, and that he would write her from Gibraltar the next day. As the squadron filled its sails, Decatur signaled that the intelligence received was that three of the Algerine frigates were off Alicante.

When the squadron touched at Gibraltar, the six ships tacked into the bay and circled the harbor, reuniting with the *Ontario*, *Torch*, and *Spitfire*, which had beaten them there after the storm. Lewis went ashore for intelligence of which way the Algerines had sailed once they passed the Straits. According to Midshipman Joseph Nones in the *Guerriere*, British naval officers, so recently the Americans' implacable enemy, provided Lewis with the latest word. The Algerine ships were close by, all right, under their most famous captain, or *raïs*, a legendary corsair named Hamidou.

Hamidou's origins were unclear. Some said he was the son of a tailor in Algiers, others that he was a Kabyle, one of the mountain tribesmen, but in either case, he was not a Turkish janissary. Instead, he had risen on merit from cabin boy to the ranking naval officer of the Algiers regency. On May 28, 1802, he captured a 36-gun Portuguese frigate by flying British colors as he approached in his own frigate, then running up the Algiers flag at the last minute before opening fire and leading a murderous boarding party that swept away the Portuguese opposition. It was a cunning *ruse de guerre* that Hamidou used often. He not only was unafraid to fight European ships, but was also a skilled prize taker: the Algerine prize registry lists thirty-one captures Hamidou made starting in 1797, and he earned a fortune rich enough to buy a splendid villa and gardens outside Algiers. For a brief period in the late 1790s, the dey made him the *wakil el kharf*, or minister of marine, for the regency, and yet in 1808 he was exiled for more than a year, during which time he lived in Beirut, before reconciling with the dey. Hamidou then received command of a squadron of ships, sailed them into the Atlantic in 1810, and won a major fleet action against the Tunisian navy in 1812. According to Elizabeth Broughton, the daughter of the British consul, Hamidou was "not the most rigid observer of the [Koran], as he sometimes chanced to drop in when my father was at the dessert, and never was so bigoted and unsocial as to refuse . . . a few glasses of Madeira." She thought he was extremely handsome, but noted that as an Algerine native, he was the subject of envy and jealousy from the Turks, and he "fully returned their antipathy." Another account described him as having blond hair and blue eyes, with a mustache but no beard. He was the dey's greatest fighting sailor, and in June 1815, he had briefly sortied out through the Straits of Gibraltar with a squadron of Algerine warships. Why he turned around will perhaps never be known; perhaps he sensed the approach of an enemy. Whatever the reason, the British naval officers were only too happy to tell the Americans that the Algerines had just returned to the Mediterranean through the Straits.

William Lewis dashed off another note to Fanny that he expected the squadron to find the enemy either off Cape de Gata, the famous white chalk bluffs known to be used as a landfall by the Algerines, or further along the coast of Catalonia. Lewis had been told that there were thirteen Algerine warships, and he hoped the U.S. warships would give a good account of themselves.

A tale long told, possibly true, but most likely legend, is that a number of British officers and citizens, along with an American gentleman residing at Gibraltar, clambered up the Rock of Gibraltar to better view the spectacle of a large U.S. naval squadron circling the bay. The British officers asked the American gentleman the name of each warship, and as he strained his eyes and pretended to give authoritative answers, more and more people crowded around him to hear. The first frigate, he said, was the *Guerriere*; the second was the *Macedonian*; the third, the *Java*; the next ship was the *Epervier*; "[t]he next, Sir, is"—"O damn the next," one officer responded, after hearing the names of all of the former Royal Navy ships now flying the Stars and Stripes.

Decatur had time at Gibraltar to write a short note to the secretary of the navy. He announced that the squadron had arrived at the Rock on June 15, after a passage of twenty-five days and after touching at Cadiz and Tangier. He recounted that gales in May had separated four of his ten ships from the rest, but that, except for the *Firefly*, they were at that moment "rejoining." From the information gathered ashore, Decatur learned that the Algerine warships had returned to the Mediterranean, where he would "proceed in search of the enemy forthwith." Obeying Lord Nelson's adage to "lose not an hour," Decatur circled the harbor and signaled his reunited nine-ship squadron to follow him out to sea, almost leaving Peter Potter stranded. The *Spitfire* had arrived in Gibraltar two days before, and Potter was touring the town when Decatur arrived and signaled to depart. Borrowing the fee for a boatman from the U.S. consul because he had forgotten to bring a penny with him, Potter was able to catch and clamber aboard the *Spitfire*, already under way.

The Americans did not have long to wait to find their enemy. Off the southern coast of Spain, the waters were crowded with shipping. The Cape de Gata was a rendezvous site for the Barbary cruisers. The Algerine *raïs*es had learned how to make the meridian observation of the sun, and the tables necessary to determine the latitude had been translated into Arabic, but Barbary seamen were littoral sailors, uncomfortable out of sight of land. This seems a strange failing for the corsairs, who, after all, had struck terror for centuries throughout Europe with raids into the Irish Sea and as far north as Scandinavia, but by the early nineteenth century, their navigational skills had atrophied. With their reliance on sailing from land-fall to landfall, the Algerine cruisers' positions and courses became predictable, and Decatur aimed to follow them back along their return course. Noah, who had sailed near the Cape de Gata en route to taking up his consular position at Tunis, described the cape as "formed by rocky mountains, which rise one above the other, in perpendicular ascent from the shore: the cape is composed of several head-lands, which break into small bays." The Algerines had made a habit of sailing over from Algiers, "conceal[ing] themselves, by the rocky promontories, near the shore, which is bold, and affords good anchorage."

Midmorning on June 17, the American squadron was abreast of the Cape, and about twenty miles offshore, but scattered over a large area, scrutinizing all the strange sails visible in the western Mediterranean, the wind blowing a steady breeze from the north northwest, when a lookout of the *Constellation* spotted a large warship, sailing along by herself. She was a mile or two off, sailing leisurely under topsails alone, and although she flew the Union Jack—Hamidou's standard ruse—no American was fooled into thinking she was English. Warships in that era often flew the flag of a neutral country or the enemy so as to keep their true identity secret for as long as possible. But based on the ship's rig and the cut of her sails, her course, and the way she was handled by her crew, experienced sailors often sensed what was afoot. Captain Gordon of the *Constellation* signaled to the flagship, "Enemy to the Southeast." Captain Lewis, at his post on the quarterdeck of the *Guerriere*, asked Commodore Decatur if the squadron should make all sail and chase. At that moment, the *Constellation* was to starboard of the sloop of war *Ontario*, a half mile ahead of the brig *Epervier*, and ahead and to port of the *Guerriere*. The rest of the Americans were scattered far behind. The ship, an Algerine vessel later identified as the *Meshuda*, apparently took the warships bearing down upon her as British, and as she was flying British colors (Algiers was at peace with Britain), she did not try to flee. Decatur realized that the squadron was slowly gaining on the enemy, and instead of making more sail, he ordered the signal "Clear for Action" made to all his ships, and then "Do Nothing to Excite Suspicion." Lewis wrote that the *Meshuda* "had no suspicion that we were enemies. [Captain] Gordon was a little ahead of us & asked permission by signal to speak [to] him & bring us intelligence, which I answered with 'No.'" It is hard to understand what information Gordon possibly hoped to gather—it is hard to believe he wanted to come near enough to hail the stranger to verify her nationality instead of trying to blow her out of the water.

At that moment, the signal halyard of the *Guerriere* broke out the flags for the signal to the *Constellation* to "Tack and Form into Line of Battle." That signal meant that each ship would change her angle of sailing to the wind and form into line with the other ships of the squadron, the classic battle formation for a fleet under sail, but unnecessary against one ship, which would be allowed time to try to escape while the squadron began its intricate pirouetting to get into line. The errant signal from the *Guerriere* has never been satisfactorily explained, but its causes are not hard to surmise. Lewis was in his second month in command of a frigate and had never commanded a ship in battle. Although he presumably had the navy signal book in hand when ordering the colored flags raised, in the excitement of imminent combat, he may have either mistakenly ordered the wrong flags or given the correct flag numbers but did not hear the lieutenant or midshipman repeat to him incorrectly the flags he was about to lift up the halyard. Leaving aside fault, U.S. Navy officers had little experience in using signals between ships in a squadron. Decatur's ships had put to sea less than one month before, and in the just-ended War of 1812, the navy had generally been able to slip its warships through the British blockading squadron rarely and singly: there had been little opportunity to practice signaling between ships operating together, and still less under the stress of battle situations. Finally, signaling problems were the norm, not the exception, in combat situations in that era. As Michael A. Palmer argues convincingly in *Command Under Sail*, "misunderstood, misinterpreted, wholly missed signals and missed opportunities, [were] a hallmark of a signals-based system of command."

Lewis did not realize the flag error at the time, but he later wrote privately that to any experienced commander, the signal was obviously a mistake. How Gordon would react to this signaling foul-up might prove crucial. There was no line of battle, the Americans being spread out in a cruising formation, and if the *Constellation* slowed down to maneuver into a nonexistent line, precious distance would be opened between the Americans and the Algerine. The safety of the port of Algiers lay nearly due east, almost a straight-line course with a following wind.

Lewis watched what happened. The *Constellation* maintained her pursuit, approximately one mile behind the chase, but, "[w]hether this [the signal] irritated the peevish little man [Gordon], or what other motive actuated him I can't tell, but he shewed American colours & gave the alarm to the Turk." George Hollins, a fifteen-year-old midshipman aboard the *Guerriere*, recounted in his memoirs fifty years later that the *Constellation* hoisted the Stars and Stripes as she surged forward. The "Algerine, as he turn'd out to be, took the alarm, and was immediately in a cloud of canvass, having evidently been prepared for any emergency. We had everything secured for [a] fight & it took some time for us to make sail." The log of the *Torch* bears the notation "At 1 PM the Strange Frigate Wore to the South & East [toward Algiers] and made all Sail to affect her Escape." Alexander S. Mackenzie, an eyewitness as a midshipman in the squadron, and later Decatur's biographer, complimented the Algerine seamanship, observing, "Quicker work was never done by seamen."

But the American warships were greyhounds, and they were soon hard on the enemy frigate's heels. The whole U.S. fleet wore and gave chase. The topmen on each warship raced up the shrouds and onto the yards at dizzying heights above the decks, untying the sails, which billowed out in huge canvas parabolas as they caught the westerly breeze and were sheeted home. Decatur did not need to order all sail now; the captains understood what was at stake. Lewis saw the 46-gun *Meshuda* make "off in a moment with all sail, & soon left the Constellation. We [the *Guerriere*] gained on him, however, very fast; & should have been alongside in a few moments, when he altered his course (or doubled as sportsmen term it), which obliged us to manoeuvre also. We lost ground in doing this. He now steered in such a way as to give Gordon an opportunity to begin the action, but at long shot." The *Constellation* opened fire from its starboard battery despite the range, and several shot were seen to smash into the *Meshuda*'s upper deck. One of the *Constellation*'s shots badly wounded Hamidou, probably from a splinter. But he resolutely refused to leave the deck, and instead had a chair brought up so that he could direct his ship sitting down. Finding herself hounded on her course, the *Meshuda* wore ship again—in other words, changed course from roughly southeast to northeast—which had the effect of bringing the wind from over their right shoulders (starboard quarter) to over their left shoulders (port quarter). With the ships turning at nearly the same time, the *Ontario* and the *Guerriere* were closer to the *Meshuda* than the *Constellation*. The *Ontario* flew ahead, and the *Torch* log recorded "the *Ontario* passed [the *Meshuda*'s] Larb[oar]d. beam, took a position on her fore & raked her Severely" with one broadside, although the momentum of the *Ontario*, or perhaps an error of seamanship from Jesse Duncan Elliott, carried her past the Algerine cruiser and out of a position where her guns could bear.

Lewis narrated that the *Guerriere* closed with the *Meshuda*, and "[w]e were in pistol shot [range] astern of him, where he fired at us with his musketry, while he returned the fire of the *Constellation* with his cannon. We waited until we could get alongside, which soon happened, & then poured in our broadside." At such close range, less than one hundred feet,

Peter M. Potter's sketch of the U.S. squadron's chase of the *Meshuda*. The *Guerriere* is close on the *Meshuda*'s starboard quarter, and the *Constellation* is far to port, which contradicts the notion that Decatur cut in between the *Constellation* and the *Meshuda* to deprive Captain Charles Gordon of fame and glory. From the diary of Peter M. Potter in the National Archives, Washington, D.C.

the massed cannon of the *Guerriere* tore apart the *Meshuda*'s deck, masts, and rigging. A 42-pounder carronade shot from the *Guerriere* literally cut Hamidou in two as he was trying to encourage his men. Many of the men of the *Meshuda* fled the maindeck, desperately seeking shelter below deck from the tremendous destruction from the American cannon. About one minute later, the *Guerriere* reloaded and fired off another enormous broadside, but at this second volley, one of the 24-pounder gundeck cannon exploded at its breech, killing three of its crew and wounding another thirty. Distracted by the explosion and carnage amidships, the *Guerriere* passed ahead of the *Meshuda* and fell off to a position off her starboard bow, and although she fired more broadsides at the *Meshuda* for a few minutes longer, her fire slackened and was ineffective. Lewis was quite disappointed, clinically noting that the *Guerriere* "only fired eight broadsides, & those badly; at least I was disappointed in the effect which I looked for. Our men were in too much hurry, & too eager to have good aim." At the same time, not a single cannonball from the *Meshuda* struck the *Guerriere*.

The *Meshuda* had one trick left to play: she put up her helm to try to pass by the *Guerriere* and escape. But hard on her heels came the 18-gun *Epervier*, which packed a heavy metal punch with her eight 32-pounder carronade broadside. John Downes brought his brig just astern of the mighty Algerine frigate, taking a firing position within a stone's throw off her stern cabin ports. As the *Epervier* opened fire, Downes backed and filled his sails, emptying the wind, to stay right off the stern of the much larger *Meshuda*. Lewis remarked that "Downes manouevred prettily in the *Epervier*," and Alexander Mackenzie recounted that Downes handled her "with such tact and seamanlike dexterity" that it was if he were putting her through her paces in practice, and not all the while firing at close range. Downes "gave him one or two broadsides well directed," wrote Lewis. At that range, few shots could have missed; 32-pound cannonballs tore into the unprotected stern quarters of the *Meshuda*. Decatur remarked that he had never seen a vessel more skillfully handled nor so heavy a fire kept up from so small a ship. The other light vessels all fired off shot, too, as Lewis put it, "for the sake of flashing powder"; the *Torch*'s log indicates that she commenced firing at 1:35 p.m. "from the Long Gun & kept up her fire, when an opportunity afforded." The *Epervier*'s fire provided the coup de grâce, and the *Meshuda* surrendered. From the first shot to the last, the entire action took about twenty-five minutes.

A contemporary rendering of the capture of the Algerine frigate *Meshuda* by the American squadron. Painting by an unidentified Algerine artist, 1815. From the collection of The New-York Historical Society.

People aboard the *Constellation* saw the chase and the battle quite differently. Joseph Causten was Captain Charles Gordon's clerk, and he had grown fond of his captain, confessing before the squadron assembled in New York of his affection for "*this good man.*" As captain's clerk, Causten's battle station was by the captain's side on the quarterdeck, taking notes and making a chronology of the action for the ship's log and, if necessary, the captain's report, and Causten was presumably in as good a position to observe the battle as any man in the squadron. Causten credited the *Constellation* alone for bringing the *Meshuda* to bay, and his account mentions nothing about hoisting American colors by mistake or the *Meshuda* changing course to flee. In a narrative impossible to square with those of Lewis, Hollins, Mackenzie, Potter, and the log of the *Torch*, Causten wrote that the *Meshuda* had "mistaken us for English and ran us down as friends, and absolutely was not at quarters, or any way prepared to fight when we brought her to action"; after the battle, when the Americans prize crew boarded the Algerine frigate, Causten found tampons still plugged into many of the muzzles of her cannon. Unlike the scattered shots that Lewis saw, Causten asserted the *Constellation* pummeled the *Meshuda* with four or five broadsides for a full fifteen minutes before the *Guerriere* came up. To Causten, Gordon was on the verge of his victory at last—the Algerine frigate surely would have struck her colors with her admiral dead, her crew scattered, and "all her Rigging & sails absolutely in ribbons." Causten claimed that as the *Guerriere* closed the distance, Decatur signaled "Cast to Starboard" to the *Constellation* to allow the *Guerriere* to administer the final blow. Even so, Causten stated that the *Guerriere*'s guns fired wildly, inflicting "no injury whatever." The *Epervier* then "ranged up under [the *Meshuda*'s] stern & gave her a couple of raking broadsides with her carronades," which essentially ended the fight. Causten claimed that he later heard John Downes say—presumably in private, to Gordon and his amanuensis, Causten—"he never saw a ship so shamefully manoeuvred, & so miserably fought in all his life as the Guerriere."

While there is no assertion in any of the accounts that is so internally inconsistent or obviously contrary to known facts to discredit Causten's account, the consistency and weight of the private, unpublished letters of Lewis, the private notebook of George Hollins, the diary of Peter Potter, and the official log of the *Torch* suggest that the regard Causten felt for his ship and his captain got the better of the truth. Indeed, in a private letter recounting the battle, William Shaler wrote that the *Guerriere* "was the only Ship engaged," suggesting that the word in the officers' mess of the *Guerriere* was that the *Constellation* contributed little to the overall American success.

The victory cost few American lives. Four sailors on the *Guerriere* had been wounded by enemy musket balls, fired from marksmen at the bulwarks and in the masts of the *Meshuda* early in the action. The only other American casualties were from the *Guerriere*'s exploding gun. Decatur rather coldly worried that the problem of bursting cannon in the navy was so endemic that the accidents "would be injurious to the service beyond the loss of the men occasioned thereby." He remarked that the men manning the nearby guns were steady, "altho many of them were much burnt." Lewis, echoing his commodore, concluded, "So much for our contract artillery! The effect produced . . . is beyond the loss of a few lives. It will by & by destroy the confidence which men should have in the sufficiency of the weapons with which they fight, and the bravest man will go into action trembling with the apprehension that the first discharge of his gun will blow him to pieces."

Before William Lewis and Jacob Jones departed with the prize to Carthagena, Decatur called all the captains of the squadron together. Selecting two ornate swords from the *Meshuda*, Decatur gave Lewis one and Downes the other, honoring them for their contributions in the battle. To each of the other captains and to the officers of the *Guerriere* he gave souvenirs, ranging from beautiful pistols to a curious-looking musket for the lowly Midshipman Nones (who, years later, donated it to the Peale Museum of Philadelphia).

If Decatur meant this scene to inspire a "band of brothers," it sadly miscarried. The navy in the sailing era was rife with simmering rivalries, as well as deep affections, between and among officers. They were competing for promotions, public acclaim, and sometimes prize money, and recognition by their peers was crucial to their self-regard. William Lewis wrote Fanny that Charles Gordon had reacted with "envious irritation" to Decatur's singling Lewis out. Gordon's modern chronicler, William L. Calderhead, has written that there was no evidence that Gordon took exception to the *Guerriere*'s alleged maneuvering in between the *Constellation* and the *Meshuda*, which that historian called a "serious breach of courtesy" and a victory "stolen from [Gordon]." In fact, Gordon took Lewis aside and privately accused him of purposely making the signal to "Tack and Form into Line of Battle" to deprive Gordon and the *Constellation* of the lead honor in taking the Algerine ship, and claimed that Lewis was so greedy for promotion that he would try to deprive other vessels from participating in the victory. He downplayed what the squadron had won, asserting "there was no honour to be had in a contest with such a miserable enemy." Lewis would not let the rebuke ruffle him, chalking up the comments to Gordon's sour disposition. To Lewis, Gordon had blundered and could not be trusted to close properly. Lewis had directed the *Guerriere* with skill. It was not a question of "courtesy" in some chivalrous sense but a question of fighting a close action against a desperate opponent.

Gordon's insult fell far from the mark. The *Meshuda* was no miserable enemy. She was outnumbered and smothered by the squadron, but for all that, she was as big as any of the American frigates, and well led by Hamidou, an experienced, savvy seaman. Although hardly remembered today, the *Meshuda* was the last frigate the United States Navy captured in battle in the sailing era.

Decatur's June 19 report to Crowninshield was stingy with praise. Terse, as was his habit, the entire report consisted of seven sentences. Decatur credited the capture to the squadron, "which fell in with and captured, an Algerine frigate of 46 guns," which was accurate as far as it went, and he mentioned the number of casualties and enemy prisoners. But the only ship named was his own. Decatur recounted that "from her favorable position," the *Guerriere* was able "to bring the enemy to close action," and after firing two broadsides, most of the enemy crew scurried for protection below decks. Decatur spent more ink on the bursting of the cannon than he did on the battle itself. There was no mention of the *Constellation* running the *Meshuda* down or hitting her first, presumably because Decatur wanted no mention of Gordon's gaffe in raising American colors. Yet there was also no mention of John Downes and the *Epervier*. Decatur could not square his spare account with the fact, which he also stated, that the *Meshuda* surrendered "after a running fight of 25 minutes." Some historians have attributed Decatur's omission of mention of any other ship or captain as evidence of his supercharged ego and his craving for the adulation of the American public and politicians, particularly after the loss of the *President*. That explanation seems superficial. After previous battles, when his own place in the American naval pantheon was less secure, Decatur had been generous with praise. Perhaps a better explanation was his desire not to add to the evident ill-feeling among his captains by publicly singling out some but not others.

On Sunday, June 18, the *Macedonian* sent her stream cable back to the *Meshuda* and took her in tow. Jacob Jones was almost the only captain who had missed the combat the day before, having been chasing down unknown vessels inshore in the *Macedonian*. Tow or no, when his lookouts found a strange sail inshore at 6:30 p.m., he cast off the cable and set sail to intercept the stranger. Jones ordered a lieutenant to hoist the signal "Brig Inshore Positively an Enemy," which caused the lighter ships in the squadron, such as the *Torch*, to make all sail and stand in for Almeira Bay in support. At 8:00 p.m., the wind died, and the *Torch* put out her sweeps and "pulled in Shore the Strange brig in Sight coming up fast," as her log recorded. Lieutenant Wolcott Chauncey cleared for action, but the brig *Spark* signaled (presumably with lights from her masts) at 11:00 p.m. that the strange sail was not an enemy. She turned out to be a neutral, an

English merchant ship, and the *Torch* put her sweeps back in the water to claw away from land. The wind being nonexistent and then fluky, it was only at noon the next day that the *Macedonian* was able to tack back to the prize frigate and take her back in tow. Late in the afternoon, a Spanish pilot came aboard to steer the *Meshuda* into Carthagena, but the wind died to a calm, and Jones ordered out the frigates' three cutters and whaleboat to kedge and tow the prize into the harbor. The *Meshuda* finally was safe in Carthagena, and the *Macedonian* headed back to sea. At four-thirty, her signal midshipman reported a signal from Decatur relayed by the brig *Flambeau*, ordering the *Macedonian* to rejoin the squadron with all possible dispatch. At seven, her log recorded, "[H]eard a cannonading to the N.E." The *Macedonian* had missed another battle.

The squadron had found another Algerine cruiser, this one a brig sailing close to the Spanish shore. Since fighting the *Meshuda*, Decatur had spread his squadron to search for the enemy, recognizing that the other Algerine ships supposedly were off the Catalonian coast. It was crucial to intercept the Algerines at sea, where they could be sunk or captured, and either way, denied to the dey as a weapon for future attacks. Decatur had his smaller ships, which drew less water, sweeping closer to shore, and the larger, deeper-draft frigates out to sea. At four o'clock in the afternoon on June 19, a clear, bright day with a pleasant breeze from the southwest, the sloop of war *Ontario* spotted a strange sail ahead, close to the Spanish coast, which she assumed was Algerine, and gave chase right into the shore. The strange brig drew less water than the U.S. sloop of war, and the *Ontario* flew the signal "Breakers," indicating that she was dangerously close to running aground. The small fry, the *Epervier*, *Spark*, *Torch*, and *Spitfire*, took over. Decatur signaled "Danger," which Chauncey in the *Torch* took to mean the danger from shoals, and he immediately had the *Torch* haul off from the chase. Peter Potter on the *Spitfire* was amused that three American ships flew British colors but that the strange brig had the U.S. ensign and pendant flying over her. At 6:00 p.m., the *Torch* recorded in her log that the strange brig had anchored, although in fact she had run aground between the watchtowers of Estacio and Albufera, and she defiantly raised the Algerine flag. Again, Wolcott Chauncey ordered the *Torch* to stand in, to sail at the Algerine brig. Again, however, he was stymied by a signal from Decatur, "Give Intelligence of the Strange Sail." The four U.S. warships stood off, and the *Torch* at least came within hailing distance of the *Guerriere*. Chauncey and Decatur managed a few words. They

Peter M. Potter's sketch of the attack on the Algerine brig *Estedio*. From the diary of Peter M. Potter in the National Archives, Washington, D.C.

may have spoken about the risks of the shallow water and how to fight the Algerine brig, but Potter in his diary recorded that "being on the Spanish coast & under the guns of a town with [the] Spanish Kings colours flying, it was necessary to be cautious." Whatever the hailing might have been, the result was that Decatur ordered the small vessels to stand in and engage the enemy. At this word, Potter recorded that the crew of the *Spitfire* gave "3 cheers [as] we pushed towards her."

As the four small U.S. ships moved in, several small boats put off from the Algerine brig to land some of her crew on Spanish soil, a risky operation under fire. The senior officer of the four American ships was John Downes in the *Epervier*. According to Potter, Downes hailed the other captains, "I am going to anchor near her, the other vessels may come up as they can, but not a gun is to be fired until I anchor." Downes, conscious of the surf and shoals, wanted to place his ships where they could enfilade the brig with their cannon but not run their own ships aground. As Peter Potter put it in his diary, "We now took a situation to blow her to pieces as we expected she would never strike [her flag]." Two more boats put off from the brig to bring the Turkish officers ashore, and the *Epervier* opened fire. A lucky shot smashed into one of the boats, sinking her. At six-thirty, the *Torch* "came to anchor within Musket Shot of [the brig] having nearly a raking position with the *Epervier* on his Starboard beam; we immediately commenced firing," as did the *Spitfire*, first with her two long guns and then with her broadside. Potter heard the "whistling of his balls," the

Algerine brig returning fire. A half hour of firing forced the enemy brig to surrender.

Robert Stockton, the first lieutenant of the *Spitfire*, asked Captain Dallas if he could board the enemy, and when Dallas agreed, Peter Potter found himself in a boat with Stockton and six marines rowing across, with the cannonade still going on practically over their heads. Potter hoped for the honor of being first to board the enemy, but the marines could not row fast enough, and boats from the other U.S. ships beat them. The brig turned out to be a 22-gun cruiser called the *Estedio*. Potter called it a "Scene of Splendour & disorder," and he was appalled to see American sailors running amuck, taking pistols and cutlasses as souvenirs, the petty looting so widespread that the lieutenant who was put in command of the prize could "get very few to attend" to their duties. Potter learned later that the men who boarded the *Estedio* were permitted by their officers to take what they wanted, and one lucky sailor seized a purse filled with gold coins. Potter, armed with a sword, went below, and discovered about sixty Algerine seamen hiding. He wanted to get them unarmed and on deck to be secured by the marines. Not knowing any language in common, he waved his sword and shouted at them, trying to intimidate them, but when they realized that Potter was not going to have them massacred, the Arab seamen prostrated themselves, kissing his hands and feet. Twenty-three Algerines were found dead on board, and the U.S. sailors captured eighty, dispersing them among the squadron. That night, the American sailors were able to float the brig off the shore, aided by the tide and heaving overboard almost all the *Estedio*'s cannon, and they sailed her out under the Stars and Stripes. Decatur wrote Secretary Crowninshield that there were no American casualties in the action against the *Estedio*, nor were any of the American ships damaged. He reported that the *Estedio* was five years old, bigger than the *Epervier*, and "perfectly sound."

Decatur ordered the *Estedio* sailed into Carthagena for a prize court adjudication, loading aboard the captured men from the *Meshuda* and the *Estedio*. They would be held as prisoners until the United States made peace with Algiers, but Decatur did not want them in his ships. Densely packed into his ships, they might pose a health risk to his own crews, or they might try to overpower their marine guards and try to seize one or more U.S. ships; at the very least, they would consume much of the squadron's precious food and water. The easiest and safest thing for him to do was to send them to Spain, where the U.S. naval agent could worry about where they might be held and fed.

Decatur's squadron off Algiers. Engraving by N. Jocelin. From Gardner W. Allen, *Our Navy and the Barbary Corsairs* (1905), author's collection.

More importantly, Decatur decided that it was unlikely that the American squadron would find any more Algerine warships at sea, but if his squadron sailed to Algiers immediately, it might cut off any Algerine ships at sea returning to their base of operations. The losses that the dey's fleet had sustained, plus the risk that the others would be destroyed as they made there way back to Algiers, Decatur hoped, would bring the dey to terms. If not, Decatur planned to bombard the batteries and sink any shipping in the harbor. But Decatur wanted a quick result: scurvy, that dread disease of sailors, caused by a lack of vitamin C from a diet without fresh fruits and vegetables, had made its appearance in many of the ships of the squadron. The telltale signs of scurvy were pains in the limbs, teeth falling out, and lethargy. After five weeks at sea, the water on the ships was also getting foul, Potter noting in his diary that it "unfortunately [was] getting an oddish twang."

The squadron arrived off Algiers on June 28. Charles Bell, a midshipman from North Carolina, kept a journal aboard the *Macedonian*. He noted the arrival of the squadron off Algiers and described what he could see, and what he had been told about, the city:

> Algiers is built on the declivity of a Mountain facing the sea; the prospect is very beautiful. The harbour has a mole 500 paces in length; extending from the continent to a small Island where there is a castle and large Battery. It is said to contain 120,000 inhabitants[,] 15,000 houses & 107 Mosques. It is not above a mile and a half in circuit, and is walled. The streets are extremely narrow. There [*sic*] public baths are large and handsomely paved with marble.

Centuries of bombardments and threatened bombardments had made the seaward defenses of Algiers formidable. The city itself was not walled toward the sea, but nearly 200 cannon were mounted along the coast outside the town and along the waterside within the walls. Another 200 cannon were massed on an island in the center of the mole, arranged in tiers; the "lighthouse battery" contained 62 guns, and 112 more cannon formed batteries to the south and west of it. Some of the guns fired through embrasures, others through casemates, arched openings in five-foot-thick stonework. Altogether, there may have been as many as 450 cannon able to fire on an attacking squadron. Just how formidable those batteries were at the moment Decatur's squadron arrived is unclear; thirteen months earlier, when Keene reconnoitered the place for Noah, he suggested that many of the cannon were poorly mounted and indifferently served by the Algerine soldiers.

Vue du Port et d'une Partie d'Alger. Lithograph by Genet from a painting by Bagot. In Adrien Berbrugger, *Algérie historique, pittoresque et monumentale* (1843), Special Collections of The Johns Hopkins University.

When the squadron came into Algiers, Decatur signaled the other ships in the squadron to "Preserve [Their] Present Stations," and the log of the schooner *Torch* dutifully reflected that Captain Chauncey "Took in Top Gall[an]t Sails, brailed up the Foresail & hauled down the Jib of Jibs & backed d[ow]n Main Topsail." The *Guerriere* flew the Stars and Stripes from her stern. Following the instructions of Secretary of State Monroe, the flagship broke out the blue flag with yellow cross of Sweden at her maintop and a white flag of truce at her foretop, and she fired a gun to the leeward to ensure that everyone ashore knew that the Americans had come to parley through the Swedish consul. At noon, a small boat came out of the harbor carrying the Swedish consul, Johan Norderling, and the port captain of Algiers.

They came aboard the *Guerriere*, and Decatur ushered both men into his great cabin. Decatur asked where the Algerine fleet was, because he knew that the Algerines did not stay at sea long, and because he suspected that Algiers had sent out a fast vessel from Gibraltar to warn of the approach of the American squadron. The Algerine port captain replied that the Algerine fleet had no doubt found refuge from the American squadron and was safe in some neutral port. Decatur replied, "Not the whole of it," and described how the squadron had captured both the *Meshuda* and the *Estedio*. The beautiful frigate about them, with all her masts and yards in place, the ropes Flemish-coiled and the brass polished, hardly had the look of a ship that had fought an action less than two weeks before. The Algerine port captain suggested that Decatur lied in stating that he had captured the *Meshuda*. According to Midshipman George Hollins, who was present, Decatur quietly passed the word for the senior surviving lieutenant from the *Meshuda*. "When the officer entered the cabin, & the [port captain] saw him he rushed at him [and] seized him by the beard. I was about to jerk him down to his feet when Decatur interfered & prevented it." Decatur merely reported that "[t]he impression made by these events [the information about the captures] was visible and deep." The Algerine port captain turned to Decatur and Shaler and requested the terms and conditions on which the Americans would make peace.

Decatur and Shaler handed the port captain two letters, one from President Madison and the other their own, to deliver to the dey. The Algerine port captain then requested that hostilities should cease during the peace negotiations and invited the American commissioners to come ashore to negotiate, their own personal security and freedom of movement guaranteed by the Algerine minister of marine—as Norderling personally confirmed. The Americans rejected both suggestions, insisting that all negotiations would occur aboard the *Guerriere* and that hostilities would continue. Not agreeing to a truce may have seemed like poor etiquette, but it gave the Americans bargaining leverage. The ships of the Algerine navy were at sea, and both the dey's negotiators and the Americans knew that if they returned with Decatur's squadron in Algiers harbor, they would likely be captured or sunk. As Potter noted in his diary, Decatur told the Algerine negotiators, "I do not want peace myself but it is my orders to treat [for peace]. My officers have come out to fight and put themselves in practice." The Swedish Consul and the Algerine port captain then departed back to Algiers.

The Decatur-Shaler letter to the dey was brief. The commodore and the diplomat informed the dey of their appointments as diplomatic commissioners with Algiers and noted that they were ready to open negotiations to restore peace between the two countries. They stated that they had instructions to "treat upon no other principle, than that of perfect equality, and on the terms of the most favoured nations. No stipulation for paying any tribute to Algiers, under any form whatever, will be agreed to."

Madison was almost as succinct in his letter, and he made America's point with great clarity:

JAMES MADISON, PRESIDENT OF THE UNITED STATES,
TO HIS HIGHNESS THE DEY OF ALGIERS

Your Highness having declared war against the United States of America, and made captives of some of their citizens, and done them other injuries without cause, the Congress of the United States at its last session authorized by a deliberate and solemn act, hostilities against your government and people. A squadron of our ships of war is sent into the Mediterranean sea, to give effect to this declaration. It will carry with it the alternative of peace or war. It rests with your government to choose between them. We persuade ourselves that your Highness, contrasting the miseries of war, with the advantages resulting from a friendly intercourse with a rising nation, will be disposed to return to those amicable relations which had so long subsisted between our two countries, and thus meet the views of this government, whose leading principle is peace and friendship with all nations. But peace, to be durable, must be founded on stipulations equally beneficial to both parties, the one claiming nothing which it is not willing to grant to the other; and on this basis alone will its attainment or preservation by this government be desirable.

I have authorized William Shaler, one of our distinguished citizens, and Commodore Bainbridge and Commodore Decatur, commanders of the fleet, to conclude a peace with your Highness. They will send this letter to you. I make this communication from a sincere desire that the honourable opportunity which it affords to your Highness to prefer peace to war will be improved. Written at the city of Washington, this twelfth day of April, A.D. 1815.

> *James Madison*
> By the President
> *James Monroe*
> Secretary of State

The dey of Algiers, named Omar, was Greek by birth and had become dey only a few months before, at age forty-three, after more than thirty years as a janissary, and after rising to the position of *aga*, or commander in chief, of the army. George Campbell Smith had provided America with intelligence of the new dey's succession to power. In a letter to a Salem friend dated April 12, 1815, he reported that on March 23, Dey Hadji Ali was assassinated by his janissaries and replaced by his first minister, leaving Algiers in "tumult and consternation," but the new dey, Mohammed Khaznadj, served for only sixteen days before he, too, was murdered by the janissaries, with the result that Omar, the *aga*, took over. Shaler described Omar as about five feet ten inches tall, with a dark complexion, a "shining black beard silvered with grey," and dark, expressive eyes. Shaler came to respect him as a man of "natural good sense, quick perception, and great dignity of character." Omar rarely looked at the person to whom he was speaking, and then only furtively, and he spoke on most subjects with diffidence, aware of his lack of worldliness. A thoughtful man, Omar could be agreeable, even friendly, but when displeased was by turns angry, gloomy, and forbidding. Western diplomats never lost sight of his ruthlessness: when he became dey, Omar put to death all the women of the seraglio of Hadji Ali, a predecessor dey, for reasons that no foreign consul could discern.

On June 30, the Swedish consul and the Algerine port captain returned to the *Guerriere*. The dey, the Algerine port captain stated, would negotiate on the basis laid out in the Decatur-Shaler letter. Shaler and Decatur handed over a draft treaty from which, they said, they would not deviate in substance, drafted by Shaler on the voyage out from New York. By its twenty-two articles, the dey would agree to free the American prisoners in Algiers without ransom, pay $10,000 in compensation for the brig *Edwin* and her cargo, give favorable treatment to American ships in peacetime and in wartime, allow American warships and privateers to sell their prize vessels and cargo at Algiers in wartime, and, most importantly, forgo tribute from the United States forever.

After reading the draft, the Algerine port captain complained about the article that required the restitution of property, alleging that such a demand had never before been made on Algiers and that the property taken from the *Edwin* had been dispersed. Decatur and Shaler refused to budge, answering, "As it was unjustly taken it must be restored or paid for." The Algerine port captain also protested with great feeling the article calling for the end of annual tribute. It was not the amount or the value that he was particular about, he told Shaler and Decatur, but the need to receive something annually from the Americans that would add to Omar's security. He suggested that the dey would be content with just a little gunpowder from the Americans every year. Decatur replied, "If you insist upon receiving powder as tribute, you must expect to receive balls with it." Hearing that, the Algerines gave up on annual tribute.

The Algerine port captain then asked whether, if Omar signed, the *Meshuda* and the *Estedio* might be restored to Algiers. The initial reaction of Decatur and Shaler was to refuse. Those warships not only represented the glory won in the campaign but also would mean prize money to every man in Decatur's squadron. More importantly, having just captured them, why should the ships be given back? The port captain then argued that it was not Omar but the former dey, Hadji Ali, who had declared war in the summer of 1812, which he acknowledged was unjust and unprovoked. According to Midshipman Hollins, who claimed to have heard the conversation, Decatur then asked why Algiers had gone to war in 1812. The port captain replied that Hadji Ali had followed the advice of the British consul, who had said, "'We will take all their (the American) Men of War & you [Algiers] can take the Merchant Ships.'" The port captain added, "'& now instead of the result being as they promised you (the Americans) have brought out three of their (the English) ships [the *Guerriere*, *Macedonian*, and *Epervier*] & whip us with [them]." Nevertheless, he told the Americans that if Omar was to make peace and restore the captives without ransom, he needed some palpable gain, such as those two warships, to save face. This was literally a matter of life and death for Omar, as the two recent assassinations of deys plainly suggested.

Decatur and Shaler withdrew to consult in private. They undoubtedly considered a number of matters. For one thing, if they were to agree to return the ships, would they then open the door to other demands needed to save the dey? More important, the Algerines were believed to be masters of duplicity, willing to make agreements and break them as they found convenient; should an American commodore return to a possible future enemy its most powerful warship? What about the risk of loss—what happened if the *Meshuda* and *Estedio*, then at Carthagena, hundreds of miles away, sank on the passage back to Algiers or came under fire from a third country? And then, of course, there was the more personal concern: the ships were prize to the United States Navy. If their seizure was held valid by an admiralty court, everyone who took part in the respective captures stood to gain a share. As squadron commander, Decatur had the most to gain. His private interest, and that of every man in the squadron (except Shaler, his diplomatic entourage, and the army artillerists) was in the balance against the diplomatic interest. On the other hand, Decatur and Shaler realized that the need for Omar to save face also served the interests of the United States, for without this dey on the throne, the chance that any treaty would be obeyed was slight. As Decatur phrased the matter in his report to Crowninshield, the dey had "earnestly requested" the return as "it would satisfy his people with the conditions of the peace." Crowninshield's April 15 orders had provided for this sort of contingency, allowing Decatur to "dispose" of any vessels he might capture that would be "unsafe" to send home in the way he felt most expedient.

Instead of taking time to weigh the alternatives, Decatur closed the deal. Shaler later wrote of how fast events had passed before them, and the willingness of Algiers to so readily accept the terms of the treaty he had drafted gave him pause. Historian Roy Nichols asserted that the return of the two ships was a "concession . . . made at Decatur's insistence and against Shaler's better judgment." In *Advance Agents of American Destiny*, Nichols insisted that there was "friction between the two men at every step." According to Nichols, Decatur was overbearing with Shaler, Norderling, and the port captain. Decatur had donned his dress uniform, a gold-trimmed navy blue coat and white trousers, with the Order of the Cincinnati hanging from his lapel. According to Nichols, Norderling thought Decatur was imperious and strutting. Nichols even claimed that Norderling referred to him as "Bashaw Decatur" to Shaler, both a cutting insult from a European consul at Algiers and an indication that relations between Decatur and Shaler may have become strained, because Norderling hardly would have insulted Decatur to his co-negotiator if he did not sense that Shaler thought similarly.

In fact, Shaler did not disagree with Decatur that the two ships should be returned to Algiers as a gesture for securing a peace treaty. A memorandum in Shaler's handwriting in his papers, labeled "Note for Conference with Como: Decatur," indicates that he disagreed with Decatur on only one point: Decatur promised that the American obligation to return the two captured Algerine vessels would be "faithfully performed," which smacked of literal compliance, whereas Shaler advocated "the most liberal interpretation" of American obligations.

Not only did Decatur and Shaler agree on substantive points, but Nichols seems to have misread Norderling's July 3, 1815, letter to Shaler. In that letter, written in French, Norderling focused on the dey's anxiety regarding the American commitment to return the *Meshuda* and the *Estedio*, and Norderling's own anxiety for his country's interests and his own person if the Americans did not follow through with their promise. Norderling refers to Decatur as "Commodor Decatur" and as the "head of your squadron" ("Chef de votre Escadre") and, near the end, asks Shaler to give his respects to Decatur ("Mes devoirs, à Monsieur le Commodor"). Norderling does not call him "Bashaw Decatur," nor is there any suggestion of disrespect, which of course would have been shockingly undiplomatic between diplomats who had known each other for only a few days.

Decatur decided that to clinch the peace, he would give the prizes back to Algiers. If the object of the United States was to secure a favorable treaty, the two ships were merely the necessary grease to lubricate the deal. The United States Navy had already proven its superiority over the Algerines—in his diary, Potter expressed amazement that the Algerine navy was "a mere burlesque" with "miserably contrived" equipment, poor gunnery, and poorly disciplined crews. If the navy needed to take, sink, or burn those ships again, Decatur must have been supremely confident that it could do that job. He reported to Secretary of State Monroe that "considering the state of those vessels, the sums that would be require to fit them for a passage to the United States, and the little probability of selling them in this part of the world," it was "expedient" to make them a gift to the dey in their "as is" condition. Decatur was adamant that the ships were, and would be seen as, a gift, and refused make their return appear as an article in the treaty.

The Algerine port captain then asked for a truce to consider the terms, which Decatur and Shaler refused, as they had refused the offer of a truce two days before. They reported to Monroe that the Algerine port captain "even pleaded for three hours. The reply was, 'not a minute; if your squadron appears in sight before the treaty is actually signed by the Dey, and the prisoners sent off, ours would capture them.'" The most the Americans would agree was that hostilities would cease when an Algerine boat returned to the *Guerriere* with a white flag flying, once Norderling pledged not to hoist the white flag unless Omar signed the treaty and the prisoners were actually in the boat with him. With that, the Algerine port captain and the Swedish consul went down the side of the American frigate into their waiting boat and set sail for the five-mile trip back to Algiers.

While Decatur and Shaler waited for the dey's decision, with a white flag of truce flying from the *Guerriere*, the rest of the squadron lay off the city, standing in toward the harbor and then wearing ship to reverse course, returning further out to sea, essentially in a holding pattern. At one-thirty that afternoon, the *Epervier* hoisted signal flags reporting that her lookouts had spotted a strange sail. Thirty minutes later, Decatur ordered the other ships of the squadron to chase. The *Torch* made sail and surged eastward where, at 3:00 p.m., her lookouts found the stranger, a schooner, sailing close to the shore but to windward of Cape Metefor. At three-thirty, the ship being chased hoisted the green and white flag of Algiers and hoisted sail after sail to try to slip into the harbor. The *Torch*, along with the other American warships, tried to cut her off. "Standing in for Algiers," her log reads, "Squared the Yards, Set the Square Sail & Top Mast Stay Sail & Main Top gall[an]t Sail." Decatur then signaled to all his ships that the stranger was "Positively Enemy." Despite the tentative treaty, there was no truce between the United States and Algiers, and the Algerine schooner could become another prize.

From the *Guerriere* and the dey's castle, dozens of American and Algerine telescopes trained on the chase saw the American warships gaining on the schooner. Less than three hours after the Algerine port captain had left the *Guerriere*, a boat pulled off from shore under a white flag. As the U.S. warships closed on the schooner, the boat slowly sailed out from the port toward the *Guerriere*.

According to Peter Potter, Decatur signaled to the ships pursuing the Algerine sail to "Come Within Hail." The schooner *Spitfire* came under the *Guerriere*'s stern. Over his taffrail, Decatur hailed Alexander Dallas, "Take a position on my weather bow & follow my motions. You are not to commence hostilities until I fire." Dallas answered, "Very well, sir." Decatur explained, "A boat is now putting off from the town with a white flag flying. If they have signed the conditions I dictated we shall not be under the necessity of flogging this dirty fellow."

The boat from Algiers, white flag flying, crept closer, finally coming within hailing distance. Decatur spotted the Swedish consul and called out, "Is the treaty signed?"

"It is," replied Norderling.

"Are the prisoners on board?"

"They are."

"Every one of them?"

"Every one, Sir."

With that, Decatur rasped out the order to hoist the signal "Peace," so that the naval commanders would not fire on the Algerine schooner, and they let her pass unmolested into Algiers harbor, leading Peter Potter to remark ruefully in his diary, "How unlucky that this peace was not delayed one day."

The boat came alongside the *Guerriere*. James Pollard and the men from the *Edwin* came aboard—George Campbell Smith, the master; Francis Garcia, the first mate; Samuel Larabee, the second mate; David Allen, a New Hampshire man who had shipped at Malta; Thomas Lewis and Daniel Glover, both listed as "boys" from Salem; Elias Currel and George Pettle, both of Beverly, Massachusetts; and the cook, Peter Blay, laconically listed as "black." According to Peter Potter, the Algerines so feared an American attack that they ordered the prisoners, who had been moved three miles outside of the city, to run the whole distance down to the port, without time to get their clothes or meager belongings, and jump into the boat that was to take them out to the *Guerriere*. They were a pitiful sight, haggard and emotionally spent by their three years of bondage. Some kissed the American flag; others simply wept. Midshipman Nones, who talked to them while they were quartered aboard the *Guerriere*, wrote that they told him that they were "cruelly treated, half starved and worked daily beyond Endurance, and when Nature claimed even a momentary truce—the Bastinado—played a cruel & a prominent part across their backs & soles of their feet." Now they were going to go home.

On July 3, Norderling returned from his garden outside the city, hoping to find Shaler at his new consular residence in Algiers, but learned that he was back aboard the *Guerriere*. He wrote Shaler in French that the dey had signed the peace treaty and had "scrupulously fulfilled the conditions to date," and that he awaited Shaler to present himself at the palace. Omar had told Norderling that he wished to hear from Shaler that Decatur fulfilled his promise to return the two prizes. Indeed, the dey was obsessed about their prompt return, as he claimed to be beset by inquiries from the families and friends of the Algerines captured by the Americans. He suggested through Norderling that Decatur send a ship away, out of sight of the city, even if it really didn't go to Carthagena, so that he could tell his countrymen that the Algerines would soon be home. As the intermediary between the United States and Algiers, it was critical for Norderling that the Americans live up to their side of the deal; he relied, he told Shaler and Decatur, on the honor of the United States government and the men's personal honor so that he, his family, and Swedish trade would not be exposed to the wrath of the dey. Omar had assured him that very morning that the two Spanish prisoners (the vice consul and a merchant) would be freed upon their request to smooth over the deal with Spain. Norderling was clearly anxious about being at risk and nervous that the Americans would not deliver what they promised.

Shaler went ashore to receive $10,000 compensation for seized American property. Shaler then found a residence to serve as the consular mission. On July 4, 1815, Decatur and Shaler wrote to Monroe on the course of their twenty-four hours of diplomacy. They observed that the Algerines "now show every disposition to maintain a sincere peace with us, which is, doubtless, owing to the dread of our arms; and we take this occasion to remark that, in our opinion, the only secure guarantee we can have for the maintenance of the peace just concluded with these people is, the presence in the Mediterranean of a respectable naval force."

Yet there was some muted criticism of the treaty from officers in the squadron, who thought that Decatur and Shaler had been too lenient. An unnamed officer of the *Constellation* wrote home that

> [t]hough an honorable [treaty], and on such terms that with propriety it could not be rejected—for the dey granted every demand made, still I think the commodore was rather hasty. Had we cruized six weeks longer we should have destroyed the whole of their navy: placed it entirely out of their power to commence for many years any depredations on our commerce, and finally made peace on the same terms we have it now. But peace with this people was certainly the most desirable *object*, and as we have it on our own terms, we should not complain.

Similarly, Peter Potter, who chronicled the entire 1815 campaign in his diary, confided there, "How unfortunate that we granted so comparatively lenient terms to these rascals. The Commodore I understand regrets it very much & has expressed his conviction that he could have obtained the release of every Christian captive!" Even Shaler, writing in his memoir, *Sketches of Algiers*, a decade later, expressed misgivings. The two U.S. naval victories over the *Meshuda* and *Estedio* "completely confounded" the Algerines, and events occurred so quickly thereafter that Shaler himself "could hardly realize them." He could scarcely believe that Algiers agreed to "the terms of the peace which we dictated, almost without discussion"; to Shaler, it was "incomprehensible." So quick and complete was the peace that Shaler, a diplomat, "regret[ted] that our instructions did not justify our inflicting upon them a more exemplary chastisement."

The criticism that the United States was too lenient in making peace—a criticism that, according to Peter Potter, Decatur shared—was perhaps natural for men who, expecting a long and difficult campaign, had won easy victories, but it is wide of the mark. Omar was willing to make a quick peace on American terms precisely because he wanted to preserve his fleet; with his fleet destroyed, the dey might well have ordered his soldiers to man the batteries at the fort and defied the Americans to attack. Without mortar vessels, a line of battleships, or a ready invasion force, the ensuing campaign likely would have bogged down. The Algerines would have been rendered powerless to capture merchant shipping for a time, but the political settlement desired in Washington would likely be no closer to reality, and the Algerines could always buy more ships to replenish their corsair fleet, even assuming the European nations would not make outright gifts of them or provide ships as tribute (as the United States had once done). As the publisher of the officer's letter observed, the other side of the coin was that Decatur "wished to avail himself of the first moment of terror to extort his own terms."

Decatur wrote Crowninshield the next day, July 5, his first dispatch since the capture of the *Meshuda* and *Estedio*. He reported sending the prizes into Carthagena, and the arrival at Algiers on June 28. He noted:

> Finding the Algerine squadron to be still out, and knowing they had been at sea a longer period than usual, and that a despatch boat had been sent to Algiers to inform them of our arrival in the Mediterranean, I thought it probable that they would seek shelter in some neutral port. It seemed, therefore, a favorable moment to deliver a letter from the President to the Dey . . . which would afford them an opportunity to begin a negotiation, if they thought fit. A negotiation was accordingly opened, and a Treaty of Peace was dictated by us, and finally concluded in twenty-four hours. . . .
>
> This treaty, possessing all the favorable features of those which have been concluded with the most favored nations, and other advantages conceded to us only [the U.S. was given the exclusive right to sell prizes at Algiers], I flatter myself will be considered honorable to the United States, particularly when we compare the small force employed on this occasion with the formidable expeditions which have often, and without success, been sent against Algiers. It has been dictated at the mouth of the cannon, has been conceded to the losses which Algiers has sustained, and to the dread of still greater evils apprehended; and I beg leave to express to you my opinion, that the presence of a respectable naval force in this sea will be the only certain guarantee for its observance.

Decatur decided to send the *Epervier* home with Pollard and the captives from the *Edwin*, the treaty, and his dispatches to Monroe and Crowninshield. He used the opportunity to reward the officers in the squadron. He gave Lieutenant John Shubrick, a protégé who had served under him as second lieutenant of the *President* and as first lieutenant of the *Guerriere*, the command of the *Epervier*. Decatur rewarded Downes by moving him from the *Epervier* to the command of the *Guerriere*. Decatur had long before promised William Lewis the chance to go home to his wife, and Decatur sent him as a passenger in the *Epervier*, placing his dispatches to the secretaries of state and the navy in Lewis's hands for delivery, along with captured battle flags from the *Meshuda* and the *Estedio*. Decatur closed his dispatch to Crowninshield commending Lewis and recommending him to the notice of the government. Decatur clearly hoped that sending Lewis home with triumphant news, and with his endorsement, would lead to Lewis's immediate promotion to captain.

With Lewis as a fellow passenger in the *Epervier* went his brother-in-law, Lieutenant Benedict Neale, the first lieutenant of the *Constellation*, who had married Mary Whittle in a double ceremony in Norfolk with William Lewis and Fanny. Lewis closed his letter to Fanny by noting that he expected to sail soon:

> I pray to Heaven it may be so; for my Dearest love, you don't know how much I desire to see you. Let what will happen, I shall return to you soon. . . . I expect to be with you by September, or October at farthest. . . . I tell you again, that I have nothing to live for in this world but you. I am more unhappy than I can describe, when I suffer myself to think that by some evil chance or other, I might lose you. Farewell my dear.

The log of the *Macedonian* on July 8 noted, "At 5 P.M. . . . Standing out of the bay of Algiers the Brig *Epervier* bound to America with the Articles of Peace."

Fanny Lewis never heard from William Lewis again, nor did her sister Mary see Benedict Neale come home. They waited for the *Epervier* in vain. Their father, Conway Whittle, sought information from anyone who might know something or be able to comfort his daughters. He tried writing Tobias Lear. On October 12, 1815, Lear wrote back that he had no good news. He reported that in a letter dated July 15, James Simpson, the United States consul at Tangiers, had mentioned that the *Epervier* had sailed from there two days before. Lear hoped that Lewis, Neale, and the others would be found safe, but the "late disastrous Gales at sea gives cause to fear the worse." William Lewis had stayed with the Lear family at

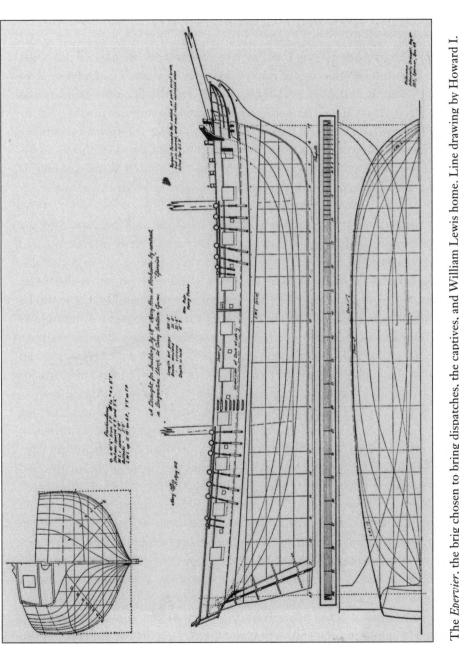

The *Epervier*, the brig chosen to bring dispatches, the captives, and William Lewis home. Line drawing by Howard I. Chapelle. From Chapelle's *The History of the American Sailing Navy* (1949), author's collection.

the consulate in 1807, when they came to know his "amiable heart." The Lears had never met Fanny but expressed their "[s]incere prayers that her suffering may be relieved by the safety of her excellent husband." The last probable sighting of the *Epervier* was on August 8, when another vessel reportedly saw her making for Charleston, hundreds of miles off the coast, laboring under double-reefed topsails in heavy weather. The *Epervier* never made it home. It has always been assumed that the *Epervier* foundered in the "disastrous Gales," perhaps a hurricane that swept out into the Atlantic. Along with Shubrick, Lewis, Neale, and other veteran naval officers whom Decatur thought he was rewarding by sending them home early, the crew of the *Edwin*, the people for whom the United States of America had gone to war, so recently freed from slavery, were all lost at sea.

ALTHOUGH THE PROMISE TO RETURN the *Meshuda* and the *Estedio* to the Algerines was deliberately kept out of the treaty, Stephen Decatur had given his word that the ships would be restored. During the negotiations, Shaler expressed the view that "the most liberal interpretation should be given to the promise to restore the Captured vessels, and that it would be good policy to do it with all the dispatch consistent with the other objects of the squadron." Decatur, however, thought there was "no necessity to conciliate these people by any extraordinary exertion." Decatur asked Shaler, who had gone ashore to establish the United States consulate, to inform the dey that the ships would be delivered "as is" to Algerine officers as they lay at Carthagena. Decatur promised to provide an escort for the restored Algerine ships, "*not* to protect them against the hostilities of any other power, but sufficient to take the crew on board from the dangers of the sea." Yet Decatur had heard that the Spanish authorities had cast doubt on the legality of the seizure of the *Estedio*, which, they asserted with good reason, was within Spanish territorial waters. If there was one principle of the law of nations that every sailor knew, it was the principle that the territorial domain of a sovereign state extended as far as a cannon-shot would reach over the adjacent waters, generally understood to mean three miles out to sea from the land, whether or not cannon were actually mounted. Decatur stated that the United States did not admit that the *Estedio* had been within Spanish waters, but wanted to put the question to rest. He suggested that Shaler encourage the dey to release the Spanish vice consul and a merchant, both confined in chains; Decatur expected that, in exchange, the king of Spain would release the *Estedio*, and he, on behalf of the United States, would abandon any claim against Spain "of

any nature growing out of her capture in the vicinity of the Spanish coast."
By July 5, he sent the schooners *Torch* and *Spark* to Carthagena carrying
the Algerine captains sent by the dey to bring back the two ships. The
Algerines had been instructed to repair them, and Decatur confided to
Shaler that, after the hammering they received two weeks before, it would
take considerable time and money to make them seaworthy.

In fact, the Algerines sailed the *Meshuda* back to Algiers, arriving on
July 23. But the Spanish balked at releasing the *Estedio*, again asserting
that she had been pursued into Spanish territorial waters and captured
within sight of a Spanish battery and the Spanish flag. The Spanish authorities decided to hold on to the brig, at least until they could sort out
their own claim. Of course, this made little sense because the United States
was not claiming the *Estedio* for itself—in other words, it had abandoned
the idea that she was a valid prize—but rather asked that the brig be returned to the Algerines, whatever the legality of the initial seizure. The
Spanish authorities rather obtusely decided that there were international
law implications and detained the brig to figure out what they should do,
or, in the words of Thomas Gamble, the commander of the *Spark*, so "the
legality of her capture can be ascertained by a Court of Justice, as they
please to term it." With an eye toward the American commander with
whom they were dealing, a man who had made his name by sailing into
Tripoli harbor to burn the *Philadelphia* under the guns of the bashaw's
massed batteries, the Spaniards not only took possession of the *Estedio*,
but, in Gamble's words, "secured her near the Arsenal, apprehensive I
presume that some attempt would have been made to take her out."

Why did Spain wish to make things difficult for the United States? The
United States minister to London, John Quincy Adams, was approached
by the Spanish ambassador to Britain on July 13, the day after the London
newspapers first reported the capture of the *Meshuda*. The Spaniard questioned Adams as to the movements and intentions of Decatur's squadron,
suggesting that U.S. naval forces would not be allowed into Cadiz and
hinting that Spain regarded relations with the United States as being in a
"state of hostility." According to the Spanish ambassador, the Bourbon
royal court in Madrid was incensed by the perceived slight to their minister to Washington, who had not been recognized by the Madison administration because Napoleon's brother, Joseph Bonaparte, had been crowned
king in Madrid in 1809, and ruled until toppled by the British army. Adams
told the ambassador that the king's ambassador had been recognized upon
the restoration of the Bourbon monarchy. Yet Adams realized from the

conversation, as he confided to his diary, that "Decatur may meet with some difficulty there."

Adams's only private source of information was a letter from Shaler written off Cadiz on June 13, which of course was before the lightning victories of the squadron. In a letter dated July 25, in his neat, beautiful penmanship, Adams offered congratulations to Shaler and expressed his "ardent hope that you will accomplish the glorious object of discovering to our Country, and to the civilized world, the only tribute which it becomes the honour of a powerful Christian Nation to pay to the Pirates of Africa." The defeat of Napoleon at Waterloo, Adams concluded, while freeing the British navy for possible mischief against American interests, should not affect Shaler's "transactions" in Algiers; all the European powers professed friendliness to the United States and specifically "towards the warlike part of your expedition."

In the meantime, Shaler took up his duties as consul general. He called on the dey, to whom he presented a jewel-encrusted sword as a gift of the United States, and despite the abandonment of tribute in the new treaty, he distributed $17,000 in gratuities to high and low Algerine officials, including Omar's barber and cooks. He found Algiers to be a strange if exotic place, his social relations limited to the other foreign consuls, but at least his residence looked out over the sea, and from his terrace he had a commanding view of Algiers harbor.

Chapter Five

Unfinished Business

AFTER MAKING HIS TREATY, Decatur and some of his officers and men went ashore to see the sights and scenes of Algiers. Norderling entertained four of the U.S. captains at dinner on July 2, and when Decatur went ashore, the Algerine authorities respectfully saluted him with five guns from the fort. But even with the American slaves now freed and safely aboard the squadron, the squalor of the European slaves working at the mole depressed the American sailors. One Venetian slave—"in most wretched condition" according to Peter Potter, with chains attached to his legs— managed to escape and jumped into one of the *Guerriere*'s liberty boats at the mole. The overseer with an armed party approached the American naval officer in charge at the landing and demanded the return of the slave. The officer, without orders, did not know what to do, and surely did not want to create an incident in a foreign and hostile port; he gave up the man, despite his screams and begging for help. This incident unsettled the American sailors and disturbed Decatur, who then gave orders, which he made sure reached every ship in the squadron, "that should another slave ever reach our boats, he should be protected at all hazards."

On July 8, Decatur's squadron left Algiers for Cagliari in Sardinia to take on water and gather fresh provisions to counter the scurvy that had appeared in his squadron. The word among the squadron was that they were ultimately bound for Tunis, because near the end of the War of 1812, Tunis had delivered into British hands two British merchant ships taken by an American privateer and sent into Tunis as prizes. "This,"

Potter confided to his diary, "I understand is the cause of our visit. I hope they will be in a bad humour & give our Commodore a saucy answer," because Potter, like many in the squadron, relished the idea of a fight. On July 14, the U.S. ships dropped their anchors in the broad bay of Cagliari. Potter wrote in his diary that because the U.S. sailors had spent time on the Barbary coast, the Sardinian authorities ordered the U.S. ships to remain in quarantine for five days, with no personal contact allowed with anyone ashore, which worried Potter, since the *Spitfire* was down to her last four days of water. The next day, Decatur signaled that the *Spitfire* would be allowed to water immediately, and she sailed across the harbor to anchor near the watering hole, but the Sardinians still refused to touch anything from the Americans, even money, which the sailors had to place in a jar of vinegar in order for the local officials to retrieve it. The Sardinians were afraid of the plague, typhus, and other contagions, and the Americans hoped that submersion in vinegar would satisfy their hosts as some sort of primitive disinfectant. An officer of the *Constellation* wrote that Cagliari was "a poor miserable place, and although I was tired after our long cruise, of the ship and *sea*, still I preferred being actively employed out, than remaining in Cagliari." Potter used similar terms, calling Cagliari "truly a miserable place. Beggars, marchionesses, pimps & cavalieros are the natural productions of the place." Decatur and Gordon went ashore to be introduced to the queen of Sardinia (the king was away in Turin), but Potter was not so impressed, calling the queen "old & ugly." When Cagliari fired off a 21-gun salute for the absent king's birthday on July 24, Decatur ordered the *Guerriere* to answer the royal salute gun for gun. The squadron completed watering and buying food, and stood out to sea on the evening of July 24, with Decatur signaling "Rendezvous Tunis."

Decatur had led the squadron into the Mediterranean, taken two prizes, and finished negotiations with Algiers so quickly that Mordecai Noah, the consul at Tunis, had no knowledge of what happened until Decatur himself appeared. Noah had learned that the bey of Tunis had ordered out his fleet, not against the Americans, but to cruise for Sicilian and Neapolitan ships, and perhaps those of Hamburg, Denmark, and Holland. Noah hurried to the palace and visited the prime minister, Soliman Kya. Noah advised him to prevent the Tunisian ships from sailing, warning that Decatur's squadron was in the Mediterranean and might detain or attack any of the bey's warships on account of the declining relations, which then would assume an unpleasant form. Soliman Kya said he regretted the differences and hoped that the two countries would be reconciled, but he would not use his influence to prevent the fleet from going out.

On the afternoon of July 25, the six ships left in Decatur's squadron (*Guerriere, Macedonian, Constellation, Ontario, Flambeau* and *Spitfire*) came to and anchored in Tunis Bay. "Nothing can be more welcome to a Consul in Barbary," Noah wrote in his *Travels*, "than the sight of a fleet, bearing the flag of his nation; he feels, that surrounded by assassins and mercenaries, he is still safe and protected."

Noah had never gotten accustomed to life in Tunis and found the city unsightly and unsavory. The city contained 150,000 people, crammed into a walled area less than five miles across. Noah described the place, with streets

> so narrow, that in many of them, four persons can scarcely walk abreast, they are not paved, and are filthy in the extreme; the houses are built of mud, and white washed, nearly all of one story, with a terrace, on which the inhabitants walk, and frequently sleep. In the centre of the town, the Bey is building a palace, the architecture of which is very heavy; some of the chambers, however, are splendidly furnished. There are two or three spacious Mosques, finished with marble, found among the ruins of Carthage and Utica. . . . Under the palace, a range of stores or shops is erected, these are narrow, yet lively, and contain fine goods. Most of the shops in Tunis are like closets, in which the owner sits cross-legged, with his few articles before him; and to exclude the rays of the sun, the streets are covered with vaulted roofs, which gives to them an appearance of subterranean passages. . . . A canal, containing all the filth of the city, runs under the northern and eastern wall, the odour from which is insufferable—in fact, the salubrity of the air, which is also rendered more pure by the aromatic herbs, burnt in their baths, is the only preventive to contagious disorders. Take the city altogether, it is mean and filthy, the beautiful country in the vicinity, alone renders a residence even tolerable.

A diplomatic incident had rocked Noah's brief tenure at Tunis. In February 1815, an American privateer brig called the *Abellino*, carrying 6 small cannon and seventy-six men under a Captain Wyer, arrived at Tunis after a twenty-nine-day cruise from Boston. She was the first American privateer since the start of the war to challenge the British in the Mediterranean. Noah arranged for the *Abellino* to pass through quarantine, and rode down to meet Wyer at the goletta, a small port area built on a narrow strip of land separating the shallow Lake of Tunis from the sea. The *Abellino* turned out to be a new, coppered brig whose keel had been laid only sixty days earlier. Noah had just learned of the signing of the treaty of Ghent in December 1814, two months earlier, which provided that Anglo-American hostilities should cease in the Mediterranean in four weeks' time. Noah satisfied himself from looking through the *Abellino's* papers that she was sailing under real articles, while for his part Wyer wanted to find out if he could use Tunis as a base of operations and as a place he might send in any British ships taken as prizes. He already had taken a British schooner off Cape de Gata and ordered her into Tunis with a prize crew. Noah recognized that the British had warships at Gibraltar and Malta, that the U.S.-Tunisian treaty prohibited the sale of prizes, and that Tunis would not want to destroy her relations with England by allowing the Americans to use its port as a safe harbor. Nevertheless, Noah told Wyer that he would try to handle the delicate task.

An apocryphal story, repeated in a number of the histories of the Barbary wars, holds that the British consul got wind of what Noah was trying to do, and protested to the bey that the British-Tunisian treaty contained language that the bey's ports should not be used for prize adjudications and sales in "any war between England and any other Christian nation." The bey was persuaded until Noah showed him a copy of the United States Constitution and stated that in the United States, all stood equal, regardless of belief, and thus America could not be called a "Christian" nation. The bey agreed in astonishment (and later supposedly pocketed his fee). The reality was more prosaic. In fact, Noah himself recounted in his *Travels* that he made the round of the ministers, and after carefully delineating the argument for allowing the *Abellino* to sell her prize cargoes in Tunis, all of which was received with grave faces, he gave assurances that each minister would receive a *douceur* to sweeten the process, and then he received permission for the privateer to land and sell the merchandise.

Wyer sailed off and began to terrorize British ships. The *Abellino* did the circuit of the Mediterranean, sailed up the Adriatic, looked into Smyrna, touched at Marseilles, and crossed back over to Tripoli and Tunis. British warships often tracked her, but Wyer succeeded in escaping every pursuer. The *Abellino* took several prizes, allowing some to ransom their worth to avoid capture, and giving some back to the English as being unworthy of further attention or as cartels carrying the prisoners he had accumulated. But two of the more valuable prizes Wyer decided to send into Tunis. The first was an English schooner called the *Dunster Castle*, with a cargo of oil and fish, and the second was the merchant brig *Charlotte* from Trieste, carrying currants and fustic (a yellowish dye from fustic wood). Noah saw the two English merchantmen come into the harbor, one actually dropping her anchor, both close to shore. But H.M.S. *Lyra*, a Royal Navy brig the two prizes had evaded to get into Tunis, sent armed sailors into Tunis harbor in boats, forcibly cut out both ships, and sent them to Malta.

Noah sent a letter to the bey's prime minister narrating what had happened under his very eyes. He asserted that the bey had not lifted a finger to protect the American-controlled ships, despite a specific treaty stipulation that obligated him to protect American vessels within the territorial waters of his regency and under the cannon of his batteries. Indeed, under the law of nations, belligerent acts within the territorial waters of neutrals were strictly forbidden. Noah duly made a claim on the bey for $46,000 in Spanish currency, the value of the prizes, and for the value of their cargoes. The bey refused to recognize the claim. In Noah's words, the bey's minister "ridiculed the idea of paying for these vessels, contending, that we had been in the habit of paying them for their friendship and forbearance, and this accident, which they could not prevent, they would not answer for."

With the American squadron appearing almost providentially, Noah went down to the quays to take a boat out to visit Decatur. En route, a messenger delivered a letter from Decatur, announcing the peace with Algiers and asking Noah for a report on the state of U.S. relations with Tunis. Noah carried with him just such a report, outlining the basic facts of the *Abellino* and her prizes, and Noah's suggestions for a plan of action. The Tunisian minister of marine lent Noah the bey's personal barge to take him out to the *Guerriere*. The squadron lay off Cape Carthage, and as the boatmen rowed Noah out in luxury, he was thrilled to see the "commanding sight" of the graceful American warships. Within an hour, he clambered aboard the *Guerriere*, greeted by the lieutenants, Downes, and Decatur in full uniform, sideboys in white gloves and bosuns' whistles screeching, the marines drawn up in double lines, and cannon firing off the five-gun ceremonial for a consul, a vastly gratifying greeting to the thirty-year-old diplomat. After an exchange of pleasantries, Decatur brought Noah down into his great cabin and handed him a sealed letter.

The letter was from Secretary of State Monroe, dated April 25, 1815, and read in its entirety:

Sir,

At the time of your appointment, as Consul at Tunis, it was not known that the RELIGION which you profess would form any obstacle to the exercise of your Consular functions. Recent information, however, on which entire reliance may be placed, proves that it would produce a very unfavorable effect. IN CONSEQUENCE OF WHICH, the President has deemed it expedient to

revoke your commission. On the receipt of this letter, therefore, you will consider yourself no longer in the public service. There are some circumstances,
too, connected with your accounts, which require a more particular explanation, which, with that already given, are not approved by the President.

Noah was flabbergasted. As Noah himself wrote, his being Jewish "was
known to the government at the time of my appointment, and it consti-
tuted one of the prominent causes why I was sent to Barbary." Indeed,
Noah's religion was known to everyone in the administration. President
Madison wrote Monroe on April 24, 1815, about a number of diplomatic
issues, and noted casually that "Tunis will be vacated by the Jew. . . . In
recalling Noah it may be well to rest the reason pretty much on the ascertained prejudices of the Turks against his Religion, and it having become
public that he was a Jew, a circumstance which it was understood at the
time of his appt. might be [awkward]." There is no record of any complaint by the bey about Noah, much less on account of his religion, but
Madison and Monroe needed a reason to fire Noah besides the fact that
he had failed in his confidential mission of ransoming the *Edwin* captives
and had made public the United States's role in the ransoming effort.

But the idea that Noah's Judaism was "awkward" in Tunis can be traced
to another source. Johan Norderling had written his old friend Tobias
Lear a long letter on April 9, 1814, even before the Keene mission failed,
almost certainly the first letter to arrive in Washington about the mission.
Norderling castigated Noah, whom he had never met, as a clumsy ama-
teur for publicizing what clearly was intended as a secret mission, and for
relying on Keene, and did so in grossly anti-Semitic language. Norderling
began his letter with objections to the appointment of "Mr. Moses M.
Noah (what a sweet Jewish name!)," and mocked Noah's appearance at
the Gibraltar synagogue. Norderling suggested that it was humiliating for a
Turkish ruler to have to deal with a Jew as the representative of a sovereign
nation. In Colonel Lear, Norderling had a kindred spirit, since Lear filled
his journals with anti-Semitic invective. Lear undoubtedly shared the
Norderling letter with his friend the president, Madison having come to
rely on Lear informally about relations with the Barbary regencies.

Noah thought himself absolutely blameless on all counts—his religion
was not known in Tunis, despite all his palaver before leaving Washington about enlisting the help of local Jews—and his expenses were all legitimate. He had an attack of nerves sitting in Decatur's presence, reading
the letter sacking him. But he had an immediate problem: if he told Decatur
what the letter stated, Decatur would of course no longer deal with him as

consul—indeed, might leave him to the mercies of the bey. Besides, Noah felt that he had a duty as the American official on the scene who knew what had happened to the *Abellino*'s prizes and knew what should be done. Noah glanced at Decatur and realized that Decatur did not know what the letter contained. "[W]ith apparent indifference," Noah wrote, he folded up Monroe's letter, "put it in my pocket, and then proceeded to relate to Commodore Decatur the nature of our dispute with Tunis." He handed Decatur his report.

Noah's report summarized what had happened, emphasizing the violation of the U.S.-Tunisian treaty and the loss of the two ships. He then formally requested Decatur to enforce "the respect due to our rights and treaties, as you may deem proper to afford." In disposing of the cargo which had landed, Noah described a fraud perpetrated on the rightful American owners by a company of local Jewish merchants, under the protection and with the approval of the bey's son Sidi Mustapha, who purchased the cargo at a price vastly below its worth. Noah ended his report with the comment, "For the satisfactory adjustment of this claim, some interference appears equally necessary." Noah urged Decatur to send a letter demanding immediate compensation from the bey, and not to land to negotiate. Decatur took umbrage at Noah pedantically laying out what he should do, and disabused Noah of any idea that he was under his orders. Noah backed down, suggesting that his only desire was to best serve his country, and Decatur agreed to write the letter.

Dealing with Tunis presented vastly different issues than dealing with Algiers. The United States had formally declared war against Algiers, and Decatur had specific guidance from two cabinet officers, Crowninshield and Monroe, as to how he should fight and negotiate with the dey. Tunis was different. The premise when he had sailed was that Tunis was friendly, and Decatur even had in his desk a letter to the bey from Monroe expressing the friendship of the United States and asking for support for the squadron. No war had been declared, Decatur had no instructions, and Washington was four thousand miles and two months' sail away. More to the point, when Decatur arrived off Algiers, the Algerine fleet was at sea, but when he came to off Tunis, the harbor contained not only its protecting batteries but also three frigates and several smaller vessels, nearly a match on paper for Decatur's squadron.

Decatur did not hesitate. Indeed, he provided a classic example of American gunboat diplomacy, using force or threatening force by the country's armed ships to punish illegal acts overseas without a formal declaration of war or specific authority from the executive authority of the nation. In some respects, Decatur set the standard for a hundred years of gunboat diplomacy: his demands invariably were brief and polite but barely concealed an unmistakable lethality.

He wrote the prime minister of Tunis:

U.S. Ship Guerriere
Bay of Tunis, July 26, 1815

SIR:

I have the honor to enclose to your Excellency a dispatch from the department of State, of the United States, by which you will perceive the friendly disposition of my Government towards the Bey and Regency of Tunis. When the dispatch was written, it was believed that an equally friendly disposition existed on the part of Tunis. With surprise I understood, on my arrival in the Mediterranean, that the treaty existing between the two countries had been violated on the part of Tunis first, by permitting two vessels, which had been captured by an American Vessel, to be taken out of the port of Tunis by a British Cruiser and secondly, by sanctioning a company of Jew Merchants, subjects of Tunis, in taking the property of an American Citizen at their own price and much below its real value.

In consequence of this information as soon as we had obtained Justice from Algiers for her aggressions, I hastened to this port with the power and disposition to exact from this Regency an observance of our treaty. I now require an immediate restitution of the property, or of its value. Your Excellency will perceive the necessity of the earliest attention to this communication, and of making known to me the decision of his Excellency the Bey with the least possible delay.

I have the honor to be, with great consideration, your Excellency's most ob: servt,

Stephen Decatur
Commander, &c.

The next morning, the Tunisian minister of marine sent for Consul Noah, having read the letter from Decatur. He was, in Noah's words, "in no very pleasant humour."

"This is not a proper and respectful manner of doing business," the minister told Noah. "Why does not your Admiral make his complaints to the Bey in person? Why does he demand the payment of us for prizes, which the British have illegally carried away, and demand an answer forthwith? We are not accustomed to be treated in this manner; there was a time when you waited our pleasure to establish a treaty, and paid us for it, and gave us presents whenever we demanded them, and all within my recollection."

Noah calmly stated that the measures Decatur proposed were indispensable, that the minister must have anticipated them, and should have paid compensation as Noah had requested before Decatur's ships arrived; now it was too late. The minister considered his arguments but insisted that the bey would not pay. Noah departed.

Despite that stance, the minister-general of the bey wrote a response to the American demand in the Italian-Arabic lingua franca, addressed to "the Illustrious Signor" Decatur. Existing among Decatur's papers is a rough translation of the letter. Decatur himself spoke Italian and probably could read it. His translation of the letter shows cross-outs and interlineations as he tried to understand the tone as well as the substance of the communication. The minister-general made clear that Tunis wished to maintain the friendship between the two countries and that the bey had authorized him to clear up the difficulties with "what is sought and pretended" in Decatur's demand. The minister-general claimed that everything already had been resolved with Noah. First, the bey would make immediate restitution of the value of the goods of the prizes "bought by a company of Jew merchants, our subjects." However, the prizes taken away by the English warship presented a different story: the minister-general stated that it had been agreed with Noah that the bey would be allowed one year to make demand on the British government for the entire sum, and if he was unable to effect reimbursement from the British king, then the bey would acknowledge the debt. After his "correct explanation," his highness the bey "will not believe, nor be persuaded that you will annul or disapprove a compact solemnly made according to the Law of Nations."

In the meantime, Noah learned through some Christian slaves that the Tunisian prime minister consulted with the Dutch consul, Nyssen, who had been born in Tunis, was fluent in Arabic, and seemed more devoted to the interests of Tunis than to those of Holland. Nyssen told the bey that Decatur had no authority to declare war and would not dare to begin hostilities—that, in essence, the Americans were all bluff—and that he should resist the United States demands. Noah picked up his pen and wrote Nyssen, warning him to not interfere with the concerns of the United States. He noted wryly that if the bey refused American demands, the naval squadron would attack, and within twenty-four hours of the event, the bey would order Nyssen's head cut off for giving such wrongful advice.

The Tunisian minister sent for Noah again. He asked Noah how it was that he could be so calm, having previously been so loud and insistent on

the need for reparations. Noah replied that he no longer needed to protest because war was imminent unless the demands were met; that, having
conquered Algiers, the squadron was ready to fight; and that fighting for
American rights was better than standing by a treaty that Tunis did not
respect. A report reached the palace at that moment that a small boat had
put off from the *Guerriere* with four sailors aboard. A man in the bow had
a lead and was charting the depth of the channel as it came up the harbor.
The rumor swept the palace that the man with the lead, dressed in plain
sailor's clothes, was Decatur. Noah did not know if the rumor was true,
but the report, he observed, "served to create a great alarm."

Part of the mythology of the navy holds that the Tunisian minister then
said to Noah, "I know this admiral; he is the same one who, in the war with
Sidi Jusef, of Trablis [Tripoli], burned the frigate [the *Philadelphia*]."

"The same," answered Noah.

"Hum! Why do they send wild young men to treat for peace with old
powers? Then, you Americans do not speak the truth. You went to war
with England, a nation with a great fleet, and said you took her frigates in
equal fight. Honest people always speak the truth."

"Well, sir, and that was true. Do you see that tall ship in the bay flying
a blue flag? It is the *Guerriere*, taken from the British. That one, near the
small island, is the *Macedonian*, was also captured by Decatur on equal
terms. The sloop near Cape Carthage, the *Peacock*, was also taken in battle."

The Tunisian minister laid down his telescope, sat down on his cush-
ions, and combed his beard contemplatively. Tunis decided to accept the
American ultimatum.

The reality was less dramatic but just as pointed. Decatur, claiming he
was "indisposed," but perhaps keeping himself aloof from negotiations so
that the janissaries could not size him up if fighting ensued, sent Captains
Gordon and Elliott ashore with a number of midshipmen from the squadron to wait on the bey and learn his answer to the American challenge.
Noah arranged for a Turkish bath to accommodate the Americans, who,
after forty days at sea, looked forward to a good steam, Turkish tobacco,
and fresh coffee. Noah then took the two captains with him to the palace
to learn the decision of the bey on the American ultimatum. The palace
was packed with the curious, and the bey had in his entourage his two
sons, Hassan and Mustapha, whom Noah described as "active and insolent." Gordon, the senior officer, stepped forward. Noah commented that
Gordon, "a short man, worn down by illness," did not make the "impres-

sive figure" that was so important to the Turks. The bey looked down at him "with the utmost indifference."

"Who are you?" asked the bey.

"I am second in command of the squadron, Sir," said Gordon, "and I am here to know whether you are ready to do us justice."

"Why does not your Admiral come on shore? Why am I treated with so much disrespect by him?"

"He will not land, Sir, until you decide to pay the value of these vessels, which you permitted the British to take from us," Gordon replied.

Mustapha then interrupted in a tone Noah thought was insolent and threatening, but before he could express himself fully, Elliott interposed, "We did not come here to be insulted. This interview must be cut short. Will you, or will you not, pay for these vessels? Answer nothing but that."

"Well then," Mustapha replied with a furious look, "we will pay for them, but have a care, our turn comes next," suggesting that Tunis would have some sort of revenge. But Mustapha was all bluster. The Tunisian navy had been whipped by Hamidou and the Algerine fleet in 1812, and the Americans, who had just captured two ships of the Algerine navy and killed Hamidou, were at his doorstep with a powerful squadron and were ready to fight. The bey could not afford to have his navy destroyed by Decatur.

"Tell your Admiral to come on shore," said the bey. "I'll send the money to the Consul. I am a rich Prince, and don't value it—go."

Yet in fact there was some hesitation. The bey asked for one year in which to pay compensation, which the Americans categorically refused. The bey then suggested that he would pay for the value of the ships, but the Jewish merchants who had bought the cargo should make compensation for that. The Americans agreed. On July 30, 1815, Decatur, resplendent in his full uniform of navy blue cocked hat and coat, both trimmed with gold, and white trousers, landed with a number of his lieutenants and midshipmen and walked up to the American consulate. The various foreign consuls accredited to Tunis came to pay their respects and offer congratulations on Decatur's twisting of the bey's tail. Amidst the party, the bey's brother arrived with the coin to pay the compensation. He reputedly flung the money onto the floor and berated the British consul with the words, "You see, sir, what Tunis is obliged to pay for your insolence. You should feel ashamed of the disgrace you have brought us. I ask you if you think it just, first to violate our neutrality, and then leave us to be destroyed or pay for your aggressions."

Noah gave a receipt, witnessed by Decatur, that he had received as agent for the privateer the sum of 46,000 Spanish dollars. Predictably, the merchants, who agreed to pay 44,000 piasters for the merchandise, "had time allowed them, and after the squadron had departed, [Noah] could not obtain more than one-fourth" of what was due. Their bills of exchange were protested and remained unpaid. When Noah decided he could no longer remain in Tunis (not being the consul), Decatur was angered at what he took to be Noah's weakness. Six weeks after the departure of Decatur's squadron, Noah sought an audience with the bey and announced his departure. He began the long journey home aboard a French frigate bound for Toulon. He had served as United States consul to Tunis for ten months.

But that lay in the future. Decatur had won a complete diplomatic victory without firing a shot. It was not lost on anyone in the squadron that his demands were made, as one officer put it, "before their walls, in sight of six frigates, as many corvettes and brigs, with fifty gun-boats capable of acting in two harbors." Decatur gave his officers a day of rest and relaxation ashore. Noah recorded that he escorted them on a visit to the ruins of Carthage, and then the officers, like any tourists, bought gifts, shawls, pipes, and other "articles of utility and curiosity."

From the *Guerriere*'s great cabin on the last day of July 1815, Decatur penned another laconic report to Secretary Crowninshield. Without flourish, he informed the navy secretary of the situation Noah had reported to him, his demand upon Tunis, and the bey's rapid agreement, resulting in the money actually paid over to Noah. He announced that his squadron would proceed to Tripoli, where he would provide Crowninshield "with early information of [its] further proceedings."

ON AUGUST 2, 1815, the squadron sailed for Tripoli. On August 5, the Americans arrived off the city, "where," as one naval officer put it, "we had a similar ceremony to perform [as at Tunis], and which was conducted in the same smooth, cool, decided way, without any palaver, which would leave room to doubt that we should do as we said." The U.S. consul at Tripoli was Richard B. Jones, who told a story almost identical to that of Noah's at Tunis. Jones reported to Decatur that the *Abellino* had captured two English merchant vessels and sent them into Tripoli, where they were seized by the British brig *Paulina* under the guns of the fortress of Tripoli, ostensibly neutral in the Anglo-American war, after they had sought protection under the U.S.-Tripoli treaty. Jones hoped that Decatur had "come fully prepared to demand and obtain ample satisfaction" in a matter in which Tripoli had flagrantly violated international law, "call[ing] for the most prompt and energetic conduct on the part of the United States, which will not only convince this Power, but all others, that our rights and privileges cannot be invaded with impunity." Like many of his officers, Decatur was willing to push matters, making it clear that if Tripoli wanted war, his squadron would oblige. A letter sent home from the schooner *Flying Fish*, reprinted in the newspapers, captured the mood of the U.S. officers. "Our *saucy* squadron," the anonymous correspondent wrote, "is before Tripoli, demanding satisfaction for some aggression committed on some of our people there; and unless atonement is made, Decatur is determined to punish her."

Similar to his letter to the Tunisian minister, Decatur's August 6 letter to the prime minister of Tripoli was without bluster but was no less menacing. He noted that he had been officially informed that the bashaw and his government had allowed a British warship "to take from out of his harbor, and from under the guns of his castle" the two prizes, and had refused a request for protection from the privateer "lying in his waters," violating the treaty between the two countries. "As soon as I had settled with Algiers for her aggressions," Decatur pointedly observed, "and with Tunis for a similar outrage to the one now complained of, I hastened to this place with a part of the squadron under my command." Although he referred to using force to exact satisfaction for the American losses, Decatur said that he would follow the "invariable rule" of American foreign policy by first making a demand for justice. He asked for the immediate restitution for the two prizes in the amount of $30,000, as well as the loss sustained by the cruiser. The prime minister would understand, Decatur suggested, the need to make known the bashaw's response "with the least possible delay." Although Midshipman Hollins engaged in slight hyperbole in stating that Decatur "gave them one *hour*" to pay, he was not far off.

Following his diplomatic practice, Decatur refused to go ashore, where he would have seemed to be waiting on the bashaw and where there was always the possibility of an assassin or an assault. The first response of Tripoli was warlike. The bashaw assembled his troops and manned the gun batteries at the water's edge. Over the night of August 6–7, the cannon from the Tripolitan forts blazed away, without hitting any of the U.S. warships. Peter Potter thought the cannonade was meant as a demonstration to the offshore Americans that "they are ready to receive us . . . [T]he sponges & rammers of their guns are visible 2 feet above the parapets & all the forts [are] manned." The American squadron did not move. The

Tripolitans then tried to temporize. On August 7, 1815, Hamed ben Mustaffi, one of the bashaw's ministers, acknowledged the receipt of Decatur's letter, and in the Italian-Arabic lingua franca suggested on one hand that the American prize retaken by the English would not have occurred if the ship had not entered Tripoli against the common usages of Tripoli and other nations, and yet on the other hand that Jones had proven the value and seemed satisfied when the bashaw was willing to pay 9,000 Spanish dollars. Hamed ben Mustaffi appealed to the desire of both countries to maintain their friendship. Decatur played his cards slowly, giving nothing away, and maintained his demands. The bashaw sent the governor of Tripoli as his emissary to negotiate with Decatur. The governor came aboard the *Guerriere* and asked the Americans to lower the demand to $25,000, all the ready specie the bashaw claimed to have. In exchange for accepting less than full monetary compensation, Decatur, who learned from Consul Jones that there were no Americans held as slaves in Tripoli, demanded that ten Christian slaves be delivered to him. Decatur understood the symbolism, which would echo throughout Europe, of the young republic freeing Christian captives and returning them safe to their countries in Europe, in the face of the resigned attitudes assumed by their own governments towards Barbary slavery. Decatur specified that the released Christians be Danes and Neapolitans, meant as a public gesture of appreciation for the help the Danish consul had provided ten years before to the captured officers and crew of the *Philadelphia* during their sixteen months of captivity, and the logistical help afforded to the American squadrons by the kingdom of the Two Sicilies. Potter saw them come aboard the *Guerriere*. In his diary, he mentions a Danish boy and girl, a woman with her three daughters, and a man who had been captive for twenty-six years. Decatur insisted on one more act of symbolism: since the bashaw had forced Jones to lower the American flag at the consulate, Jones would now rehoist it to a 21-gun salute from the bashaw's palace, and a band would play "The President's March" and "Yankee Doodle." The Tripolitans agreed to all Decatur's demands. Why they capitulated so quickly is a mystery. Surely the presence of a large American squadron, battle-tested and just outside the port, was impressive. And the Tripolitans remembered Decatur as the man who had destroyed the captured *Philadelphia* ten years before. The bashaw and his advisers must have considered that fighting meant the likely destruction of his navy, the blockading of his port, and a dangerous threat to his regime; but if the Americans were paid off quickly and departed, Tripoli's navy would be intact, the harbor open, and the ability to seize and hold for ransom other countries' mariners preserved. For that, $25,000 and ten Christians was a small price. To Crowninshield, Decatur could not help repeating that "[a]ny attempt to conciliate [the Barbary rulers] except through the influence of their fears I should expect to be in vain."

Having freed eight Neapolitans, Decatur decided that the United States squadron would deliver them home. The same day, August 9, 1815, Decatur's squadron sailed for Sicily. On August 12, the squadron arrived off Syracuse, on the east coast of Sicily, where the Americans spent a disappointing four days, because they were not allowed to come ashore because of "practique," the lengthy quarantine of all people who had been to the Barbary coast. One American naval officer wrote that the priests exercised authority at Syracuse, and they were "so superstitious that they will have no communication [i.e., contact] with any vessel less than thirty days after leaving the coast of Barbary." The squadron then sailed off to Messina, near the northeasternmost point in Sicily, across from the Italian mainland, where they arrived on August 20. Decatur landed his eight rescued Neapolitans there. After ten days at Messina, Decatur led the squadron to Naples, passing Stromboli, where Midshipman Bell in the *Macedonian* jotted down in his log that he saw the volcano belching lava at night, and Capri. The squadron dropped anchor the next day, September 6, in the beautiful bay of Naples, about a mile off the city. Decatur sent the two Danes ashore to the Danish consul-general, who arranged their safe passage home, and informed the foreign minister of the kingdom of the Two Sicilies that he had secured the release of the Neapolitan captives from the bashaw and safely delivered them at Messina. To Decatur, it was a "small service," a gesture of "the grateful sense" the United States felt for the kingdom's assistance to the American navy and nation ten years before. In fact, it was a magnificent symbolic gesture not lost on anyone in Europe. Decatur received not only the written thanks of the foreign minister, the marquis di Circello, but an invitation to call upon the king at his palace, the Villa of Portici, overlooking the splendid panorama of the Bay of Naples, where he received royal thanks for his act of humanity. Decatur wrote Secretary Crowninshield of his hope that the "successful result of our small expedition" would "induce other nations to follow the example; in which case the Barbary states will be compelled to abandon their piratical system."

With his mission accomplished, the cruise of Decatur's squadron took on something of a triumphal procession. The squadron left Naples on

September 13, was off Cagliari in Sardinia on September 19, and spent three days at Carthagena in southern Spain. They put to sea again, passed the Cape de Gata, and arrived at Malaga, Spain, on September 30, where Decatur learned that Bainbridge had entered the Mediterranean with the second squadron. The next day, Decatur ordered all the other ships of his squadron to sail to Gibraltar to rendezvous with Bainbridge, who by prior design succeeded him as commander of the combined U.S. naval squadrons. He alone delayed, bringing up the rear in the *Guerriere*.

The *Guerriere* finally turned westward, tacking against a headwind toward Gibraltar. On October 5, 1815, her lookouts spotted a number of ships making their way on a converging course—the rest of the Algerine navy. This chance meeting provided a fitting symmetry to the earlier fight against the *Meshuda*. Here were a swarm of sloops of war and frigates bearing down on the single, powerful American frigate. From Decatur down to the youngest powder boy aboard, none of the Americans knew whether the Algerines would respect the treaty their dey had signed just three months before, and they probably half expected that the Algerine *raïs* would open fire if he thought he could overwhelm the lone American frigate. But the *Guerriere* did not flinch. Decatur would not commit the cardinal sin of unpreparedness for which he had condemned James Barron in the *Chesapeake* almost ten years before: Decatur ordered John Downes to clear the ship for action, had the marine drummers beat to quarters, and then had the crews run out the *Guerriere*'s guns. The gun crews opened the gunports, rolled the mammoth 24-pounders back, took out the tampons, primed the guns, loaded them with roundshot, and stood ready to open fire. Decatur, a captain given to rhetoric and theatrical displays of leadership, called the ship's crew aft, where he could address them from the captain's customary position on the quarterdeck. He told his men:

> My lads, those fellows are approaching us in a threatening manner. We have whipped them into a treaty, and if the treaty is to be broken let them break it. Be careful of yourselves. Let any man fire without orders at the peril of his life. But let them fire first if they will, and we'll take the whole of them.

Decatur sent his men to their battle stations. Silence reigned. On came the Algerine fleet, four frigates and three sloops of war. They might have passed the *Guerriere* miles to windward, but they took in their topgallant sails and courses (they furled the highest and lowest sails on their ships' masts), a sign they meant business, for sailing warships classically went into battle only with topsails (the midlevel sails on the masts), which still hung down on each mast. Then the Algerines scrambled to form their ships into two parallel lines of battle. In the sailing era, these ominous moments developed with heart-pounding slowness, even on converging courses. While the Algerines formed a line, Decatur had the *Guerriere* pass to windward of them, weathered them, and later wrote that he "could have beaten the whole before their line could have got up." Nearer and nearer came the Algerine ships; they would pass the *Guerriere* downwind at point-blank range, and Decatur did not know whether their intentions were hostile. The ships began to pass. One after another sailed by the *Guerriere* without a sound, but without the flash and smoke of a broadside, either. The most weatherly Algerine ship tried to veer across the *Guerriere*'s bow to cross upwind of her but couldn't, and just had time to change course back to pass just downwind of the American frigate's lee, or else, Decatur declared, he would have "run him down." Instead of the accepted hail of "What ship?" the call came over the water from the *raïs*, "*Dove andante?*," "Where are you going?," which was none of the *raïs*'s business and was considered rather discourteous between naval officers. Decatur answered immediately in the same tone, "*Dove mi pace*," "Where I please." With that, the Algerines sailed on, and Decatur and the *Guerriere* continued on their way to Gibraltar.

Chapter Six

The Return

WILLIAM BAINBRIDGE arrived at Carthagena with the second squadron on August 5, thirty-four days out from Boston. Crowninshield had sent him his sailing orders on June 17, the very day Decatur's squadron mauled and captured the *Meshuda*, a fact that no one in the United States could possibly have known for weeks to come. Crowninshield's orders were clear and decisive. Bainbridge was to sail to the Mediterranean with the ships ready for sea at Boston, following the orders the department had sent to Decatur, as well as the State Department's directives for concluding a peace treaty. Lest there be any doubt, the "object of the expedition," Crowninshield explained, "is to obtain an honorable Peace with the Dey of Algiers, with whom we are at War, or to destroy his Fleet, Blockade his Ports, cut up his commerce, in short to practice against him and his people all the rigour of civilized Warfare, until he is compelled to make a Peace." In Washington, the administration had heard rumors that one or more of the European nations might have declared war against Algiers, and the Dutch specifically were said to have sent a powerful squadron to fight. If the rumors proved true, and not knowing in mid-June that Decatur would soon conclude a peace treaty with Algiers, "should it become a question of policy, or an object of importance to your success, to act in consort with [the Dutch fleet], you are permitted by the President so to act in consort with any naval power at war with Algiers in any manner which shall be best calculated to effect the object of the enterprize, taking care to preserve to yourself and your Government the proper rank and respect." Secretary

Crowninshield's directive was the first time in United States history that the navy had been allowed to sail and fight as part of a multinational force. The rumors were not far wrong. The Dutch had a squadron sailing about the western Mediterranean, looking to fight. Indeed, a year later, John Quincy Adams, the United States minister to the British court, had a conversation with the Russian ambassador, who asserted that the Dutch wanted "concerted operations," Spain had actually proposed that "a joint naval armament" be fitted out to act against the Barbary states, and while the czar had not quite signed on for Russia, he recognized "the inconvenience of partial operations and negotiations, which, by making peace for one or two nations, would immediately have the effect of producing hostilities against others."

If the European world was starting to coalesce against Christian slavery in Islamic North Africa, the United States had somewhat unrealistic expectations of assistance from the other Barbary regencies. In his June 17 orders, Crowninshield asserted to Bainbridge—ironically, as it turned out—that "no doubt is entertained" that Tunis and Tripoli, as well as "the different courts of Europe," would "render you every assistance that friendly nations ought to do." Before Decatur's squadron had sailed in May, naively relying on traditional notions of friendly neutrality, Monroe had given Shaler letters of introduction to the rulers of Morocco, Tunis, and Tripoli, asking each to provide "hospitality" to American warships needing supplies or sanctuary during the "just and necessary war" declared against Algiers. Monroe's letters obviously were not percipient. Crowninshield informed Bainbridge that Decatur was allowed to shift his commodore's pennant to a smaller ship and return to the United States, along with enlisted men from the squadron whose terms of service had expired. Expecting that it would be up to Bainbridge to make a treaty with Algiers, when "your Fleet thereby [would] be released from the blockade of [Algiers's] ports, it might not be amiss to sail with your ship & two or three frigates &c. and pay a friendly Visit to Tunis & Tripoli avoiding even a suspicion of hostility, it would shew you[r] force & be a just inducement for these People hereafter to respect our rights." Finally, Crowninshield ordered him to leave a frigate and two smaller vessels "to cruize within the Streights," and return with the rest of the fleet to Newport, Rhode Island.

When Bainbridge acknowledged his orders on June 25, his letter had a tone of self-righteousness and sense of himself as a victim; it was filled with rationalizations cushioning against a possible failure of his mission. Leaving aside the ships in Decatur's squadron that he would inherit, Bainbridge was bringing out the 74-gun ship-of-the-line *Independence*, the sloop of war *Erie*, the brig *Chippewa*, and the schooner *Lynx*. They would be joined by the frigate *Congress* after she delivered the new American minister to Holland, the frigate *United States*, two brigs, a bomb vessel, and store ships from the United States as soon as they were ready. Bainbridge promised his "best exertions," but the force under his command, he opined, was "too small to make much impression on the strong batteries" protecting Algiers. He wished that five or six mortar vessels had been fitted out to bombard Algiers, but he noted that he had not been "consulted, or even informed of the preparations and arrangements made relative to the force employed in the Mediterranean service untill [*sic*] the receipt of my sailing instructions." Bainbridge wrote that his squadron would "do as much as is Practicable for such a force to do." Bainbridge got his ships to sea on July 1, the day after the dey had agreed to a treaty at the mouth of Decatur's cannon thousands of miles away. After making sail, Bainbridge wrote a final note to the navy secretary that he was on his way, and thus he was spared another embarrassment: from all of Bainbridge's complaints and cavils about the *Independence*, the ship that Bainbridge had spent years building and desperately wished to take to sea, Crowninshield concluded that she might be unfit for sea because with all her heavy cannon mounted she lay too low in the water. Crowninshield wrote Bainbridge that if four other captains concurred with Bainbridge, he could send her back into the navy yard to be dismantled or cut down (razéed) into an overlarge frigate, and Bainbridge could pick a frigate as his flagship for the Mediterranean. Luckily for Bainbridge, he sailed before the letter arrived.

When Bainbridge's squadron arrived off Carthagena on August 5, the Spanish authorities required him to remain in quarantine for six days. In the harbor, he found the *Spark* and *Torch* from Decatur's squadron, from which he learned of Decatur's success against Algiers. He wrote Crowninshield that "[p]eace having taken place with the Regency of Algiers it only now remains for me to obey your instructions of shewing this Ship and several others of the Squadron of[f] Tunis and Tripoli." Bainbridge was dejected that all the fighting and diplomacy with Algiers was already over, but for the moment he acted graciously toward Decatur, whom he had superseded as commander in the Mediterranean. Bainbridge wrote Decatur that if it would be "more gratifying" for him to return to the United States in the *Guerriere*, Bainbridge would take pleasure in agreeing to the arrangement.

Richard McCall, the United States consul in Carthagena, kept Shaler abreast of developments. Bainbridge had brought word that a third squadron was forming up in the United States, commanded by Isaac Chauncey in the second American ship-of-the-line, the 74-gun *Washington*, with a number of bomb vessels, although everyone realized that it would not sail if the news of Decatur's victory over Algiers reached home quickly. After speaking with Lieutenant Commandant Gamble, McCall wrote that Bainbridge's ships would call at Algiers, Tunis, and Tripoli, showing the flag at each place and reminding the dey, bey, and bashaw of the reach of U.S. power. Gamble passed word that the bulk of the fleet would return home in October 1815, and that the Navy Department wanted Bainbridge to leave a frigate and two smaller vessels on station in the Mediterranean.

But the effort to have the Spaniards give up the *Estedio* had become increasingly frustrating. McCall fumed that "these foolish negotiations are abominable & subject us to very considerable inconveniences." He expected Bainbridge to demand the vessel and take her by force should the Spanish refuse. But McCall was wrong. Bainbridge did not want to risk war with Spain to rescue a prize sent in by Decatur.

The failure of the Spanish to turn over the *Estedio* put William Shaler in a difficult position. Omar accused the Americans of lying and cheating him. He demanded to know when he would get his *Estedio* back from the Spaniards or an equivalent brig from the United States. Decatur himself was rather blasé about Shaler's predicament. He wrote Shaler that he had thought it "probable" that the Spanish would be difficult about the brig, which was why he had been "so particular" in insisting that the brig would be turned over in whatever shape it was in, and that an Algerine captain go over to Carthagena, where the *Estedio* was "regularly delivered to him & receipt obtain'd, the Algerine colours hoisted, & they [the *Estedio* and *Meshuda*] in all respects became Algerine vessels, as they were in the exclusive possession of the Dey's officers & crews." Decatur insisted that "we have complied fully with our engagement with the Dey & can in no wise be responsible for the Spanish aggressions on the Regency of Algiers." Decatur was sorry for the difficulties Shaler faced so soon in his tenure but knew that Shaler recognized he would not "repose on roses" in a diplomatic posting such as Algiers. This was slight solace to Shaler, who could do nothing except write home for instructions and wait for support from any American warships that fortuitously might arrive.

By early September, Bainbridge had taken his squadron around the Mediterranean. On September 6, he forwarded letters to Monroe in Washington that Shaler and Decatur had negotiated a treaty with Algiers. He also heard a rumor that the bashaw of Tripoli and Consul Jones had had a "misunderstanding"; sensing the chance of a fight, he wrote that with the *Independence* and four ships of the squadron, he had called at Algiers "to exhibit this additional force off there, presuming it would have some wait [*sic*] in preserving the peace which had been made (for the only mode of convincing these people is by occular [*sic*] demonstration)." He then sailed his squadron to Tripoli, where he learned that Decatur had been there first and "had adjusted our differences which existed at that place. Our Consul at Tripoli informed me that that the exhibiting of our Naval force before Tripoli had produced a most favourable change in the disposition of the Bashaw for preserving the peace with us." While off Tripoli, Bainbridge learned that the bey of Tunis was "restless towards the U.S.," and he "immediately proceeded with the vessels with me for that place," only to learn that Decatur had pacified the bey. Having "exhibited the Force under my command to all the Barbary powers (and which I believe will have a tendency to prolong our treaty with them)," Bainbridge declared that he would "leave one Frigate and two smaller vessels in these seas, and to return with the remainder of the Squadron" to America. He could not help adding that his squadron had not "had an opportunity of doing more than shewing its force off the Barbary ports, and exercising in the evolutions of naval service. I beg leave thru' you to assure the President that had occasion demanded, or an opportunity afforded, that the Gallant Officers and men under my command, would have proved that devotion to their Country which our small Navy has so often exhibited."

Ten days later, Bainbridge wrote William Shaler directly. He apologized that when his squadron was off Algiers, he could spare no time to visit because he needed to be off to Tripoli. It would have given him "infinite pleasure," he noted, "to have . . . shaken you by the hand." What Bainbridge called the "very unexpected Peace" Shaler and Decatur made rendered it impossible that he would be able to visit. But he left some advice for Shaler and for American foreign policy. "I am decidedly of opinion," he noted, that the "security of our Treatys [*sic*] with Barbary depends on having a marine force near them. The force I leave, will be ready to act on any emergency, and the rapidity with which an American Squadron can move from the U. States to the Mediterranean sea, if fully impressed on the Respective Governments of Barbary, ought to prove a Check on their Cupidity." The ships Bainbridge left behind in 1815, including Charles Gordon in the *Constellation*, began the permanent

American naval presence in the Mediterranean that has continued for nearly two centuries and now is known as the Sixth Fleet.

By early October 1815, Bainbridge had returned to Gibraltar, with all the ships of his, and Decatur's, commands. But where was Decatur? Decatur's triumphs and the "very unexpected Peace" had preempted any glorious role for Bainbridge, and all that had been left for him was to dutifully follow in Decatur's tracks to each of the Barbary ports, showing the flag and America's first 74-gun battleship. But Decatur had not written him, and as Decatur gallivanted around the western Mediterranean on his victory lap, Bainbridge prepared to sail his fleet home. On October 5, he ordered his fleet to prepare to depart for home. On October 7, the *Independence* lifted her anchors and began to make sail, followed by the rest of the fleet. As they began to make their way out of the great anchorage, their lookouts spotted the *Guerriere* coming into Gibraltar. Decatur had arrived just in time to catch them before they began the journey home.

It was a dramatic and emotional moment. As the powerful frigate rounded Europa Point and made her way into the enormous bay, she made the recognition signal for Bainbridge in the *Independence* and began to fire the cannon salute for a commodore, which the *Independence* duly returned. Decatur, decked out in his best uniform, descended into his gig and began to be rowed across to visit Bainbridge in the *Independence*. Decatur's visit to the flagship marked his subordination to the senior officer. Yet Bainbridge, who just weeks before had courteously written Decatur that he

Commodore Bainbridge's squadron sailing from Gibraltar. From the Naval Historical Center, Washington, D.C.

could take the *Guerriere* home instead of a sloop of war, now could not stomach the idea of greeting Decatur and tried to snub him in full view of the entire fleet. He did not back his ship's sails to slow down even temporarily; the *Independence* held her course, clearly trying to avoid a meeting. But Decatur's oarsmen were able to hook on to the flagship's chains, and Decatur clambered up the side of the *Independence*. The two captains had not seen each other for years, but their meeting was brief and icily formal. Bainbridge brought Decatur down into his cabin. What they said there will never be known, but based on what her husband told her, Susan Decatur many years later stated that Bainbridge never even asked how Decatur was or offered him a drink or the "slightest hospitality." After Decatur departed, he and Bainbridge would not meet again for five years.

Years earlier, Bainbridge himself had regarded Decatur as the bright light of the new navy. But with the Algiers war over, he realized that Decatur's bright light had darkened his own hopes of fully retrieving his reputation. It was a bitter pill that Bainbridge took as another humiliation. Unfortunately for him, the adulation for Decatur had only just begun.

Decatur had written to John Quincy Adams while en route to Tunis, with the news of the treaty signed with Algiers. In his September 11 reply, Adams, temperamentally cold and reserved, congratulated Decatur, expressing the hope that the peace "may prove permanent as it is glorious. It is to be hoped that the lesson which you so promptly and so opportunely gave to that Power, will make a durable impression upon its future policy, and I most ardently pray that the example which you have given of rescuing your country from the disgrace of a tributary Treaty, may become an irrevocable Law for all future time."

Decatur sailed home in the *Guerriere* and arrived at New York on November 12. He had been away from America for a mere 187 days. In that time, he had sailed across the Atlantic, captured the flagship of the Algerine navy in a battle that killed its famous commander, directed the squadron's capture of another Algerine cruiser, negotiated a peace treaty in forty-eight hours with Algiers that met all the criteria laid down by the secretary of state, including the freeing of the *Edwin*'s captives and the perpetual abandonment of tribute, demanded and received compensation for losses to Tunis and Tripoli, freed a handful of Danish and Neapolitan captives and set eight of them ashore in their native country, and sailed back across the Atlantic. Decatur reported his arrival to the Navy Department immediately. He noted that Bainbridge had departed with the fleet thirty-six hours before him but that the *Guerriere* passed the squadron. He informed the secretary that the *Epervier* had passed through the Straits of Gibraltar on July 14, "and from the length of time which has elapsed, I fear she is lost."

Ironically, because of the disappearance of the *Epervier*, just about the last people to learn of what happened on the Barbary coast were the Americans. Rumors that Decatur had captured Algerine ships and had made a successful peace with Algiers began to appear in American newspapers in early September, but the reports were confused and sometimes contradictory. Just before Decatur himself arrived in New York, duplicate copies of his dispatches arrived at the Navy Department. His return caused a sensation. One of the navy commissioners, Commodore David Porter, sent his effusive congratulations on "the brilliant, comet-like expedition to our old friends. You have done more in a few months than all Europe have been able to effect in ages, and have given a lesson not only to Christendom, but to the Barbary States that will not soon be forgotten." In his restrained, gentlemanly way, Crowninshield informed Decatur that he had placed Decatur's dispatches before the president, who warmly expressed his approval, to which the navy secretary added his own "cordial sentiments" and congratulations. James Monroe, who had belatedly received the July 4 Decatur-Shaler letter with the account of the negotiations and Decatur's gunboat diplomacy, wrote that the expedition was not only "glorious to yourself and honorable to yourself and to the officers and men under your command," but also "very satisfactory to the President." But the greatest accolades came from the newspapers, which, whether they reflected or anticipated public sentiment, put Decatur into the pantheon of heroes. In a piece republished to a national audience, the *Boston Gazette* referred to the "*electric shock*, as was never before discharged from a Christian battery," that Decatur had inflicted on Algiers, Tunis, and Tripoli. Observing that the treaty he had forced upon Algiers vindicated American honor, brought indemnity for past losses, and ensured security for the future, the *Gazette* called Decatur the "champion of Christendom."

Bainbridge and the ten ships of his fleet—three became separated on the voyage home—arrived at Newport, Rhode Island (where Crowninshield had provided as his return port in his orders in June), on November 15, three days after Decatur's ship had come to in New York. Not knowing that Decatur had beaten him home, as he had beaten him in everything else, Bainbridge reported that "[a]s I was standing out of the Bay of Gibraltar, the Guerriere, Como. Decatur, was going into that Port" for supplies.

Aware of how prickly Bainbridge was, the civilian leaders lavished him with praise. On his cruise, Bainbridge had shown the flag off Algiers, Tunis, and Tripoli, and initiated the permanent United States naval force in the Mediterranean to maintain its treaty rights and preserve peace. Crowninshield congratulated him upon his safe return and the "successful result of the Expedition to the Mediterranean." A week later, Crowninshield acknowledged three more letters from Bainbridge, which he had submitted to President Madison, who gave his "entire approbation." The president, Crowninshield stated, fully appreciated Bainbridge's services and knew that if circumstances had required him to fight, Bainbridge "would have added to the lustre of your fame & nautical reputation, and fulfilled the high expectations of your Country & Government." Crowninshield had done his best to sugarcoat the obvious disappointment Bainbridge felt by showing that the commander in chief himself respected his abilities.

But the balm did not suffice for Bainbridge's ego. Bainbridge asked to be reappointed to command of the Boston (Charlestown) Navy Yard, but Crowninshield stopped him short. Isaac Hull had been ordered to take command at Boston without any "stipulations to relinquish it to you or any other Officer" because Crowninshield had assumed that "the uncertainty of the operations in the Mediterranean . . . induced a belief that [Bainbridge] would be absent one or two years at least." The upshot was that the secretary refused to displace Hull. Bainbridge would remain for the time being in command of the *Independence*, afloat at Boston.

What Crowninshield did not state explicitly but what everyone knew was that Hull had exchanged a seat as a navy commissioner for the Boston Navy Yard post, and that Crowninshield had asked Decatur to take what had been Hull's seat on the board. Decatur accepted the nomination, which finally fulfilled Susan Decatur's hopes to bring her husband ashore, away from danger and into Washington society, and he thanked the president for the honor. Before the end of the year, Decatur's nomination had been sent to the Senate and confirmed, and Crowninshield presented him with his new commission.

President Madison presented his seventh annual message, the equivalent of the State of the Union address in recent times, to the United States Congress on December 5, 1815. His first words dealt with developments in the Mediterranean. "The squadron in advance on that service, under Commodore Decatur," Madison noted, "lost not a moment after its arrival in the Mediterranean in seeking the naval force of the enemy then cruising in that sea, and succeeded in capturing two of his ships." The president praised the "high character" of Decatur, which was "brilliantly sustained" in the close action with the *Meshuda*, and then lauded the peace he made. Madison praised, too, "the judicious precautionary arrangements" Bainbridge made with the Mediterranean squadron, which, Madison thought, "afford[ed] a reasonable prospect of future security for the valuable portion of our commerce which passes within reach of the Barbary cruisers."

Along with the praise and the honor of a seat on the Board of Navy Commissioners, Decatur and the men of his squadron received cash. Decatur retained his friend Littleton Waller Tazewell, one of the great maritime lawyers and Supreme Court advocates of the early Republic, to represent the interests of his squadron. Tazewell wrote Crowninshield on February 1, 1816, that he sought fair compensation for his clients' relinquishing of their rights to the *Meshuda* and *Estedio*, a "mere act of justice, required by existing laws, and in exact conformity with its already settled practice in previous similar cases." He did not comment, of course, that because the *Estedio* had been captured in Spanish territorial waters, no admiralty court would have found her to be a valid prize. Tazewell demonstrated with lawyerly precision the logic of the matter and the precedent set in early cases, including one involving John Rodgers as a commander in the Mediterranean. By invoking the case of Rodgers, the president of the navy commissioners, Tazewell subtly and diplomatically countered any impulse the navy might have had to contest the claim. As to the amount, Tazewell breezily conceded that, once the administration acknowledged in principle that compensation was due, he would agree to any methodology that the navy desired to determine the amount. He suggested that the *Meshuda* and *Estedio* were worth at least $200,000 and that the captors were collectively entitled to one-half of the value because the American squadron was of superior force to the Algerines. Crowninshield passed Tazewell's letter along to Treasury Secretary Dallas, who in turn submitted it to Congress with Crowninshield's recommendation to pay the $100,000 prize money figure suggested by Tazewell, noting that President Madison concurred. Congress duly voted the money to Decatur and the officers and men of his squadron. Under the prize money law, Decatur received 15 percent of the net proceeds, or approximately $15,000.

Decatur had received fame, the applause of his president and countrymen, a high administrative position in the navy at the seat of the government, and a dollop of cash. Bainbridge was left to brood on how the fates, or Decatur, had worked against him.

Chapter Seven

The British Bombardment
and an "Occular Demonstration"

THE WHIRLWIND of naval and diplomatic action by the United States against Algiers, Tunis, and Tripoli caught the European nations completely off guard. News of Decatur's lightning success against Algiers, considered the foremost Barbary power, arrived after the allied coalition had beaten Napoleon at Waterloo, marched into Paris, and convened again on methods to secure the peace and security of Europe. At first, the proof provided by the Americans that Algiers was a weak despotism, and not the all-powerful threat imagined for centuries, had little effect except with newspapers. British newspapers had a field day, railing that the Americans had triumphed while the great powers of Europe—specifically, England—continued with the tribute racket. One of the great political essayists of the early nineteenth century was William Cobbett, an Englishman who had spent several years in the United States, the editor and scrivener of a polemical Federalist newspaper in Philadelphia in the 1790s aptly named *Porcupine's Gazette*. He had reestablished himself in England, lambasting the excesses and inequalities of British life and touting himself as a friend of American liberty. On July 15, 1815, he wrote a column praising "the signal triumph of America, which her invincible fleet has just obtained over the European pirates. This great achievement of the real sons of liberty . . . does not, I dare say, go down well with our corruptionists. . . . While all the regular governments of Europe were acknowledging their *inferiority*, by sending annual presents to the dey of Algiers, the Americans fitted out a squadron to annihilate this *royal* pirate . . . and the extirpation of the royal nest of African pirates, is an act which will be recorded in the page of history to the eternal honor of the American people, while the long endurance of this haughty and barbarous race, will for ever reflect disgrace on the nations of Europe." From far-off Copenhagen the U.S. minister to Denmark, J. M. Forbes, sensed the increased reputation of America in Europe and wrote Shaler that "the favorable impression throughout Europe is of great value to us. The glory with which we have covered ourselves is heightened by the dark cloud of Shame which covers the great powers of Europe in their tame submission to the Piracies of those unprincipled barbarians."

The British foreign secretary, Lord Castlereagh, had raised the idea of suppressing the black African slave trade to the foreign ministers of the other powers in conference in Paris after Waterloo. After a fifteen-year debate prompted by abolitionists such as William Wilberforce, the British Parliament had banned the slave trade in 1805. But France, Spain, and Portugal, the principal traffickers in black Africans, saw Castlereagh's overture as English hypocrisy. The British loftily assured the rest of Europe that they had stopped the slave trade because of its immorality, but the other European foreign ministers suspected some unknown mercantile motive. Instead, they raised the seemingly more immediate issue of the Barbary powers, which held two thousand European Christians as captives. They asked why Britain, supposedly so concerned with morality, had done nothing to abolish white slavery in North Africa. Castlereagh had no principled answer, and the other countries widely believed, as Benjamin Franklin had put it twenty-five years before, that British trade indirectly benefited from Barbary seizures of poorer countries' ships and seamen. With Napoleon returned to exile and Europe at peace, the Barbary states were no longer important to England for food or supplies. But what Decatur's squadron had done loomed large in British thinking. As Edward Brenton, a British naval captain in the Napoleonic Wars and later a historian, wrote in 1825, British opinion and policy could not accept "that England should tolerate what America had resented and punished." The British government decided to send a fleet to visit the Barbary regencies and, through diplomatic muscle or force, secure the release of white Christian slaves.

In charge of the fleet against Algiers was a famous British admiral, Edward Pellew, recently ennobled as Lord Exmouth. Pellew, born in April 1757, first saw combat in the American Revolution on Lake Champlain in 1776 as a teenage midshipman, and then on land in command of a brigade of seamen in the Saratoga campaign of 1777. He became renowned as a frigate captain in the French Revolutionary Wars. His most famous exploit came in January 1797, in command of the 44-gun frigate *Indefatigable*. In company with another English frigate, in the darkness and monstrous seas off Ushant, Pellew engaged a French ship-of-the-line, the *Droits de l'Homme*, over the course of eleven hours, until the French battleship foundered and sank with a terrible loss of life. He was promoted to more important commands, leading a squadron in the Channel fleet, the British fleet in the Indian Ocean, then the North Sea fleet, and in 1811 the Mediterranean fleet. In early 1815, when Napoleon returned from Elba for the Hundred Days campaign, Exmouth landed troops at Marseilles to lead an allied army from horseback against the French army. He was an active officer constitutionally unable to delegate authority, a hearty seaman famous throughout the British navy for his boast that, even as a doughty aging admiral, he could beat any topman in a race to the mainpeak and back down to the deck. In a nation that gloried in its navy, Exmouth was in 1815 one its most prominent admirals, recognized as a thorough professional, but he was no Nelson: he had few followers, he did not have Nelson's way of imparting his philosophy or strategy over dinner or walks on the quarterdeck, and his men followed him because he was their superior officer, not because he inspired them.

The British Admiralty did not recall Lord Exmouth from the Mediterranean after the fall of Napoleon and Decatur's triumph. Instead, he was ordered to negotiate the release of Christian slaves from the Barbary regencies. The Mediterranean squadron wintered at Livorno, and the five ships-of-the-line and seven smaller vessels sailed for Algiers on March 23, 1816, arriving the next day.

Admiral Lord Exmouth, who was ordered to deploy the British fleet against Algiers after Britain decided to no longer "tolerate what America had resented and punished." Engraving by Turner from a portrait by Sir William Beechey. From Edward P. Brenton, *The Naval History of Great Britain* (1825), author's collection.

The dey knew that Lord Exmouth had orders to ransom the slaves and negotiate treaties on behalf of the weaker Mediterranean kingdoms, Sardinia and Naples. The king of Sardinia agreed to pay $500 for each Sardinian held in slavery, as well as making the customary presents; over two years, the Neapolitan monarch agreed to pay $1,000 for each of his subjects held in captivity, or more than $1 million, the payments being guaranteed by Britain. Whatever merit these deals had as humanitarian gestures, they showed that there were still buyers in the market for kidnapped European mariners, and the British were willing to give their bond to clinch the deals. On these terms, Exmouth ransomed 357 Sicilians and Neapolitans and 51 Sardinians and Genoese. In addition, 23 other captives of different nationalities were released without payment as having been under the protection of England at the time of their capture. Exmouth paid the "market price," but after years of diplomatic half-measures and uncertain negotiations, he made the captives' release a reality. The ransomed slaves were taken aboard four transports accompanying the squadron to return to their native countries. Not all the slaves could leave, however. The Neapolitan government was so poor that it could not put all the capital up at once; 714 Sicilians and Neapolitans were left in captivity until their ransoms could be paid. However noble and magnanimous it was for Britain to negotiate on behalf of weaker European nations for the release of their captives, for the greatest European power to conduct ransoming negotiations did nothing to discourage white slavery, and only brought derision on the heads of the British. Alexander S. Mackenzie, a midshipman in the U.S. Mediterranean squadron, saw the British officers leaving Algiers "insulted by the populace, which threw dirt and stones at them." On April 7, 1816, Exmouth's fleet sailed for Tunis.

Immediately after Lord Exmouth sailed away, the dey looked for a pretext to raise tensions with the United States. Perhaps Omar felt that he had successfully extorted money from the British and felt emboldened to reopen the issue of tribute with the Americans; perhaps he needed to show belligerence to shore up his standing among the janissaries. In any event, he decided to make the missing *Estedio* a means to make new demands on the United States. The Spanish government had finally allowed the brig to return to Algiers on March 17, 1816. Nevertheless, the dey declared the Shaler-Decatur treaty violated by the United States and thus null and void because the Americans, not the Spanish, were supposed to have given back the *Estedio*, and according to Omar's logic, the Americans still owed him an equivalent brig. As Charles Gordon, commander of the *Constella-*

tion, a frigate left in the Mediterranean as part of the permanent squadron when Bainbridge sailed home, put it, Omar "discovered a high tone . . . on the old subject of the damn'd prize Brig." Then Shaler gave Omar another opportunity to create dissonance. Shaler produced the official copy of the Decatur-Shaler treaty, which had been brought out to the Mediterranean by Captain Oliver Hazard Perry in the frigate *Java*, with the news that the United States Senate had ratified it, and presented it to the dey for an exchange of ratified copies, a ceremony that apparently had never taken place before because Algiers hardly had an equivalent legislative body. Omar discovered that his own copy differed from that ratified in Washington. In the presence of both Shaler and Norderling, the dey had the Turkish text of the treaty read and retranslated into English, and Shaler was "much surprised to find the promise to return his ships, and to give a consular present introduced into his instrument as a treaty stipulation." Shaler only could respond that his copy—the English-language text—was binding because it had been translated to Omar through his interpreters and fully explained to him in June 1815, and that the dey "well knew that it was impossible for [Shaler] to obtain any positive assurance of the fidelity of its translation into the Turkish language." In a stroke of wiliness, Omar returned his copy of the Decatur-Shaler treaty to Shaler on April 6, 1816, telling him that it remained unratified by Algiers. With no treaty of peace, it was unclear whether, legally, Algiers was at war with the United States. Shaler gathered himself and asked for another interview with Omar so that he could send Washington the latest news. The dey refused to meet, but Shaler had an audience with the Algerine minister of marine, who accused Shaler of deception about the brig. The *Epervier* had been sent home with the signed copy of the treaty, as well as Shaler's and Decatur's dispatches, and when she was lost at sea, it took time for a duplicate copy to get to Washington and be ratified. The minister denied that the *Epervier* had been lost at sea, and claimed that Shaler relied on the loss of the *Epervier* as an excuse for inaction, equivocation, and failing to make an explanation for the *Estedio*. The minister's tantrum was hostile enough that even a cool character such as Shaler fled the consulate and had himself rowed out to the American squadron to seek refuge.

Upon Bainbridge's return to the United States in October 1815, John Shaw had become the commander of the U.S. naval squadron. Shaw brought together all his captains to plan a response. He prepared for battle and developed a plan to send the squadron's small boats into the harbor with 1,200 sailors and marines to set fire to the dey's warships as they lay moored within the mole. Part of the attacking force was to scale the water batteries, spike the guns, and prevent the rest of the raiders from being annihilated as they boarded and burned every ship. Shaw placed Charles Gordon in command, and Oliver Hazard Perry, the hero of the Battle of Lake Erie, was to be second in command. According to Mackenzie, who was there, "every officer and man became a volunteer; scaling and hook ladders were speedily made, cutlasses and pikes ground [sharpened], and firearms put in the highest order for service." But Shaw, like Decatur before him, decided to hoist the white flag and Swedish colors to call in help from Consul Norderling. With Norderling's advice, Shaw wrote the dey demanding an explanation.

The next day, Perry went ashore with Norderling to hand-deliver Shaw's letter to the dey. Omar recounted the "pledge" of Decatur, which he "viewed equal to an article of the treaty and which had not been fulfilled consequently the treaty was violated by us." Although Spain had turned over the *Estedio* to Algiers, Charles Gordon somehow was won over to the dey's view, later writing that "every rational man must allow that it is us who have acted wrong by Commo. Decatur's violating a sacred pledge, which was in every respect regarded as an article of [the] treaty." Gordon thought that the diplomacy would result in the United States giving Algiers a brig, "and then [they would] make war with them and take her away again." As Gordon recounted, Omar told Perry:

> I have received no brig from the Americans. I made the Spaniards give up the Algerine Brig for a number of Spanish subjects I seized for the purpose. And all I now ask for is the fulfillment of Commodore Decatur's pledge to reconcile my subjects to the treaty which I made, I have waited for you to hear from your President and nothing is done. I therefore consider the treaty as null and void. Still I am not disposed for war unless you wish it. Your consul can come on shore under the old treaty or we can remain neutral until you hear from your Government. In the meantime, you will be respected as tho[ugh] at peace . . . . But if your Squadron departs without communicating on the subject, I shall consider it a commencement of hostilities and act accordingly. But this treaty must be fulfilled or a new treaty must be negotiated.

In short, the dey wanted to extort a brig from the Americans or return to an annual tribute system. Perry left without delivering the Shaw letter, as he did not feel it proper to have to explain American policy. Shaler wanted the navy to make the night assault on the mole, writing Perry that "a glorious occasion offers." Gordon thought that if the night had not had a bright moon, the navy would have launched its attack on the harbor shipping—although he observed that the dey had mustered crews aboard each of his warships in the harbor and "all his batteries fill'd with men." After another meeting with his commanders, however, Commodore Shaw wrote Omar the next morning that the Algerine position would be conveyed to the president because the United States Constitution did not allow a commodore to decide on making war. The Americans regarded the treaty to be fully in effect, and the treaty provided for three months' notice before commencing hostilities. Shaw added, however, that the squadron was prepared to meet any hostility by the Algerines. Captain Perry delivered Shaw's letter to the dey, bringing Norderling along for help. Omar again told Perry that the United States had broken the treaty by not returning the *Estedio* and her crew; the United States could respect the three-month notice period to get advice from President Madison or begin hostilities immediately, although he did not want war and promised that while an appeal to Madison was pending, he would respect the existing treaty and Shaler could return ashore unmolested. Perry rejected the notion that the United States had violated the treaty but, despite himself, was impressed by the dey's dignity and lack of bluster. Shaler landed and reoccupied the consulate, and the American commanders agreed to convey a letter from Omar to James Madison.

Ignorant of American institutions, Omar's April 24, 1816, letter was rather quaintly addressed to "his Majesty, the Emperor of America, . . . our noble friend, the support of the kings of the nation of Jesus, the pillar of all Christian sovereigns, . . . elected amongst many lords and nobles, the happy, the great, the amiable James Madison." Omar noted that the year before, Algiers had restored to the United States through Decatur "all that he demanded from us." His one condition for entering a new treaty, he claimed, was that his frigate and sloop of war be returned. Decatur had "given his word to send back our two ships of war, and not having performed his promise, he has thus violated the faithful articles of peace which were signed between us, and by so doing a new treaty must be made." Instead of the Decatur-Shaler treaty, Omar proposed renewing the treaty signed during the reign of Hassan Pasha in 1795, in other words, a return to tribute. Omar asked Madison to respond immediately, but "immediately" in the days where mail went by sailing ship meant a delay of many months.

Dey Omar's letter arrived in the midst of a Washington summer. Madison was at his estate, Montpelier, in Orange, Virginia; Monroe sent a copy southward and gathered the cabinet for an informal meeting to discuss the American response. They agreed that the Decatur-Shaler treaty needed to be upheld, and the dey needed to ratify it, before the United

States could even consider any claim for reparation for the supposed injury sustained for the detention of the brig by Spain. For an anxious government, the benefit of having a squadron in the Mediterranean was recognized for the first time. Monroe wrote that the naval force there, especially when augmented by Commodore Isaac Chauncey in the 74-gun *Washington*, would "probably be sufficient to secure a compliance with our demands." In Washington, the administration already knew that Spain had allowed the *Estedio* to sail to Algiers, but Monroe suggested to Madison that, as secretary of state, he should call in the Spanish minister in Washington to determine whether Algiers had given Spain any consideration for the brig, "not by way of implication against his government, but to obtain such evidence as to enable [the Madison administration] to refute any insinuation of the Dey to that effect." Yet Monroe could not help commenting that by first raising the issue of the capture being in her territorial waters, and then balking at returning the *Estedio* to the Algerines, even when the United States had asked her to, Spain's conduct had been "disrespectful, disingenuous, and unfriendly."

IN THE MEANTIME, the British squadron reached Tunis. Lord Exmouth made a demand for the freedom of the Christian captives. He was able to ransom 524 Neapolitan and Sicilian slaves at half the price paid at Algiers, and the bey agreed to turn over 257 Sardinians and Genoese without payment. Exmouth asked the bey to discontinue enslaving captives. After some hesitation, he agreed. This did not mark the end of ransoming per se in Tunis, but ameliorated the worst aspects of it; the Tunisians promised to treat Christian captives as prisoners of war.

Exmouth's squadron then sailed for Tripoli on April 24. In his negotiations there, he sought and received the same terms as at Tunis. He bought the freedom of 414 Neapolitans and Sicilians for 50,000 Spanish dollars, and persuaded the bashaw to release 140 Sardinians and Genoese without ransom. He even cajoled the bashaw to free 14 Romans and citizens of Hamburg as a personal favor.

On leaving Tripoli, Exmouth's fleet returned to Algiers. The ministry in London had just digested the news that in the treaty with the United States the year before, Omar had agreed to a provision that a nation at war with the United States would be prohibited from selling its American prizes in Algiers, but that the United States might sell its prizes in Algiers. That clause seemed to give the United States an advantage over Britain, which had recently been at war with her transatlantic "cousin" and, for all they knew, might be in the future. The Admiralty sent Exmouth and his fleet back to Algiers to protest. En route, on May 5, 1816, he wrote the prime minister, Lord Sidmouth, that he would have been "more heartily glad should I have been [ordered to] put down for ever all these [Barbary] States," but, even so, the government "deserve[d] immortal Honor" for securing the release of all Christian slaves. Exmouth hoped that the British "have finally smoked the horrors of Christian Slavery, and that it has been attained by pure Conviction and fair reasoning from a People who have been supposed never to reason or hear reason. . . . We have released 2500 poor Creatures and left the Dungeons empty—I hope for ever."

In London, Lord Castlereagh called in John Quincy Adams to assure him that the British naval operations off Barbary were not directed against the United States. In an anteroom at the Foreign Office, Adams stated half in jest to Lord Melville, the first lord of the admiralty, that Exmouth had been making peace for Naples and Sardinia, and with the sequel to the *Estedio* and the prize clause issue, a quarrel for the United States. Melville replied that Britain did not intend trouble for the United States. Adams replied that, should there be a quarrel, if the United States had merely one-third of Britain's naval force, "the Christian world should never more hear of tribute, ransom, or slavery to the African barbarians." Castlereagh then ushered Adams in and reiterated that the British had no intent to create problems for the United States with Algiers. Castlereagh allowed Adams to read Exmouth's instructions, Exmouth's report from Algiers dated April 17, 1816, and the promise of Mohammed Bashaw, the bey of Tunis, to put an end to the slavery of Christians. Adams thanked Castlereagh but urged him to compel Algiers to stop its practice of kidnapping Christians and holding for them for ransom. He observed that Britain was powerful enough to accomplish this goal for all humanity alone, but if she wanted to act in cooperation with other nations, Adams was confident that the United States would send a squadron to help. Castlereagh replied that the British king wished that "all the Barbary Powers should abandon altogether this mode of warfare; but he thought that mild and moderate measures, and persuasion would be better calculated to produce this effect, than force." Castlereagh made explicit the comparison of Barbary slavery and the African slave trade, and concluded that if Britain, which had outlawed the slave trade in 1805, would not go to war against Portugal or Spain to stop them from trafficking in black Africans, so too could Britain "not make War upon the Barbary States to force them to renounce the practice of making slaves of Christians, so long as they never

applied it to [British] subjects, or had given [Britain] any cause of offense."
In other words, as morally odious as slavery had become to Britain, since
the British government was not ready to use force to stop European states
from trading in black slaves, it was illogical to stop Algiers from taking
non-British white captives as slaves. Apparently thinking aloud, Castlereagh
then recalled that the Barbary regencies had been "useful friends" in the
Napoleonic Wars, supplying the British army in Portugal and Spain with
fresh provisions. Adams reminded the British foreign secretary that the
experience of Decatur's squadron proved that the Barbary regencies were
"not very formidable antagonists upon the Ocean" and that the U.S. Navy
had shown itself strong enough to protect American commerce in the
Mediterranean. Upon reading Adams's dispatch, President Madison wrote
Secretary of State Monroe that Adams's "idea of making his country the
sole champion of Xndum [Christendom] against the Barbarians, is very
heroic, but is not in perfect harmony with the sober spirit which tempers
its zeal & [e]nterprize. If we can maintain an elevated position in the Mediterranean for ourselves, and afford that example for others, it will, for the
present at least, best reconcile all our duties."

The British fleet dropped anchor off Algiers on May 14, 1816. Lord
Exmouth went ashore the following morning and had a long interview
with the dey. He protested against the article of the treaty between the
United States and Algiers that gave the United States a favored position
with regard to selling prizes. Omar replied that the protest was unnecessary, as he had already annulled his treaty with the Americans and was
about to declare war against them, since they had taken unfair advantage
of him. Exmouth then told the dey that European countries finally had
been roused against Algiers's practices of keeping prisoners in slavery.
The world was weary of the Barbary captive-and-ransom system, and the
European powers would not long allow it to continue. He asked the dey
to agree to keep captives as prisoners, as Tunis and Tripoli already had
agreed. Algiers would then have peace and could develop commercially.
The discussion lasted three hours. The dey said he would consult his divan and meet with Exmouth the following morning. In fact, Omar's intelligence and seeming moderation masked intransigence: he was powerless
to alter the system under which Algiers existed. Their stock in trade was
capturing Christians to ransom. Nothing short of defeat could alter that
system.

The next day, presumably after consulting with the divan, Omar re-
tracted all he had said. The dey finally asked for six months to send an

emissary to the sultan in Constantinople to decide. Exmouth agreed, provided that Omar would abide by the decision. The dey refused, which indicated, of course, that Omar would rely on the sultan's response only if it provided a convenient excuse. Lord Exmouth was angered by what he perceived as bad faith. He left the palace and sent the British consul to inform the dey of his intention to withdraw. There was an ugly incident, with a mob setting upon the admiral and consul, with cries of putting them to death; Exmouth's brother, Sir Israel Pellew, the captain of the fleet, drew his sword, but the push of arms and bodies prevented him from wielding his weapon. An emissary from the dey arrived and allowed the officers to pass, but the British consul was prohibited from seeking refuge in the fleet. Exmouth was appalled by the treatment. As soon as he reached his own quarterdeck, he signaled the fleet to get under way to get into position to bombard Algiers, although the wind allowed his ships only to drift over to the east side of the bay, where they anchored. For several days, war seemed imminent.

Dey Omar gave immediate orders to his provincial governors to prepare for war and detain all British subjects. On the third day of the crisis, Omar invited the British to resume discussions, which resulted in Omar agreeing to send an ambassador to the sultan in Constantinople for discussions. Within six months, whether or not he had heard from Constantinople, he promised to send an ambassador to England with full power to treat on the question of white slavery. What exactly this meant was unclear. During the discussion, the dey mentioned that he had sent messengers to Oran and Bona, but the British did not know what the orders were. He apologized and dispatched countermanding orders. There was the obvious problem: the distance from Algiers to Bona is more than two hundred miles, and the first set of messengers had three days' start.

Exmouth's squadron departed Algiers on May 20, 1816, and arrived back in England on June 24. Freeing hundreds of captives with ransom seemed disappointing and unheroic. The entire mission of the British fleet seemed anticlimactic and aroused little enthusiasm. Some thought that paying for slaves was a waste of money and encouraged the Barbary racketeering system. Increasingly, opinion hardened that negotiations with the "barbarians" was immoral and that the Algerines only respected force. A rising chorus of evangelical Christian faith in the aftermath of the Napoleonic Wars began to be heard. When the House of Commons debated the actions of Exmouth's squadron, every speaker said that the Barbary states had to relinquish the state-sponsored captive-and-ransom system, and that the British should use force if necessary. The ministry began looking for an excuse to revisit its earlier policy.

On May 23, 1816, the dey's first set of messengers with his first set of orders reached Bona, the center of coral fishing on the North African coast. For years, Algiers had licensed the right to fish the Bona coral reefs to England, and the British consul at Algiers in turn had sublicensed the right to fishermen from Corsica, Sicily, and Sardinia, who therefore were regarded as under British protection. When Omar's orders arrived to detain British subjects, Turkish troops swooped down to arrest the fishermen, several hundred of whom were on shore to hear Mass. The unarmed fishermen attempted to resist or escape, and the janissaries reportedly massacred two hundred of them.

News of the Bona massacre reached England even before Exmouth's returning squadron. The public was horrified after the press reported lurid scenes of unarmed fishermen hacked to death, which suggested that the dey was completely unscrupulous. The Admiralty immediately asked Exmouth to return on a punitive expedition. Exmouth shifted his flag to another ship-of-the-line, the *Queen Charlotte*, and prepared a new squadron.

On July 18, 1816, Lord Castlereagh called in John Quincy Adams again to assure the United States about Britain's aims in North Africa. He reported that, upon his return to Algiers, Lord Exmouth had protested article 18 of the Decatur-Shaler treaty to the dey. Omar had admitted that Algiers's century-old treaty with Britain prohibited granting the United States a more favored position, but said that he had suspended the American treaty "on account of some ship that had not been sent to him." Castlereagh asked Adams for information. Adams told him how the American squadron had captured two ships the year before and agreed to restore them as a condition of peace, but the Spanish detained the brig because she had been taken within Spanish waters. Castlereagh then asked, "Well, but if he now has got the vessel, what difficulty can remain?" Adams could only guess that the dey was using "the pretence of delay" and that in the immediate aftermath of Lord Exmouth ransoming so many European slaves, Omar had "concluded that it was time to put an end to his treaty with the United States." Castlereagh then told Adams that Tunis and Tripoli had agreed to not make slaves of Christian prisoners in the future, that the dey had balked at making any such promise, stating that the sultan would have to approve, and after the insult to the persons of the British officers and the escalation of tensions, the dey had issued orders that resulted in the Bona massacre, although he knew that Omar had tried to countermand the orders. Castlereagh told Adams that Lord Exmouth was returning to Algiers with a new squadron, although the foreign secretary would not disclose his precise instructions. He made clear that if war ensued, the British admiral had discretion to attack Algiers at any point on which he thought them vulnerable. It was now Britain's intent to represent the "general cause of Europe" against Algiers. Britain's goal was to create a multinational fleet to force the Barbary powers to stop enslaving white Christians, and at the same time the multinational fleet would abolish the African slave trade by "arrest[ing] every ship pursuing the traffic in black slaves." Castlereagh's scheme received Adams's approval. As the United States in 1808 had prohibited the slave trade by its own citizens, his country, he told Castlereagh, "could have no objection to measures which may serve to put down these odious practices, the one by the other."

By the end of July 1816, Lord Exmouth managed to get his fleet to sea. The fleet under Exmouth's orders included his flagship, the 100-gun *Queen Charlotte*, and four other stout ships-of-the-line. The battleships, in line and at point-blank range, provided the massed gunnery with which Exmouth planned to batter the seaward fortifications on the mole and on the waterside. He also had five frigates, whose job it would be to bombard the Algerine warships, and if necessary to help any of the battleships that became damaged. Exmouth also had four bomb vessels, which were meant to smash up at least part of the town of Algiers, terrorizing the population and perhaps forcing the dey to capitulate.

Ten days later, on August 9, 1816, the squadron anchored in Gibraltar Bay to find a Dutch squadron of five frigates and a corvette, commanded by Vice Admiral Baron Van de Capellan, who pledged to cooperate with the British. Exmouth decided he would use the Dutch to enfilade the Algerine batteries, to bombard them from a different angle than the English battle line. With the smaller ships, including an "infernal" and some gunboats, the British fleet numbered thirty-five vessels. There is no indication, however, that Exmouth even considered using the poison gas that Cochrane had suggested the year before.

All the professional officers recognized the potential flaw in Exmouth's plan: the assumption that he could bring this fleet into point-blank action against massed batteries without getting pummeled on the way in. Ever since Nelson had brought the British fleet into shallow water against the Danish fleet and forts at Copenhagen in 1801, causing huge casualties among his own men even as he destroyed the Danish navy, the idea of fighting land forts from wooden ships seemed an enormous risk. Exmouth seemed convinced that the British ships would be able to approach without being under fire; the Royal Navy would not have to run the gauntlet of the batteries' bombardment to get into position. Perhaps Omar had told him that in their negotiations in June. Nor did Exmouth worry about the dangers of retreating from the massed batteries; for one thing, by that time, the shore fortifications would have borne hours of intense bombardment; for another, Exmouth planned to withdraw the fleet at night.

The fleet sailed from Gibraltar on August 14, 1816, but because of the notoriously fickle winds off North Africa, only arrived off the Barbary coast on the evening of August 26. In spite of hazy weather, the fleet was seen from the shore as soon as it made its landfall. From his veranda, William Shaler saw the "whole western horizon . . . covered with vessels of war." Lookouts had been posted on the mountains, and they lit bonfires to warn the city. Alarm guns were fired by the garrison, and before nightfall, all Algiers knew that the British were coming. A lead British vessel reported that Algiers was totally mobilized to face the British: the seaward fortifications had been repaired, forty thousand troops had been brought into the city, and janissaries from throughout the regency had been recalled to man the batteries. Omar refused to release the British consul, who was confined in his own house, and eighteen British officers and sailors who had been detained as prisoners. The contrary wind died away in the course of that night, and a light westerly breeze sprang up. With a strong current, the fleet was swept toward the town, so that the leading ships were within six miles of Algiers when dawn broke.

At 5:15 a.m. on August 27, the frigate *Severn* left the fleet and went into the mole under a flag of truce. The fleet lay to, a mile and a half from the town, while a boat from the *Severn* approached. After a brief parley between Exmouth's interpreter and the Algerine port captain at 11:00 a.m., the Algerine agreed to take the English ultimatum to the dey. The ultimatum required the total abolition of Christian slavery and the repayment of the money recently paid in ransom. The British demanded an answer within three hours.

Algiers could not agree to such terms. Agreeing to return a few Americans when Decatur and Shaler made their demands was one thing; the British demand meant the total and universal end to Algiers's way of life.

Facing page *Plan of the Bay & City of Algiers, August 27th, 1816.* Painting by W. J. Pocock. From the U.S. Naval Academy Museum, Beverly R. Robinson Collection.

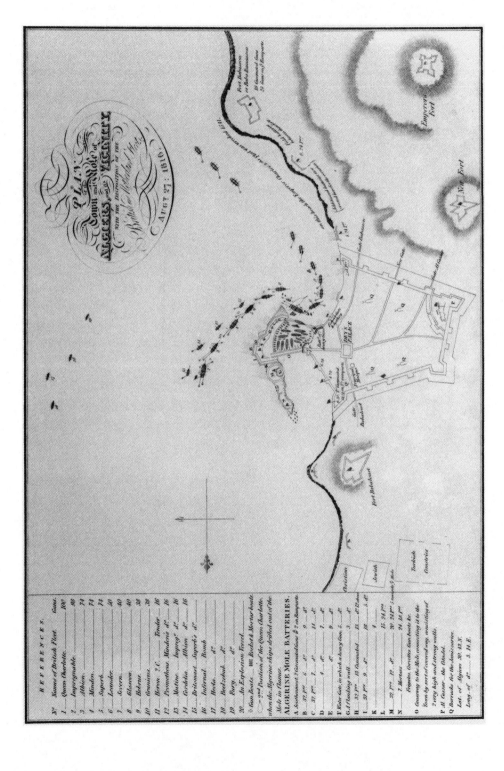

For hundreds of years, the regime had been based on a system of Christian slaves ransomed for money, and the slaves still in captivity represented hundreds of thousands of dollars in value. To give up its "piratical" system, Algiers would have little outlet for its janissaries and its privateers and would be forced to develop trade and farming. It was a vision of a world that no Turkish dey could possibly accept—or live to accept, surrounded as he was by his janissaries—particularly at the point of a Christian ultimatum.

At about two-thirty, the boat waiting near the mole hoisted the signal "No Answer Has Been Given," which was immediately repeated to the flagship. Exmouth made the signal "Are You Ready," which every ship answered in the affirmative. Exmouth ordered the hoists, "Annul the Truce" and then "Hoist the Jib." The *Queen Charlotte* paid off and stood slowly toward the mole.

According to Shaler, watching from his veranda, at 2:30 p.m. the British ships-of-the-line, led by the *Queen Charlotte*, sailed slowly and majestically closer and closer to shore, until the five battleships were "almost brushing" the batteries of the forts with their yardarms. The Dutch frigates formed a separate line, heading farther to the south. The other English ships sailed independently for their battle positions. In the face of these sudden, coordinated movements, the Algerines were paralyzed. The dey was unsure whether to open fire or how to reply. He had planned to allow the English to approach, and when they were close inshore, he meant to order his overwhelming number of janissaries to board their ships. The thirty-five Algerine gunboats lay inside the mole, their plan calling for an attack while the English crews were aloft, furling sails. Yet the cannon in the batteries on the mole were left unloaded. When the English ships began to take their positions, the Algerine gunners began to load their pieces.

The breeze died away as the *Queen Charlotte* approached the molehead. The great English warship, bristling with cannon from its three gundecks, slid slowly toward her position. There was only two feet of water under the keel by the time the anchors were dropped. The ship came to rest eighty yards from Algiers's guns. But the moment for the gunboat attack never came: there was so little wind that Exmouth dropped anchor with the *Queen Charlotte*'s sails set, and then ordered the sails clewed up (pulled

---

Facing page *The City of Algiers, in the Morning of August 27th, 1816.* Engraving by T. Sutherland. From the U.S. Naval Academy Museum, Beverly R. Robinson Collection.

up to the yardarms by ropes), not furled (which would have required dozens of men to go aloft and tie the sails). The men never left their guns. They waited until the ship was stationary, and then, in typical Royal Navy fashion, gave the enemy three cheers. After that there was silence.

Both Exmouth and the dey wished to provoke the other to fire first. But the Algerine gunners' coolness was no match for the discipline of the Royal Navy. A little before 3:00 p.m., a cannon from the Algerine fish-market battery fired, and the flagship heard the hiss of a shot passing to starboard. Then a second shot boomed past. Exmouth turned to his flag captain and said, "You may fire away now." With that, the English line began firing their massive broadsides.

Smoke billowed everywhere. With the ships fighting at anchor in a dead calm, the smoke hardly drifted. A battleship such as the *Queen Charlotte* burned more than a thousand pounds of black powder every minute during battle. Acrid, dense smoke accumulated everywhere, too thick for anyone to see much. Exmouth lost control of his ships soon after the battle began.

The battle did not go as Exmouth planned. Some of his battleships had not taken their proper positions. One anchored too far off to effectively bombard the forts. Other ships lagged behind, opening large gaps in what was supposed to be a compact line, vitiating some of the intended effect of concentrated firepower from the English cannon, or anchored on the wrong side of the line designated for the battle line. As a result, one of the strongest English battleships, the *Impregnable*, came under a withering cannonade. The Algerine fire cut her masts and rigging to pieces. At the end of the action, her crew counted 233 shot-holes, and she had almost as many men killed as all the other vessels put together. Nevertheless, the British ships fought on. With their guns firing two cannonballs at each discharge, they blasted the lighthouse battery, almost knocking it out. All told, the ship fired 7,000 cannonballs, as well as canister and shrapnel.

Meanwhile, Exmouth's *Queen Charlotte* was standing only a few hundred feet off the mole batteries, firing as fast as her gunners could prime, load, and fire. The *Queen Charlotte* enfiladed the mole from end to end. After her first broadside had crashed out, the Algerian gunboats made a brave, suicidal rush across the open water to board the lead British ships. The British gunners depressed their cannon and blew thirty-three of them out of the water. After twenty minutes' firing, the mole batteries were almost silent; after an hour, they were smashed and in ruins. At 3:35 p.m., Exmouth ordered the *Queen Charlotte*'s cannon to cease firing. As the smoke slowly cleared, he could survey at least his immediate field. At 4:30 p.m., he ordered a frigate and smaller vessels of the squadron to bombard the shipping in the harbor, with the result that by 7:30 p.m., most of the Algerine navy was on fire.

All the while, the four bomb vessels, situated almost a mile off shore, were lobbing 10- and 13-inch shells into the town behind the batteries. Most of the Algerine houses were made out of concrete and did not burn, but the mortar shells shattered roofs and collapsed buildings. For all the flashing of the huge mortars and high-arcing shells tracing the sky, little of military value was accomplished. Whether the mortars affected the nerve of Omar and his divan to maintain the fight will never be known.

At 7:30 p.m., the *Queen Charlotte* used a spring on her anchors to swing around and train her guns on the fish-market battery. An hour of bombardment damaged that fort, and the British cannonade began to slacken. It was starting to get dark. Exmouth ordered an "infernal" to blow the lighthouse battery to smithereens. Owing to a navigational mistake, the infernal exploded in the wrong place, doing no harm.

The firing began to die away. Nearly all the Alerine batteries had been silenced by 10:00 p.m., and the British warships began to cut their anchor cables and sail away, out of range. They gradually straggled out into the bay. The bay was lit by the blazing ships and storehouses about the harbor.

In his memoirs, William Shaler described how, after the one Algerine cannon opened fire at 3:00 p.m., a crescendo of massed British gunfire instantly answered:

> At twenty minutes past three, the fire of the marine batteries appears to be silenced, and hundreds of fugitives from them are seen flying along the sea-shore under the walls of this house, where many of them are mowed down by the fire of the Impregnable [a 98-gun British battleship]. The cannonade endures with great fury on the part of the British, and is returned with constancy from the batteries in this quarter. At five o'clock the fire of the marine batteries is renewed, and continued at intervals. At half past seven, the shipping in the port is discovered to be on fire. . . . At half past eight the cannonade endures. The upper part of this house is apparently in ruins; five shells have burst within its walls. At nine, the fire begins to slacken on both sides. At eleven, the growling of cannon is only heard at long intervals. At midnight, from the terrace of this house, every thing in the port appears to be in flames, and two wrecks on fire are drifting out. . . . Shells and rockets occasionally streaming across the horizon, and discharges of cannon from ships still within reach, proclaim an enemy fatigued, exhausted, but not vanquished.

By the light of the next morning, August 28, Shaler could see that the Algerines' defenses were destroyed, and they could not fight on. At noon,

Exmouth sent the dey a short message, offering him peace on the terms proposed the day before. "For your atrocities at Bona on defenceless Christians, and your unbecoming disregard to the demands I made yesterday, in the name of the Prince Regent of England, the fleet under my orders has given you a signal chastisement, by the total destruction of your navy, storehouses, and arsenal, with half your batteries. As England does not war for the destruction of cities," he wrote, he did not want "to visit your personal cruelties upon the inoffensive inhabitants of the country"; should the terms be refused, however, Exmouth promised to begin the bombardment again.

Omar finally surrendered, which was fortunate for Britain because the Anglo-Dutch fleet had fired off almost all of their ammunition. By one account, the combined fleet consumed 118 tons of gunpowder, firing off 50,000 shot, not including the 960 mortar shells lobbed into the city. By contrast, during the 1814 British attack on Baltimore, in the estimation of the commander of Fort McHenry, the five British bomb vessels fired 1,500–1,800 shells at the fort—although many burst over the defenders, 400 exploded within the fort, but only four men were killed and twenty-four wounded. Unlike what happened at Fort McHenry, the fortifications at Algiers had taken a pummeling. Omar agreed to relinquish all Christian slaves, whatever their nationality, to the British fleet, along with all the tribute he had received since the start of 1816, and to renounce Christian slavery forever. Yet for wooden warships to fight against massed stone fortifications at point-blank range was a terrible, grim experience. The Anglo-Dutch fleet lost 883 dead and wounded out of 6,500 engaged. The bombardment tested British and Dutch fortitude and discipline, and Exmouth commented in his report to the Admiralty that the "whole [battle] was conducted with perfect silence, and such a thing as a cheer I never heard in any part of the line."

On September 1, 1816, a parade of Christian slaves started to make their way down to the port. Neither the British nor the Dutch knew in advance how many people their bombardment had freed. Sicilians, Genoese, Neapolitans, Sardinians, Spaniards, Dutch, Frenchmen, Englishmen, even a few stray Austrians and Portuguese—1,642 in all, some of whom had been captive for thirty years, many in wretched physical shape— trooped down to the quays, by turns crying tears of joy and cheering the coalition sailors who were freeing them, linked in groups of ten, where smiths broke off their ankle chains. The Anglo-Dutch attack had come within a whisker of causing another massacre. At the approach of the squadron, the Christian slaves had been moved to an immense cavern at the top of the mountainous terrain on the landward side of the city, a four-hour march up the hillside. During the bombardment, the Turkish soldiers guarding the slaves reportedly began to systematically behead the Christians, supposedly on the order of the dey's chief minister, and thirty were allegedly killed before the dey countermanded the order. When the bombardment ceased, the slaves dragged themselves down to the harbor. They were welcomed aboard the British warships and returned to their native countries, where they were greeted with jubilation.

To his brother, Exmouth confided that he had never "[seen] any set of men more obstinate at their guns" than the Algerines, but they had paid for their bravery: Exmouth reported an estimate of seven thousand Algerine casualties. The massed fire of the British guns had devastated everything before them:

> Such a state of ruin of fortifications and houses was never seen, and it is the opinion of the consuls that two hours more fire would have levelled the town; the walls are all so cracked. Even the aqueducts were broken up, and the people famishing for water. The sea-defenses, to be made effective, must be rebuilt from the foundation. The fire all round the mole looked like Pandemonium.

Lord Exmouth reported to Lord Sidmouth that he had humbled his "Rascally opponent," the dey, so badly that "he would receive me if I chose it on the Wharf on his knees." Exmouth lamented his own "sad loss" of so many men, "but we were exposed to a Compleat Circle of fire." Exmouth considered the bombardment of Algiers "the happiest point of my fortunate Life," noting it had ended with "1000 Slaves [awaiting embarkation] now Cheering on the Mole." The fleet sailed for England on September 3 and arrived at Portsmouth on October 5. Exmouth never went to sea again.

IN OCTOBER 1816, one month after Lord Exmouth's fleet left Algiers, the United States Mediterranean squadron arrived there under Commodore Isaac Chauncey aboard the 74-gun *Washington*. Along with three frigates and two sloops of war, Chauncey's ship-of-the-line provided the "occular demonstration" necessary after the pummeling inflicted by the Anglo-Dutch squadron. The Algerines assumed that the Americans had come to mete out more chastisement. Their defenses lay in ruins. William Shaler went aboard the flagship, and learned that Chauncey did not have dispatches from Madison. Shaler sailed off with the squadron to Gibraltar to await the president's response to Omar's April 24, 1816, letter suggesting a return to the tribute system, and to plot negotiating strategy with Chauncey, but only after assuring the dey that the United States desired peace and that, in any event, the navy would not return to bombard Algiers without first informing Omar if the nations were at war.

On December 8, 1816, the *Washington* and the *Spark* returned from Gibraltar and anchored off Algiers. Shaler went ashore to begin negotiations, carrying Madison's letter to Omar and his own note. Madison's August 21, 1816, response to Omar began by stating that Algiers had "an erroneous view of what has passed" with Decatur. His predecessor dey had declared war without justification on the United States in 1812 and enslaved innocent Americans. Madison would not allow the dey to rewrite history:

> The moment we had brought to an honorable conclusion our war with a nation the most powerful in Europe on the sea, we detached a squadron from our naval force into the Mediterranean. . . . Our squadron met yours, defeated it, and made prize of your largest ship, and of a small one. Our commander proceeded immediately to Algiers, offered you peace, which you accepted, and thereby saved the rest of your ships, which it was known had not returned into port, and would otherwise have fallen into his hands. Our commander, generous as brave, although he would not make the promise a part of the treaty, informed you that he would restore the two captured ships to your officer. They were accordingly so restored. The frigate, at an early day, arrived at Algiers. But the Spanish government, alleging that the capture of the brig was so near the Spanish shore as to be unlawful, detained it at Carthagena, after your officer had received it into his possession. Notwithstanding this fulfillment of all that could be required from the United States, no time was lost in urging upon that government a release of the brig, to which Spain could have no right, whether the capture were or were not agreeable to the law of nations. The Spanish government promised that the brig should be given up, and although the delay was greater than was expected, it appears that the brig, as well as the frigate, has actually been placed in your possession.
>
> It is not without great surprise, therefore, that we find you, under such circumstances, magnifying an incident so little important as it affects the interests of Algiers, and so blameless on the part of the United States, into an occasion for the proposition and threat contained in your letter. I cannot but persuade myself, that a reconsideration of the subject will restore you to the amicable sentiments towards the United States which succeeded the war so unjustly commenced by the Dey who reigned before you. I hope the more that this may be the case, because the United States, whilst they wish for war with no nation, will buy peace with none. It is a principle incorporated into the settled policy of America, that as peace is better than war, war is better than tribute.
>
> Our Consul, and our naval Commander, Chauncey, are authorized to communicate with you, for the purpose of terminating the subsisting differences

by a mutual recognition and execution of the treaty lately concluded. And I pray God that he will inspire you with the same love of peace and justice which we feel, and that he will take you into his holy keeping.

Written at the city of Washington, this twenty-first day of August, 1816.

James Madison
By the President.
James Monroe
Secretary of State

The Shaler note recited that Decatur's promise to restore the *Meshuda* and *Estedio* had been met by the "actual return of those vessels to Algiers," and that the dey's claim otherwise was "unfounded." Shaler suggested that the two nations renew the terms negotiated in June 1815, with two revisions. First, the United States was willing to remove the clause that allowed the U.S. Navy to sell prizes in Algiers in wartime, as the clause was offensive to the British. Second, the United States insisted on striking from the dey's Turkish translation of the earlier treaty a clause providing for the United States to make gifts upon the presentation of a new consul to the dey. Shaler and Chauncey insisted that "no obligation binding the United States to pay any thing to the Regency or to its officers, on any occasion whatsoever, will be agreed to." To avoid a future misunderstanding based on self-serving translations, Shaler sent his note in Arabic as well as in English, and required that the dey's reply be made in English, French, Spanish, or Italian. Although Omar tried to evade acknowledging the earlier treaty in his personal negotiations with Shaler, he ultimately conceded that the Anglo-Dutch bombardment of the city had left him powerless to resist, and that he would agree to the terms. On December 23, 1816, the Decatur-Shaler treaty was "renewed."

The Mediterranean squadron kept careful watch, but the Algerines never seized an American ship or seaman again. In fact, the dey rebuilt his fleet by buying some ships from Naples and Genoa and received a gift frigate from the Ottoman sultan in Constantinople. His corsairs went out to make a few desultory prizes over the next few years—as late as October 1815, Tunisian cruisers had the audacity to land their janissaries on the island of Santo Antonio, off Sardinia, and seized 150 men, women, and children, whom they brought back to North Africa to replenish their stock of captives. Nevertheless, the end of Barbary terror was in the offing. As far as the United States was concerned, the long reign of Barbary terror was over.

Wars are always clarifying. The American 1815 campaign against Algiers demonstrated that the rising republic across the Atlantic was willing to act to protect its trade and people. The United States in 1815 was no more a fledgling experiment. Having survived its second "war of independence" against Britain, it proved able to defend its far-flung interests. The interests were both mercantile and nationalist. A vague contempt for America had arisen in Europe and North Africa as a land of calculating "Jonathans," good traders and merchants, but imbued either with Quaker principles or those of the countinghouse, calculating that paying tribute was cheaper than fighting. The Algerine corsairs expected to nab American merchant shipping and seamen, selling the vessels and cargo and extorting bribes to release the sailors. Algiers made fundamental miscalculations about Americans' willingness to put aside their commercial culture and fight. Or rather, the United States made the fundamental calculation that it was better to fight while Algiers had only ten American captives, the U.S. Navy was powerful and battle-tested, and before American merchant vessels resumed an active trade in the Mediterranean.

Even as the War of 1812 was ending, and ending with the United States unable to balance its books and its capital city burnt, the United States was able to send powerful squadrons overseas to fight a nettlesome enemy. Decatur's quick success was largely a matter of luck. He caught the Algerine navy at sea, the worst place for it against a competent foe. The United States Navy was able to capture the *Meshuda* and the *Estedio*—and would have captured the entire Algerine navy on its way back to Algiers had Omar not agreed to terms. Whether the United States would have been able to keep the peace without the forceful intervention of the British navy in 1816 will never be known. The dey searched for pretexts to overturn the treaty dictated at the mouths of Decatur's cannon, and Decatur and Bainbridge both recognized that the peace could only be kept by force or the threat of force. What Bainbridge called the "occular demonstration" given by the Mediterranean squadron might not have been enough to deter the dey from returning to the old system of capture and ransom.

But the American naval and diplomatic triumph signaled Europe that the festering, centuries-old problem of white Christian slavery in Muslim North Africa did not need to remain a fixture. The American foray proved that Algiers was hardly the power that Europe had long feared, and embarrassed the British government into action. When the British government decided to send Lord Exmouth's fleet against Algiers, the destruction of the system of white Christian slavery became one of the first, great international humanitarian causes.

Dealing forcibly with white Christian slavery in North Africa was a prerequisite for Europe and, more importantly, America, to wrestle with the far more intractable problem of black African slavery and the slave trade. Recent historians, echoing Benjamin Franklin's Historicus essay, see hypocrisy and racism in the efforts of the slave-owning Virginians Madison and Monroe to eradicate white Christian slavery at the hands of darker, Islamic people overseas, when America's own "peculiar institution" flourished on the backs of black Africans. That there surely was; Americans considered the Turks and Moors and Arabs less than themselves racially and religiously. Yet until they had resolved to confront and crush the bondage of people like them—whites, Christians, Americans— it was difficult for most Americans to think of extending the principle of abolishing slavery to people who looked so different from them.

In 1849, Charles Sumner, then a thirty-seven-year-old Boston lawyer, brought the first racial desegregation lawsuit in an American court, arguing that the spirit of America's institutions and the equal protection of the law required Boston's public schools to be open to black children. His arguments, far in advance of the times, did not prevail. Sumner lost that case, but for the rest of his life he was animated by the cause of the abolition of slavery and civil rights for black Americans. In 1853, two years after he was elected to the United States Senate from Massachusetts, he wrote *White Slavery in the Barbary States*, the first book to deal systemically with what was then the recent history of slavery in Islamic North Africa. But *White Slavery in the Barbary States* was also a polemic. Sumner anticipated by 150 years the now-standard observations of modern historians about the hypocrisy of destroying slavery in Islamic North Africa while tolerating its existence in the United States. He pointedly observed that the Barbary regencies were situated near the parallel of 36° 30', the line of the 1850 Missouri Compromise, which, he said, made Virginia, Carolina, Mississippi, and Texas the American equivalents of Morocco, Algiers, Tripoli, and Tunis. The "common peculiarities of climate, breeding, indolence, lassitude, and selfishness," he suggested, were the cause of their "insensibility to the claims of justice and humanity." Sumner, of course, became one of the stalwart Unionists during the Civil War and later a Radical Republican who pushed for the emancipation of Negro slaves and the Reconstruction of the South.

Men such as Charles Sumner found a universal theme from the 1815– 16 victory over slavery in Islamic North Africa. As Sumner put it, "Slavery in all its forms, even under the mildest influences, is a wrong and a curse."

The comparisons that Benjamin Franklin and William Eaton had drawn a half century before between slavery abroad and slavery at home were driven to their logical conclusion by abolitionists like Sumner and, ultimately, Lincoln. To view the naval and diplomatic campaigns of 1815–16 simply as an illustration of America's continuing racism and hypocrisy is historically simplistic. Rather, the war and diplomacy of 1815–16 should be seen as a way station in the gradual evolution of Western thinking that regarded all slavery as abhorrent.

Epilogue

STEPHEN DECATUR returned to the United States as one of its greatest heroes, and he always regarded the 1815 campaign as his greatest achievement. He was lionized by the public in a series of celebratory dinners up and down the eastern seaboard. In Norfolk in 1816, he responded to his hosts with a toast, "Our country! In her intercourse with foreign nations, may she always be in the right; but right or wrong, our country!" which Americans during the divisive years of the Vietnam War changed into "My country, right or wrong." Even though eighteen towns, cities, and counties are named for him across America, it is ironic that today, if he is remembered at all, he may be best known for an after-dinner toast.

Having chosen to live and work in Washington, Decatur found that paperwork, petty politics, and bureaucratic details were not his forte. But the life of a hero and naval commissioner was prestigious, well-paying, and not demanding in the peacetime navy, and his home with Susan was as close to a salon as muddy, provincial Washington had. He was admired and befriended by personalities as diverse as Madison, Monroe, John Quincy Adams, and John Randolph of Roanoke. In 1819, architect Benjamin Latrobe built the Decaturs a rather austere Federal-style brick townhouse on the corner of President's Square (now Lafayette Square), which still stands and is open as a National Historic Trust Property. But the Decaturs were not to live there long.

Commodore James Barron, the long-absent officer humiliated in the *Chesapeake-Leopard* incident in 1807, finally returned to the United States in 1818 and sought command of a ship. Decatur made known his opposition to any post for Barron, and Decatur's letters had a disdainful tone. Although Decatur easily might have avoided Barron's slow-motion steps toward calling him out to fight a duel, he allowed himself to get mired in the suggestion that he had said to others that Barron might be insulted with impunity (he did not say that, but Decatur had such an elevated sense of pride that he did not want to say that he would not have said it, either). Barron, egged on by Jesse Duncan Elliot, who hated Decatur, challenged Decatur to a duel. Understanding that a duel with a jowly, nearsighted, nearly forgotten naval officer would be senseless, Decatur's naval friends tried to dissuade him, and then begged off serving as his second.

Into this embarrassing social breach stepped William Bainbridge, who had not spoken to or seen Decatur since their strained meeting on the *Independence* in Gibraltar Bay in October 1815, but who clasped Decatur to his chest and professed his friendship in an allegedly chance meeting on a Washington street, and who soon agreed to act as Decatur's "friend." As the seconds, Elliott and Bainbridge agreed the duel would occur in a ravine off the Bladensburg (Maryland) road on March 22, 1820. When Barron breached protocol on the field of honor by speaking to Decatur in words suggesting conciliation, the seconds did nothing to intervene, perhaps for their own reasons, perhaps in rigid obedience to the code of gentlemen. Decatur, a crack shot, had decided in advance he would merely wound Barron; Barron, corpulent and wearing eyeglasses, did not have such ability with the pistol, even if he had the desire. The two duelists' shots rang out at the same time. Decatur's shot hit Barron in the hip, causing a flesh wound that bled profusely, but he lived; Barron's shot smashed into Decatur's groin, nicking his femoral artery. In agony, Decatur was carried home, where he bled to death several hours later.

Susan Decatur was so overcome that she was prevented from seeing her husband as he lay dying. Decatur's funeral two days later was attended by all of Washington, including President Monroe and the cabinet, Chief Justice Marshall and the Supreme Court, and most of the Congress; ten thousand people were said to have lined the streets.

Susan Decatur never recovered from her loss, and became increasingly spiritual, socially isolated, and impoverished. She died in 1860 in a cottage on the Georgetown College grounds.

James Barron lived on, never getting a sea command. Many years later, he was reconciled with Decatur's faction in the navy and was given a shore position. He died as the senior officer of the navy in 1851.

William Bainbridge commanded at sea and became a navy commissioner, but as he aged, he became addicted to alcohol and opiates, and died in 1833 calling for all hands to repel boarders. Several years before he died, he burned his personal correspondence. Whether Bainbridge was a Judas-like figure complicit in Decatur's death, as Susan Decatur long insisted, or merely a man who lived by a rigid code is still the subject of debate among historians.

Benjamin Crowninshield served as secretary of the navy into Monroe's administration, although after the 1815 campaign, he was mostly content to let the department's clerks run the peacetime navy. He resigned from the cabinet and returned to Salem in October 1818. He was elected to Congress (1823–30), where he had the satisfaction of serving on the House Naval Affairs Committee. In his later years, he served in the state house, representing his new home district in Boston. He died in 1851. He never lost his gentlemanly ways: when James and Dolley Madison left Washington after Monroe's inauguration as president in March 1817, Crowninshield was the only civilian friend who accompanied them as they began their trip home to Montpelier.

Captain Charles Gordon, aware that the fame he craved had eluded him, cursed that he had never been able to "whip an Englishman." He might have added that his own mistake prevented him from whipping an Algerine. His old dueling wound became infected, and he was debilitated by stomach ailments and diarrhea; in September 1816 he died ashore in Messina, Sicily.

Congress did not completely forget the loss of the *Epervier*. In March 1817, an act was passed appropriating six months' pay, as well as pay owing through July 14, 1815, to the widows and orphans of the men lost on the brig. By modern standards, the relief act was not generous, but those were harder days. In 1849, more than thirty years after the *Epervier* went down, the widow of Tobias Lear sent Fanny Lewis a locket with some of William Lewis's hair that he had given her in 1806, writing Fanny that Lewis's memory still "live[d] fresh in [her] affections."

John Downes survived the 1815 war because of his fortuitous transfer from the *Epervier* to the *Guerriere*. He was promoted to captain in 1817. From 1831 to 1834, he circumnavigated the world in the new frigate *Potomac*. On the way, in February 1832, he launched a punitive attack on the natives at Quallah Batoo (now Kuala Batu) in Sumatra for murdering, almost exactly a year earlier, American seamen of the ship *Friendship* (owned by Nathaniel Silsbee, a U.S. senator from Massachusetts and the very man who had been part owner of the *Edwin*). Downes landed the marines, stormed the local fort, and then bombarded the village, killing several hundred natives, along with the Malay pirates. Although President Jackson supported Downes, his punitive assault met with an uproar in Congress and in the press, and he never went to sea again. He died in 1855.

Midshipman George Hollins stayed in the navy. Forty-five years after serving with Decatur, he reacted to the secession crisis of 1861 by going South, and in 1862, he commanded Southern naval forces on the Mississippi. After the war, he returned to Baltimore, where he was appointed a bailiff in the city court. He died in 1877.

Mordecai Noah returned from Tunis to literary and political pursuits in New York; no one ever questioned him for continuing to act as consul after he knew that he had been recalled. In 1819, he wrote *She Would Be a Soldier, or the Plains of Chippewa*, a formulaic girl-pretending-to-be-a-boy-in-uniform play that was successfully staged in New York, and often revived in the nineteenth century, as well as a number of forgettable dramas—about one per year—many with patriotic themes such as 1824's *The Siege of Yorktown*. Throughout his life, Noah wrote about Jewish history and themes, as well as essays dealing with contemporary American politics. In 1818, he delivered a speech consecrating the new building of Congregation Shearith Israel, the Spanish and Portuguese Synagogue in New York. His speech focused on the theme of the persecution of the Jews in countries that lacked democracy. Never shy, Noah sent copies of his address to former Presidents Adams, Jefferson, and Madison, each of whom responded warmly and expressed broad support for Jews' civil rights. In his reply, Madison disingenuously informed Noah that "your religious profession was well known at the time you recd. Your Commission; and that in itself could not be a motive for your recall [from Tunis]."

The next year, 1819, Noah sent John Adams a copy of his recently published book, *Travels in England, France, Spain and the Barbary States*. In his letter acknowledging the gift, the eighty-four-year-old ex-president praised *Travels* for its "ancient and modern learning of judicious observations & ingenious reflections." Adams regretted that Noah had not traveled to "Syria, Judea and Jerusalem" as Adams would have relished reading Noah's comments more than "any traveler I have yet read." Adams then asserted, in what has been called the first pro-Zionist expression by an American statesman, "I could find it in my heart to wish that you had been at the head of a hundred thousand Israelites . . . marching with them into

Judea & making a conquest of that country & restoring your nation to the dominion of it. For I really wish the Jews again in Judea an independent nation."

Noah himself espoused the emigration of the Jews, but the Zion he advocated was an area near Buffalo, New York, which he purchased for that purpose and called "Ararat." Equally fantastically, Noah theorized in his writings that the American Indians were the lost tribes of ancient Israel. Politically, Noah became a man of some influence. As a New York newspaperman, he strongly supported Martin Van Buren. He was appointed sheriff of New York in 1821, although he lost election to the post on nakedly anti-Semitic appeals. By the 1830s, Noah was regarded as the most prominent American Jew. Noah later broke with the Democratic party and in 1841 was rewarded by Governor William H. Seward of New York with a position as a judge on the Court of Sessions, apparently the first Jew appointed as a judge to an American criminal court. He died in 1851, although the first edition of his *Selected Writings* only appeared in 1999.

William Shaler stayed as consul general to the Barbary regencies until 1830. A student of cultures and languages, he wrote "On the Language, Manners, and Customs of the Berbers," published in the American Philosophical Society's *Transactions* in 1825, and then a full-length book, *Sketches of Algiers*, in 1826. Princeton granted him an honorary degree in 1828. He was transferred to be consul in Havana in 1830 and contracted cholera and died there in 1833, at the age of sixty.

In *Sketches of Algiers*, William Shaler looked into the future. Algiers appeared "to be tottering on the brink of ruin, [which] must remove the last pretext upon which the anti-social existence of these banditti can be tolerated." He predicted that a "dissolution of this ridiculous government must necessarily follow the entire suppression of their claims to pursue the trade of pirates, which, in the natural order of things, cannot much longer be delayed." He prophesied that Britain would occupy and colonize Islamic North Africa. He was right that Algiers would not long remain in the corsair business, nor as an autonomous regency, but it was the French army that marched in and seized Algiers in 1830. They did not leave for 130 years.

Appendix I

Navy Department's Orders to Commodore Stephen Decatur

Navy Department
April 15th 1815

Sir

The Government of the United States, having declared War against the Regency of Algiers, the President has appointed you to command the Squadron immediately destined to act against that power.

You will proceed to the Mediterranean with all the United States Ships and Vessels which shall be ready for Sea in the Port of New York, and you are hereby authorized and directed to subdue, seize and make Prize of all Vessels, goods & effects, belonging to the Dey or Subjects of Algiers; and you will in your course to the Mediterranean, ascertain if possible, whether any Algerine cruisers have passed the Streights into the Atlantic Ocean, and endeavour to capture or destroy them. On your arrival in the Mediterranean Sea, you will establish and declare the Port of Algiers in a State of Blockade, and prohibit all intercourse by ingress or egress, of all Vessels, of any nation whatever, giving due publicity of the Blockade; and you will use your utmost exertions to intercept and capture the cruising Vessels which may be at Sea belonging to the Dey of Algiers, or others sailing under that Flag.

As it is considered that the Squadron at present under your command is not sufficiently Strong to attempt offensive operations against the Town and Batteries of Algiers, you may await an augmentation of force which will follow from the United States with all possible despatch and use your own discretion in directing the operations of your Squadron in such manner as to produce the most effect upon the Enemy or for the more immediate protection of our commerce to and from the ports of that Sea, and give instructions to all the commanding Officers to that effect, and establish such convoy regulations as shall be necessary to give efficacy and security to the Vessels under Convoy.

In the expenditures for the Squadron, the strictest economy is recommended and you will endeavour to controul commanders in this respect as far as shall be consistent with the good of the Service and the indispensable wants of their respective Vessels: a Store Ship will be sent soon after you, to supply the Provisions and such articles of general use as may be necessary in anticipation of your probable wants; the Store Ship will proceed to Barcelona to receive your orders.

Richard McCall Esqr. Consul at Barcelona in Spain, is appointed the Agent of this Department in the Mediterranean, upon whom you will draw for all Contingent wants of the Service; and you will be pleased to instruct the commanders to present all their indents and requisitions to you for approval without which they will not be answered. A credit will be lodged in London of Ten Thousand pounds Sterling to meet the Bills of Mr. McCall for the demands of the Squadron.

Should you find it necessary from the State of health of the crew to establish a Hospital at any neutral port, you will be governed by the actual State of things in Europe, and decide upon the most eligible station both for the health cheapness of living and general convenience.

Surgeon Jno. D. McReynolds is ordered to report himself to you for the Special service of the Hospital Establishment and his Requisitions of Medicines, Stores and Necessaries for that purpose you will be pleased to sanction, holding him accountable for the expenditure.

The Port of Cagliari in the Island of Sardinia is recommended to you as the best for the Hospital Establishment, as well as for the convenience as the friendly disposition of the Sovereign of that Island who has a Common Interest in our Success against Algiers with which Regency he is continually at War: you will of course secure the most friendly relations with the Government of Sardinia by every means in your power.

In chosing a port of General Rendezvous for your Squadron you will be governed by circumstances and your good judgement will determine that point better than it can be decided here by the Department. The Bay of Majorca in the Island of that name is said to be the best station to retire to for a Squadron Blockading Algiers as you can return to Algiers with an Easterly or Westerly wind, whereas were the Rendezvous at Gibraltar to the westward, or Cagliari to the Eastward, your Squadron might be wind bound at either while the Algerines could escape and be at Sea before you could gain the Station. There are many ports in France, Spain &c. which will afford safety and convenience, and where your Flag will be received with attention and respect.

You will treat all friendly flags with respect and give full protection to the Merchant Vessels of the United States and our commerce generally without injury to the rights of others.

Establish Blockade no further than may be necessary effectually to keep the Algerines in port and explain if necessary to the European Governments near the Mediterranean, and also Tunis & Tripoli, that your views are friendly to all powers except Algiers, and that your Government asks of them no more than justice.

The Department of State will join you in a Commission, to treat with Algiers, and you will of course obey those instructions; and either fight and subdue them, or make an honorable peace if you can.

You will caution your Officers while upon distant service so to conduct themselves in their deportment and expenditures as to gain credit for themselves and do honor to the service.

If a superior officer should supercede you in the command you may shift your Flag and return in a Sloop [of war] to New York or Philadelphia, as shall be most agreeable to you. In the event of your return to the United States, you will give the commanding officer who may succeed you copies of all orders, papers &c. connected with your command which may be necessary for his information or useful to the object of the expedition.

The Officers of the Army, when their services shall not be further required, are to be permitted to leave the Squadron and to return either to the United States, or to be landed at a port in Europe, at their option.

You will obtain Twenty thousand Dollars in Specie at New York, for the use of your Squadron for which you will be held accountable in the expenditure.

Those men whose terms of service are nearly expired ought not to be taken out in the fleet. You may recruit American Seamen, if necessary, in the Mediterranean.

The fleet now ready will consist of the Guerriere & Constellation Frigates, the Ontario and Epervier Sloops [of War], and the five small Vessels lately under the command of Captain Porter, together with the Frigate

Macedonian, if she can be equipped in time; and you will sail without any delay, so soon as the orders for the commissioners shall arrive, taking out Mr. Shaler, who is one of them; and Consul McCall who is to act as Agent for the fleet.

Such prizes as you may capture may be condemned in the courts of Sardinia and sold taking care to account strictly for the proceeds thereof; and preserve and transmit all the papers that they may be filed in our courts; and national Vessels if of consequence to warrant it, may be sent to the United States for adjudication.

You will order correct Muster Rolls to be transmitted to this Department before you Sail of each Ship and Vessel of your Squadron, regularly signed and certified by the Commanders and Pursers.

With every wish for your Success, and the most honorable result of your expedition,

I am, very respectfully,

Sir,

Your Obedient Servant,

B. W. Crowninshield

Commodore Stephen Decatur
commander in chief of the
United States Squadron destined to the
Mediterranean

New York

Appendix II

Memorandum from W. D. Robinson to William Shaler, May 9, 1815

It has been long known to all travellers that have visited Sicily, that the Manufactories of Sulphur have been attended with great risque to the Inhabitants that dwelt within many leagues of them, and it has been customary for those inhabitants to remove 8 or 10 leagues distance during the period the furnaces are burning, and even with all those precautions, some of the villages to Leeward occasionally suffer'd severely. This circumstance gave birth to the Idea that Sulphur might be efficaciously used in warfare. Lord Cochrane while Cruising in the Mediterranean made some experiments with a few hundred pounds of Sulphur, and discovered that its deleterious effects were as instantaneous as certain. At a distance of some hundred yards from the spot where he made the experiment there were several sheep and oxen grazing, but as soon as the smoke spread over them, they drop'd down in a state of *stupefaction*, and many of them *immediately died*. Lord Cochrane made a similar experiment in England with the same success, and it is known to the British Government that he made use of Sulphur (perhaps by loading and setting fire to a small vessel) in his successful attack on some Ships of War on the French coast at the *Isle of Aix*. The British Cabinet were so well convinced of its importance, that they intended to have applied it in an attempt to destroy *the Fleet at Toulon*, had not peace interrupted the project, and it was likewise contemplated to use Sulphur on a large Scale for the purpose of neutralising the batteries of *New York and other Cities on our Atlantic Coast*.

Two or three Ships laden with Sulphur would be more than sufficient to *destroy Algiers*. These vessels are to be used as fire ships. The Sulphur to be placed in *layers* between other layers *of clay & wood*. The vessels to be conducted as near as possible to the Squadron or battery, and there wait until the wind or tide enables them to float directly into the harbour, or against the batteries in question. The match to be applied at the proper moment, and if they can come in contact with the enemy at Anchor, or approach within a few hundred yards of the batteries, the effect will be inevitable. From the situation of the batteries at Algiers, and the position their squadron usually anchors under those batteries it is conceiv'd that two sulphur vessels would decide the *fate of Algiers in a few hours*, and at all events place the Squadron in our possession.

No danger need be apprehended to the Party using this plan, because in case of a sudden shift of wind, the fleet by being under sail can easily get out of the way. It may however be necessary to use due precautions, and not to start the sulphur vessels until an opportunity is offer'd of a *steady wind* blowing directly into the harbour. Should the Algerine fire red hot shot on these vessels thus floating in, so much the better.

When our Squadron arrives in the Mediterranean, the Commodore may make the experiment with facility by purchasing a few hundred pounds of Sulphur, and trying in the same way as Lord Cochrane has done, and should the result establish the facts before mentioned, there will then be no difficulty in obtaining a sufficient quantity of Sulphur to make the experiment at Algiers.

The preceding is the substance of a communication made to me by Cochrane Johnstone, and which I have thus committed to writing as a memorandum for the reflection of William Shaler Esqr who will use it as his discretion dictates, and should it turn out to be a *Practicable project*, I feel assured there are no persons better able to carry it into effect than Commodore Decatur with the gallant officers and seamen under his command.

New York May 9th 1815
W. D. Robinson

Note—we know the effects of Sulphur in destroying rats, therefore I do not see why we shall not try the principle in smoking barbarians.

Appendix III

Treaty Between the United States and the Dey of Algiers

TREATY of Peace and Amity,
concluded between the United States of America
and His Highness Omar Bashaw, Dey of Algiers

Art. 1. There shall be, from the conclusion of this treaty, a firm, inviolable and universal peace and friendship between the President and citizens of the United States of America, on the one part, and the Dey and subjects of the Regency of Algiers in Barbary on the other, made by the free consent of both parties, on the terms of the most favored nations: and if either party shall hereafter grant to any other nation any particular favour or privilege in navigation or commerce, it shall immediately become common to the other party, freely when it is freely granted to such other nations; but when the grant is conditional, it shall be at the option of the contracting parties to accept, alter, or reject such conditions, in such manner as shall be most conducive to their respective interests.

Art. 2. It is distinctly understood between the Contracting parties, that no tribute, either as biennial presents, or under any other form or name whatever, shall ever be required by the Dey and Regency of Algiers from the United States of America, on any pretext whatever.

Art. 3. The Dey of Algiers shall cause to be immediately delivered up to the American squadron, now off Algiers, all the American citizens, now in his possession, amounting to ten, more or less; and all the subjects of the Dey of Algiers, now in [the] possession of the United States, amounting to five hundred, more or less, shall be delivered up to him, the United States, according to the usages of civilized nations, requiring no ransom for the excess of prisoners in their favour.

Art. 4. A just and full compensation shall be made by the Dey of Algiers, to such citizens of the United States, as have been captured and detained by Algerine cruizers, or who have been forced to abandon their property in Algiers in violation of the twenty-second article of the treaty of peace and amity concluded between the United States and the Dey of Algiers, on the 5th of September 1795.

And it is agreed between the contracting parties, that in lieu of the above, the Dey of Algiers shall cause to be delivered forthwith into the hands of the American consul, residing in Algiers, the whole of a quantity of bales of cotton, left by the late consul general of the United States in the public magazines in Algiers, and that he shall pay into the hands of the said consul the sum of ten thousand Spanish dollars.

Art. 5. If any goods, belonging to any nation with which either of the parties is at war, should be loaded on board of vessels belonging to the other party, they shall pass free and unmolested, and no attempts shall be made to take or detain them.

Art. 6. If any citizens or subjects with their effects, belonging to either party, shall be found on board a prize vessel taken from an enemy by the other party, such citizens or subjects shall be liberated immediately, and in no case, on any pretence whatever, shall any American citizen be kept in captivity or confinement, or the property of any American citizen, found on board of any vessel belonging to any nation, with which Algiers may be at war, be detained from its lawful owners after the exhibition of sufficient proofs of American citizenship and of American property by the consul of the United States, residing at Algiers.

Art. 7. Proper passports shall immediately be given to the vessels of both the contracting parties, on condition that the vessels of war belonging to the Regency of Algiers, on meeting with merchant vessels belonging to citizens of the United States of America, shall not be permitted to visit them with more than two persons besides the rowers; these only shall be permitted to go on board, without first obtaining leave from the commander of said vessel, who shall compare the passport, and immediately permit said vessel to proceed on her voyage; and should any of the subjects of Algiers insult or molest the commander or any other person on board a vessel so visited, or plunder any of the property contained in her, on complaint being made by the consul of the United States residing in

Algiers, and on his producing sufficient proof to substantiate the fact, the commander or Rais of said Algerine ship or vessel of war, as well as the offenders, shall be punished in the most exemplary manner.

All vessels of war belonging to the United States of America, on meeting a cruizer belonging to the Regency of Algiers on having seen her passports and certificates from the consul of the United States, residing in Algiers, shall permit her to proceed on her cruize unmolested, and without detention. No passport shall be granted by either party to any vessel, but such as are absolutely the property of citizens or subjects of the said contracting parties, on any pretence whatever.

Art. 8. A citizen or subject of either of the contracting parties having bought a prize vessel condemned by the other party, or by any other nation, the certificates of condemnation and bill of sale shall be a sufficient passport for such vessel for six months, which, considering the distance between the two countries, is no more than a reasonable time for her to procure passports.

Art. 9. Vessels of either of the contracting parties, putting into the ports of the other, and having need of provisions or other supplies, shall be furnished at the market price; and if any such vessel should so put in from a disaster at sea, and have occasion to repair, she shall be at liberty to land and re-embark her cargo without paying any customs or duties whatever; but in no case shall she be compelled to land her cargo.

Art. 10. Should a vessel of either of the contracting parties be cast on shore within the territories of the other, all proper assistance shall be given to her crew: no pillage shall be allowed. The property shall remain at the disposal of the owners, and if re-shipped on board of any vessel for exportation, no customs or duties whatever shall be required to be paid thereon, and the crew shall be protected and secured, until they can be sent to their own country.

Art. 11. If a vessel of either of the contracting parties shall be attacked by an enemy within cannon shot of the forts of the other, she shall be protected as much as possible. If she be in port she shall not be seized or attacked, when it is in the power of the other party to protect her; and when she proceeds to sea, no enemy shall be permitted to pursue her from the same port, within twenty-four hours after her departure.

Art. 12. The Commerce between the United States of America and the Regency of Algiers, the protections to be given to merchants, masters of vessels, and seamen, the reciprocal rights of establishing consuls in each country, and the privileges, immunities and jurisdiction to be enjoyed by such consuls, are declared to be upon the same footing in every respect with the most favoured nations respectively.

Art. 13. The consul of the United States of America shall not be responsible for the debts contracted by the citizens of his own nation, unless he previously gives written obligations so to do.

Art. 14. On a vessel or vessels of war, belonging to the United States, anchoring before the city of Algiers, the consul is to inform the Dey of her arrival, when she shall receive the salutes which are by treaty or custom given to the ships of war of the most favoured nations, on similar occasions and which shall be returned gun for gun; and if after such arrival, so announced, any Christians whatsoever, in Algiers, make their escape and take refuge on board of the ships of war, they shall not be required back again, nor shall the consul of the United States, or commander of said ships, be required to pay any thing for the said Christians.

Art. 15. As the government of the United States of America has in itself no character of enmity against the laws, religion, or tranquility of any nation, and as the said States have never entered into any voluntary war, or act of hostility, except in defence of their just rights on the high seas, it is declared by the contracting parties, that no pretext arising from religious opinions shall ever produce an interruption of harmony between the two nations; and the consuls and agents of both nations shall have liberty to celebrate the rites of their respective religions in their own houses.

The consuls respectively shall have liberty and personal security given them to travel within the territories of each other both by land and sea, and shall not be prevented from going on board of any vessel they may think proper to visit; they shall likewise have the liberty to appoint their own drogoman and broker.

Art. 16. In case of any dispute arising from the violation of any of the articles of this treaty, no appeal shall be made to arms, nor shall war be declared on any pretext whatever; but if the consul, residing at the place where the dispute shall happen, shall not be able to settle the same, the government of that country shall state their grievance in writing, and transmit the same to the government of the other, and the period of three months shall be allowed for answers to be returned, during which time no act of hostility shall be permitted by either party; and in case the grievances are not redressed, and a war should be the event, the consul and citizens, and subjects of both parties respectively, shall be permitted to embark with their effects unmolested, on board of what vessel or vessels they shall think proper, reasonable time being allowed for that purpose.

Art. 17. If in the course of events, a war should break out between the two nations, the prisoners captured by either party shall not be made slaves, they shall not be forced to hard labour, or other confinement than such as may be necessary to secure their safe keeping, and they shall be exchanged rank for rank; and it is agreed that prisoners shall be exchanged in twelve months after their capture, and the exchange may be effected by any private individual legally authorized by either of the parties.

Art. 18. If any of the Barbary states or other powers at war with the United States, shall capture any American vessel and send it into any port of the Regency of Algiers, they shall not be permitted to sell her, but shall be forced to depart the port, on procuring the requisite supplies of provisions: But the vessels of war of the United States, with any prizes they may capture from their enemies shall have liberty to frequent the port of Algiers, for refreshment of any kind and to sell such prizes, in the said ports, without any other customs or duties, than such as are customary on ordinary commercial importation.

Art. 19. If any of the citizens of the United States, or any person under their protection, shall have any disputes with each other, the consul shall decide between the parties, and whenever the consul shall require any aid or assistance from the government of Algiers to enforce his decisions, it shall be immediately granted to him; and if any disputes shall arise between any citizens of the United States and the citizens or subjects of any other nation having [a] consul or agent in Algiers, such disputes shall be settled by the consuls or agents of the respective nations; and any dispute or suits at law that may take place between any citizens of the United States and the subjects of the Regency of Algiers, shall be decided by the Dey in person and no other.

Art. 20. If a citizen of the United States should kill, wound, or strike a subject of Algiers, or on the contrary a subject of Algiers should kill, wound, or strike a citizen of the United States, the law of the country shall take place, and equal justice shall be rendered, the consul assisting at the trial; but the sentence of punishment against an American citizen shall not be greater, or more severe, than it would be against a Turk in the same predicament, and if any delinquent should make his escape, the consul shall not be responsible for him in any manner whatever.

Art. 21. The consul of the United States of America shall not be required to pay any custom or duties whatever on any thing he imports from a foreign country for the use of his house and family.

Art. 22. Should any of the citizens of the United States of America die within the Regency of Algiers, the Dey and his subjects shall not interfere with the property of the deceased, but it shall be under the immediate direction of the consul, unless otherwise disposed of by will. Should there be no consul, the effect[s] shall be deposited in the hands of some person worthy of trust, until the party shall appear who has a right to demand them, when they shall render an account of the property; neither shall the Dey or his subjects give hindrance in the execution of any will that may appear.

Done at Algiers on the 30th day of June A.D. 1815.
(Signed) OMAR BASHAW (L. S.)

Whereas the undersigned William Shaler a Citizen of the United States, and Stephen Decatur Commander in chief of the U. S. naval forces now in the Mediterranean, being duly appointed Commissioners by letters patent under the signature of the President, and Seal of the U. S. of America, bearing date at the City of Washington the 9th day of April 1815 for negotiating and concluding a treaty of peace between the U. S. of America, and the Dey of Algiers.

Now Know Ye that we William Shaler and Stephen Decatur commissioners as aforesaid, do conclude the foregoing treaty, and every article, and clause therein contained, reserving the same, nevertheless for the final ratification of the President of the United States of America, by and with the advice and consent of the Senate.

Done on board of the United States Ship Guerriere in the bay of Algiers on the 3d day of July in the year 1815 and of the independence of the U. S. 40th.

Acknowledgments

I BEGAN RESEARCHING *The End of Barbary Terror* before September 11, 2001. I was struck by the anomaly that there were dozens of books about America's 1801–1805 wars with the Barbary pirates but little written about the last of those wars, in 1815. This was curious, because the war itself was brief, successful, and popular, and it enshrined Stephen Decatur as a popular hero. Although books about the Barbary Wars have come out at a prodigious rate since the terrorist attacks on New York and Washington, D.C., there is still little written about the last of those wars and how that era's maritime "terror" came to an end. The further I probed, the more I thought the different, and almost completely unknown, strands of the story—the *Edwin*, Mordecai Noah, the mysterious W. D. Robinson, *raïs* Hamidou and the *Meshuda*, William Lewis and his beloved Fanny, and the ironic fate of the Americans freed from Algiers—could be made into a compelling narrative. I gratefully acknowledge the help which enabled those various strands to come together in this book.

Much of my research was done at the National Archives in Washington, D.C., and at three august institutions in Baltimore—the Enoch Pratt Free Library, the Milton Eisenhower Library of The Johns Hopkins University, and the Maryland Historical Society—and I thank the librarians and archivists who provided me advice and sources at those places.

Although most of the official letters to and from Stephen Decatur are published in old government sources, I was able to read a handful of unpublished letters that his collateral descendant, Stephen Decatur Jr. of

Marblehead, Massachusetts, graciously lent me. To hold in my own hands the original letters between Decatur, Crowninshield, and Monroe was a wonderful treat. I would not have known of Mr. Decatur had James Tertius de Kay not generously provided an introduction.

The *Edwin* was an obscure merchant brig, and I was relieved and amazed at how much information the staff of the Peabody Essex Museum in Salem, Massachusetts, was able to unearth about her, as well as about Benjamin Crowninshield. Sarah Tapper, then the curator of the Decatur House Museum in Washington, D.C., facilitated my research among the original papers there, and Julie Koven of the American Jewish Historical Society in New York supplied me with the relevant papers of Joseph Nones. When the Historical Society of Pennsylvania provided me with William Shaler's papers, including W. D. Robinson's poison gas memorandum (which apparently no historian has used before), Leslie Hunt enthusiastically answered my questions about the provenance of the document and W. D. Robinson. Similarly, Virginia Steele Wood at the Library of Congress and Iain G. Brown and Colm McLaughlin at the National Library of Scotland assisted me in my painstaking but ultimately inconclusive search for clues about Robinson and his connection with Cochrane-Johnstone.

Christopher McKee, Librarian of the College and Rosenthal Professor of History at Grinnell College, made a number of what he thought were offhand suggestions, but they led me to William Lewis's letters at the College of William and Mary and to Joseph Causten's papers at Georgetown University. One of the earliest supporters of my research was Donald A. Petrie, and I am grateful for his friendship and thoughtful criticism over the years.

Several friends and acquaintances translated documents for me. Seth Winnick, a diplomat himself, ably dealt with Johan Norderling's July 3, 1815, letter, written in French, and Simona Castellani-Duncan and James Duncan translated Hamed ben Mustaffi's August 7, 1815, letter to Decatur from the idiomatic and archaic Arabic-Italian.

After I completed an initial draft of the manuscript, James Vescovi volunteered to "take a look at it," and ultimately proofread and made marginal suggestions on the whole thing, improving it considerably. I have also benefited from his humor and insight regarding ship captains, authors, publishers, and critics.

Steven Strogatz, a distinguished mathematician at Cornell, is not a historian, but he is an old friend. Based on the faith that what I wrote must be interesting, he suggested my manuscript to his publishing friend, Jack

Repcheck, who sent it to Oxford University Press. My editor at Oxford University Press, Peter Ginna, and his assistant, Laura Stickney, made numerous suggestions which have polished and focused my writing, although of course any mistakes of fact or interpretation which remain are mine.

As always, my parents, Robert W. Leiner and Mary Ann Leiner, have been warmly enthusiastic about my writing. Finally, my wife, Jill, and my sons, Ben and Josh, indulged me over the course of the nights and weekends spent researching and writing this book, by occasionally letting me wander off to a library to look through rare books or to type away seemingly without end on the computer. They still do not understand what is so interesting about sailing ships, but I love them just the same.

Source Notes

Abbreviations

AJHS = American Jewish Historical Society

ANB = American National Biography

Captains' Letters = National Archives, Record Group 45, M125, Letters Received by the Secretary of the Navy from Captains

Consular Despatches = National Archives, RG 59, State Department Consular Despatches, M23, Algiers Series, rolls 10–11 (January 3, 1808–December 9, 1817)

DAB = Dictionary of American Biography

DAFS = Dictionary of American Fighting Ships

Letters to Officers = National Archives, Record Group 45, M149, Letters Sent by the Secretary of the Navy to Officers

MdHS = Maryland Historical Society

Niles = Niles' Weekly Register

William Lewis Papers = College of William and Mary, Earl Gregg Swem Library, Williamsburg, Virginia, Conway Whittle Family Papers, MSS 76, W61, William Lewis Papers

Macedonian log = National Archives, Record Group 24, Records of the Bureau of Naval Personnel, Logs of Ships and Shore Stations, Log of U.S.S. *Macedonian* (April 5, 1815–March 12, 1816)

NA = National Archives

PEM = Peabody Essex Museum, Salem, Massachusetts

Private Letters = National Archives, Record Group 45, T829, Confidential Letters Sent by the Secretary of the Navy, February 1813–January 1840, roll 453

RG = Record Group

Torch log = National Archives, Record Group 24, Records of the Bureau of Naval Personnel, Logs of Ships and Shore Stations, Log of U.S.S. *Torch*

Introduction

"Man was born free, and he is everywhere in chains" is the first sentence of Book I, chap. 1, of Jean-Jacques Rousseau, *The Social Contract*, trans. Maurice Cranston (London: Penguin Books,

1968), 49. The religious and scriptural support for slavery is mentioned in Lewis, *Race and Slavery in the Middle East*, 3–6. Davis, *Christian Slaves, Muslim Masters*, 8, estimated the number of black Africans shipped to slavery in the New World. For broad treatments of slavery in the Islamic world, I have relied on Davis, Lewis, and Murray Gordon, *Slavery in the Arab World*. The enslaving of white Christians in the Crimea is mentioned in Colin Hayward, review of Robert C. Davis, *Christian Slaves, Muslim Masters*, in *Mariner's Mirror* 91 (Aug. 2005), 489–90.

Davis refers to specific raids throughout *Christian Slaves, Muslim Masters*, the last part of which deals with the effect of three centuries of corsair raids on coastal Italy. The notion that Barbary slavery was in part driven by revenge is in Davis, xxv. Davis, 8–23, derives the figure of 1-1.25 million white Christian slaves in Barbary.

Frank Lambert's thesis in *The Barbary Wars* is that free trade guided America's early engagement with the world and that the obstacle to free trade the Barbary corsair-states caused by capturing ships and cargoes and enslaving mariners caused friction, and not religious or ethnic hostility.

Foss's account is in John Foss, *A Journal, of the Captivity and Sufferings of John Foss; Several Years a Prisoner at Algiers* (Newburyport, Mass.: Angier March, 2d ed. 1798), 7–21, reprinted in an edited form in Baepler, 73-102.

Chapter One: The Odyssey of the *Edwin*

Details concerning the *Edwin* are in *Ship Registers* and Peabody, "Marine Notes," 147, 157, 340. Leaving Smith's cargo aside, the mercantile venture represented by the $21,920.10 of the *Edwin* and her cargo was divided between Silsbee (35 percent), Devereaux (25 percent), and Stone and Pickman (20 percent each). PEM, "Statement of Salvage." The insurance policy on the *Edwin*, signed by Nathaniel Bowditch as president of the Essex Fire and Marine Insurance Company, was issued on March 31, 1812. PEM, Insurance Policy on Brig Edwin. The British license system for American grain ships is detailed in Crawford, 165–67.

The prewar 1812 embargo, enacted by the Act of April 4, 1812, *Public Statutes*, 2:700–1, chap. 49, 12th Cong., 1st Sess., was to last for ninety days. The embargo is discussed in Brown, 98–104, and mentioned in Wills, 96.

References to the *Edwin*'s last voyage are in Noah's *Travels*, 66, including Appendix II, Declaration of William Turner, May 24, 1814. The *Edwin*'s earlier encounter with the French privateer is in Phillips, 264–65, citing *Salem Gazette*, May 26, 1807. George Campbell Smith's letters are in Consular Despatches, roll 10, T. Lear to J. Monroe, November 3, 1812, enclosing G. C. Smith to J. Gavino, August 30, 1812, and G. C. Smith to E. Fettyplace, September 30, 1812.

For background information about Algiers, its appearance, inhabitants, economy, and customs, see generally Shaler; Broughton; Barnby; Prentiss; Parker; and Spencer. Mrs. Blanckley's comments on Algiers's beauty are in Broughton, 112, 154 (entries of October 25, 1808, and October 29, 1809). All of the major sources on Algiers describe the political system, with its ruling cadre of Turkish janissaries, in similar terms. Broughton, 109, 125–26, 185 (entries of November 7, 1807, March 5, 1809, and November 16, 1810, provide details of the assassinations).

Shaler, 66–67, writes that the Jews in Algiers were allowed the free exercise of religion and their own laws in civil matters, but paid a per capita tax and double duties on every imported item. Only Jews were allowed to be brokers and moneylenders, and they dominated certain trades, such as gold- and silversmithing. But they were "a most oppressed people; they are not permitted to resist any personal violence of whatever nature, from a [Muslim]; they are compelled to wear clothing of a black or dark colour; they cannot ride on horseback, or wear arms of any sort, not even a cane; they are permitted only on Saturdays and Wednesdays to pass out of the gates of the city without permission; and on any unexpected call for hard labour, the Jews are turned out to execute it." He observed that the Jews lived in perpetual fear of attack and saw them "pelted in the streets even by children." Broughton, 108–109n., 110–11, 204–5, 230, 352–53, describes the killings of Baccri and Durand, the ransoms paid to avoid pillaging, and Jews seeking refuge in the British consulate.

For descriptions of the lives of the slaves in Barbary, see generally Barnby and Spencer. Describing the slaves as "white" is not completely accurate because a small number of the captives were black. To describe them as "European" obviously is inaccurate because the captives in this narrative were American. To describe them as "Christian" might seem to modern readers to place an undue emphasis on their religion, but ultimately, they were enslaved precisely because they came from "Christian" countries; for purposes of Barbary terror, the United States was one of those countries. Shaler, 76, notes that "private cruising" had been suppressed by the Algerine government fifty years earlier, and that slaves captured since then belonged "to the Regency." Shaler concluded that the lives of Christian slaves were no worse than those of prisoners of war in European countries. Sumner, 121–29, provides an early view of the comparative lenity of Islamic slavery, after canvassing the accounts of writers, travelers, Noah, and Shaler. Broughton, 62, 103, cites her mother's diary entries of September 26, 1807, and October 11, 1807, about the frigates arriving with captives, and at 290 quotes the dey's comments to her father.

Allison, *Crescent Obscured*, 107–15, provides a more benign view of Barbary slavery. He suggests that whether captivity meant slavery depended on "attitude" because the conditions were not harsh, just boring. This seems wide of the mark. Baepler, 28, concludes that "[w]hite slaves actually suffered greatly in captivity and were forced to live under humiliating conditions, eat rancid food, sleep with droves of vermin, bake under the desert sun, . . . and face inhuman punishments." One of the firsthand accounts of life as a captive in Algiers was John Foss, *A Journal, of the Captivity and Sufferings of John Foss*, which is also reprinted in Baepler, 73–102. Broughton, 85–86, referred to the Blanckley family's reluctance to walk down to the port.

Broughton, 5, writes of the Algerine women on the roofs, and at 21 quotes her mother's diary entry for January 4, 1807, about the wedding. Shaler, 55, describes the domestic life of Algerines.

Wheelan, 40–41, cites Jefferson's letter quoting the Tripolitan ambassador to London on the Barbary view of war. Spencer, ix, notes that the corsairs received legal sanction "through the intervention of an article of faith, that of the jihad." Davis, 6–7, refers to the Algerine corsair raids that snatched four hundred people from Ireland in 1627 and sixty people from Cornwall, near Penzance, in 1640.

Jennifer Margulis and Karen M. Poremski in their introduction to Rowson, "Slaves in Algiers," xiii–xiv, and Allison, *Crescent Obscured*, 69–85 and 92–97, detail the Barbary captive literature. Baepler, 24, estimates the number of Barbary captive editions published in America.

Eaton's comments on slavery are in a letter to his wife, in Prentiss, 154, April 6, 1799. Carey's conclusion that the Algerines were not the only barbarous people and the morality of Tyler's novel are developed in Allison, *Crescent Obscured*, 92–94. The Historicus essay is reprinted in *Franklin*, 1157–60 (published March 25, 1790); Allison, *Crescent Obscured*, 104–5, comments on it. The tribute "racket" is described in many accounts, including Parker, 7–9; Barnby, passim; Spencer, 47–50, 113–16. Spencer, ix, notes that seizing non-believers was part of *jihad* and thus supported by Islamic law. Franklin's belief that the English might be behind Algiers is in his July 22, 1783, letter to Robert R. Livingston, reprinted in *Franklin*, 1072. Eaton's observations and despair about dealing with Algerine slavery are in his September 15, 1799, letter to George Hough, in Prentiss, 163–70.

John Adams's calculus of arming or paying off the Algerines is in *Works of John Adams*, 8:410–12, J. Adams to T. Jefferson, July 31, 1786.

Jefferson's idea of a coalition of navies of minor European powers is in Field, 35, Parker, 40, and Wheelan, 52–56. The 1801–6 naval campaigns against the Barbary states have been dealt with extensively. Two of the best popular treatments are Allen, and Tucker, *Dawn Like Thunder*.

Shaler, 118–21, details the prince regent's letter to the dey, the *Allegheny* incident, and the humiliation of Lear, which Lear describes in Consular Despatches, T. Lear to J. Monroe, July 29, 1812. Lewis, *Romantic Decatur*, 159, referred to Algiers leaving American ships alone after the 1796 treaty. The capture of the three ships in November 1807 is detailed in Parker, 127–28, 343–44, and Irwin, 168–69. Waldo, 246, alleges that in 1812, the British refitted the Algerine navy with $160,000 worth of stores and equipment. That Lear knew the gist of the prince regent's letter to the dey is shown by his April 30, 1812, letter to Monroe in Consular Dispatches, roll 10. The dey's treatment of the Danish consul in 1808 is mentioned in ibid., T. Lear to Secretary of State, March 28, 1808. Lear's loan from the Baccris is in ibid., T. Lear to J. Monroe, July 29, 1812.

Niles, vol. 3, no. 22, January 30, 1813, 349, printed the "Distressing Capture" article. Lear's efforts through Norderling to ameliorate the captives' conditions are described in Consular Dispatches, roll 10, T. Lear to J. Monroe, November 3, 1812, and December 16, 1812 (enclosing G. C. Smith to T. Lear, October 2, 1812, requesting winter clothes). George Campbell Smith's March 15, 1813, letter to Lear is in Consular Despatches, roll 10. Garcia's February 26, 1813, letter is in PEM, MSS 74, Box 1, Folder 6. Norderling's letter regarding the conditions of the captives is in Consular Despatches, roll 10, J. Norderling to R. Hackley, April 19, 1813. Niles, vol. 6, no. 6, April 9, 1814, 104, notes that the captives were well supplied.

As to biographical details on Mordecai Noah, see Sarna; Cember; ANB, 16:466–67; and "Judaic Treasures of the Library of Congress: Mordecai Manuel Noah," available online at http://www.us-israel.org/jsource/loc/noah.html. His letter to Robert Smith is in AJHS, Nones Family Papers, P-5, Box 1, Folder 1.

As to the idea of Jews in early America, see Harap, 6–20. Sarna, 8–9, suggests Noah as the Jew as intermediary. Washington's address to the Touro Synagogue is available online at http://www.tourosynagogue.org/GWLetter1.html. Adams's comment is in Works of John Adams, 9:608–10, J. Adams to F. Vanderkamp, February 16, 1809. Madison's comment is in Schwartz, 65. The crucial intervention of the Baccri family of Algiers, a "remarkable gesture of faith" in the United States at a time when no one there had seen a penny of the promised American money, is mentioned in Barnby, 285.

Noah, 70, reprints Monroe's instructions to him.

Noah's retention of Keene as his subagent is in Sarna, 17, and in Noah, 71–74. Noah's contract with Keene is in Irwin, 174, and Sarna, 17. Noah, 75–76, describes the foreign assistance given to the American mission. Noah, 76, 95, 108, describes his and Keene's travel to Gibraltar and Noah's difficulty in establishing credit. Sarna, 18, describes Noah's reception by the Jewish community in Gibraltar. Noah, 109, narrates his directions to Keene. In his May 1814 letter to Noah, Keene describes the dey's statement to Ortiz and Keene, Norderling's audience with the dey, the negotiations about Walker, and the circumstances of the release of the two Americans from the Edwin's crew. Noah, 144–47, 150–51. Within that long letter, Keene provides the long quote of Baccri's audience with the dey, describes why he could not make any further headway, and describes the treatment of those captured (Noah, 147–52).

Noah's expenses for ransoming Turner, Clark, and the four Louisianans amounted to $15,074. Noah gave Keene $1,000 for expenses, $6,000 for Turner and Clark, and $6,000 for the Louisianans. Keene paid an additional $50 to the English and Spanish dragomen at their respective consulates, $1,000 to charter and provision a vessel to return with the six men to Spain, and $348 in additional lodging and travel expenses. Noah had a total of $678 in expenses to keep the six at a Cadiz tavern while he found passage for them, clothing, and their transport to the United States. Over and above the $15,074, Noah reimbursed Keene for the $2,554 he paid as a 35 percent premium on the bills discounted at Algiers; paid his own salary of $1,500; and paid a premium on the American bills discounted at Gibraltar of $4,782. Noah took some solace from the fact that, as consul, Tobias Lear paid almost $500,000 in gifts to the deys of Algiers without complaint from Washington. Cember, 55–56.

Noah, 145–48, analyzes the costs of Keene's mission, and compares the costs to those of Lear's mission. Noah, Appendix, ix, contains Attorney General Rush's opinion regarding Noah's mission and disallowing the bills of exchange.

Chapter Two: At War with Algiers

Madison's offer of the navy portfolio to Crowninshield is in Writings of James Madison, 8:320–21, December 15, 1814. Navy Department records indicate that Crowninshield signed his first order as secretary on January 18, 1815. Letters to Officers, roll 12, B. Crowninshield to R. Spence, January 18, 1815. There is no biography of Crowninshield. Sketches of his life are in *DAB*, 2:577–78; *ANB*, 5:807–8; and Edwin M. Hall, "Benjamin W. Crowninshield," *American Secretaries of the Navy*, 1:113–20. As to the family business, see Phillips, and Reinoehl, "Post-Embargo Trade." Reinoehl provides information about Jacob Crowninshield in his introduction to Crowninshield's "Some Remarks," 85–91. Some idea of Crowninshield's interests and devotion to his family can be found in "Some Mary Boardman Crowninshield Letters."

The major biographies of Decatur are by Mackenzie, Lewis, and Anthony, recently joined by de Kay, Tucker, and Allison. The account of the *President*'s attempted breakout from New York, and her battle with the British squadron, is drawn from Tucker, *Stephen Decatur*, 141–46; Allison, *Stephen Decatur*, 153–56; and my article in *Naval History* (April 2003). Decatur's January 18, 1815, report to the secretary of the navy is printed in *Niles*, vol. 8, no. 1, March 4, 1815, 424–25. Decatur's return to New London, and the reception there, is based on Mackenzie, 233–35; Allison, *Stephen Decatur*, 159; and Wilson, 114–15. *American Naval Biography*, 92, "unhestitatingly pronounce[d]" Decatur the "pride and boast of our infant navy." His leadership qualities and his relationship with his men I wrote about in *Naval History* (October 2001).

The Post Office location for Congress is mentioned in Wills, 139. Madison's February 23, 1815, paper is in *A Compilation of the Messages*, 1:554. Madison's early view of the navy is in Federalist Paper No. 41, *The Federalist Papers*, 260–61. McDougall, 43–49, discusses the American opposition to entangling alliances and the trend toward unilateralism. The April 1815 Dartmoor prison massacre is mentioned in Hickey, 306, and is recounted in Waterhouse, 155–230 (which also contains many of the official documents).

The House resolution asking for Madison's views on relations with Algiers is in *Annals*, 28:1153–54, February 15, 1815. Monroe's February 20, 1815, report is in *Annals*, 28:1192–93, February 23, 1815; and ibid., 28:1275, "Supplemental Journal" contains the House's secret proceedings. A motion to indefinitely postpone consideration of the bill lost by a 21–108 vote, and the motion to have a select committee report on the bill passed by a 79–42 vote. The creation of the select committee is in *Annals*, 28:1275–76, February 24, 1815. The "era of good feelings" denotes the time after the War of 1812 to the advent of Jacksonian America, a time supposedly of less partisanship in politics and a sense of unifying national purpose. See Dangerfield, passim. Details about Forsyth and Gaston are in *Biographical Directory*, 1048, 1079. The select committee's report is in *Annals*, 28:1277–78, February 28, 1815. The temporizing amendments were debated and voted down in ibid., 28:1278–80, February 28, 1815. The roll call on Goldsborough's amendment resulted in a 47–92 vote. The Senate proceedings are in ibid., 28:284–91, March 1–2, 1815. The act appears at ibid., 28:1943–44.

Chapter Three: Fitting Out the Squadrons

In her own time, Susan Decatur was described as an "amiable and elegant" woman, "a lady celebrated for her accomplishments, and at that time [of her marriage] a reigning belle of Virginia." "Biography of Commodore Decatur," *Analectic Magazine*, vol. 1, no. 6, June 1813, 510 and n. On Susan Decatur, see Parsons, 16; Dunne, "Pistols and Honor"; de Kay, *Rage for Glory*, 73–74; and Allison, *Stephen Decatur*, 75–77. Her personal collection of Italian and French books, described in "Scope Note," Stephen and Susan Decatur Papers, Georgetown University Library, makes clear her literacy in those languages. The anecdote about their courtship, which almost certainly came from Susan Decatur herself, is in Mackenzie, *Life of Decatur*, 134n. Decatur's October 30, 1812, letter to her is in Mackenzie, *Life of Decatur*, 371. Decatur's report of the battle with the *Macedonian* of the same date to Secretary of the Navy Paul Hamilton is in *Naval War of 1812*, 1:552–53.

Susan Decatur's February 25, 1815, private letter to Crowninshield is in PEM, Benjamin W. Crowninshield Collection. According to Dye, 74–79, William Henry Allen idolized Decatur, but W. M. P. Dunne, who at the time of his death was writing a detailed biography of Decatur, noted that his six-year relationship with Allen appears to have been a purely professional, absolutely impersonal one, and devoid of a close social friendship. Dunne, "Stephen Decatur, 1779–1820: A Critical Biography," chapter outline at 6.

Crowninshield's March 14, 1815, letter to Decatur is in PEM, Benjamin W. Crowninshield Collection. Decatur's March 20, 1815, letter to Crowninshield is in PEM, Crowninshield Family Papers. I have been unable to find the letter reflecting the "first time" Susan Decatur's worries got the better of her judgment, but the reference clearly implies the psychological trauma she felt. I also was unable to locate Crowninshield's private letter to her. In my article "Decatur and Naval Leadership," I describe the concept of "followers." Except for the bruised ribs he received from the splinter in the *President-Endymion* battle, Decatur's health was robust, suggesting that his health was a pretext, and the real reason was his wife's concerns.

Long, *Ready to Hazard*, 194, claims that Decatur did not accept any of the three options Crowninshield gave him. Crowninshield's March 24 and March 27, 1815, letters to Decatur are in Letters to Officers, roll 12.

Within a few days of his arrival back in the United States, Decatur traveled to New York to recuperate. He reported to the Navy Department only on March 6, "in consequence of a contusion of the breast received in the Action of the 15th January." Almost two months after being wounded, he reported he was "still confined." Even so, he twice asked the secretary to convene a court of inquiry to investigate his conduct in the loss of the *President*. Captains' Letters, roll 43, S. Decatur letters of March 6 and 31, 1815. Crowninshield expressed his confidence in him in Letters to Officers, roll 12, B. Crowninshield to S. Decatur, March 14, 1815. Decatur wrote that his squadron would be "able to sail before the result of [the court's] enquiry will be probably be [*sic*] known," and asked Crowninshield to allow the judge advocate to provide Decatur with a copy of the proceedings. Captains' Letters, roll 44, April 15, 1815. Crowninshield agreed to issue such an order to the president of the court, Alexander Murray. Letters to Officers, roll 12, April 18, 1815.

Dallas's letter to Crowninshield about the jealousies of the officer corps about the Decatur appointment is in PEM, Crowninshield Family Papers, March 21, 1815. The typescript copy of Mary Crowninshield's letter reflecting the Salem gossip is in PEM, Crowninshield Family Papers, MH-15, Box 11, Folder 9, Mary Crowninshield to B. Crowninshield, March 11, 1815.

Commodore Rodgers's comments about the other officers, and the appointments of Rodgers, Hull, and Porter as navy commissioners in February 1815 are in Paullin, 301–3. McKee, 183–85, describes Hugh Campbell. Murray is described in *DAB*, 7:357–58, and *American Naval Biography*, 51–64. Eaton's comment about Murray (like sending "out Quaker meeting-houses") is in Prentiss, 224, W. Eaton to J. Madison, August 9, 1802.

According to a typescript copy in the Decatur House Museum, Bainbridge's April 8 and June 5, 1815, letters to David Porter are in the New-York Historical Society, Naval History Society Collection, Misc. MSS, Bainbridge, William. Crowninshield's letters to Bainbridge of May 31 and June 16, 1815, are in Letters to Officers, roll 12. The modern biography of Bainbridge is Long, *Ready to Hazard*. The Crowninshield family's shipping interests were grievously damaged in the 1809–12 period when Bainbridge commanded the naval station at Boston. See Reinoehl, "Post-Embargo Trade."

The idea that Bainbridge was "owed" the command of the first squadron and that Decatur deprived him of it is in Long, *Ready to Hazard*, 191, 195. In *Gold Braid*, 33–34, Long goes further, asserting that Bainbridge "should have been that man"—the squadron commander—but Decatur "wrest[ed]" it from him in "a campaign as tactically adroit as it was morally shabby." In this view, Crowninshield became Decatur's pliant "minion." This view gives Crowninshield (and Madison) little credit and, more importantly, is unsupported by the evidence. In their campaign against Decatur, Guttridge and Smith, 272, begin with the theme of Decatur taking Washington Irving's advice to "whip the cream off the enterprize," which becomes a smooth transition (277) into Decatur's supposed "ruthlessness," his ability to manipulate a "pliant" Crowninshield at will, and his "brazen confiscation of personnel and equipment."

Nothing in the early months of Crowninshield's tenure as secretary of the navy supports David F. Long's claim that Crowninshield was "weak and erratic" or Guttridge and Smith's assertion that Crowninshield was "weak and indecisive." Getting the first squadron to sea was Crowninshield's priority. He made sure that Decatur received the ships, men, equipment, and supplies to get to sea quickly. An erratic and weak executive might have vacillated when approached by a powerful Republican figure such as Dearborn, but Crowninshield did not. More to the point, Crowninshield in his private letter to Decatur on March 14 set forth his organizational plan: (1) two squadrons would sail; (2) the lead squadron would contain three frigates and a half dozen smaller ships; (3) the second squadron would contain the *Independence*, another battleship if ready, and "other frigates as fast as they can be manned & prepared for Sea"; and (4) Bainbridge, who had superintended the building of the *Independence*, would "go on the service," commanding the second squadron. Crowninshield did *not* deviate from that plan both because it was a good one and because it had Madison's express backing. Over the next three months, Crowninshield put the plan into effect and showed decisiveness in directing war preparations. As Hall, 115, notes, Decatur "sailed with as clear a conception of what was expected of him as any American had ever had, and the credit was Crowninshield's."

As to President Franklin Roosevelt's selection of General George Marshall, see Larrabee, 96. Dearborn is profiled in *DAB*, 3:174–76, and his April 10 and 12 letters to Crowninshield are in PEM, Crowninshield Family Papers. Crowninshield's April 15 orders to Decatur are found in Private Letters, roll 453.

The profile of Shaler is distilled from Nichols, *Advance Agents*, 50–108. Shaler's explanation that Napoleon's departure rendered it "out of [his] power to render any useful service during the negotiation," and his explanation for leaving Ghent are in his letter to James Monroe, [] March 1815, William Shaler Papers, Collection 1172, Historical Society of Pennsylvania. His reference to Algiers as "that Den of Banditti," and his description of his warm reception in Washington is in his June 4, 1815, letter to Jonathan Russell, Shaler Family Papers, Collection 589, Historical Society of Pennsylvania. Monroe's diplomatic instructions are set forth in James Monroe to William Shaler et al., April 10, 1815, William Shaler Papers, Collection 1172, Historical Society of Pennsylvania. Consular Despatches, roll 10, contains a "List of Mr. Lear's Letters Given to Mr. Shaler on the 8th April 1815." Pleasanton's May 5, 1815, letter to Shaler regarding Shaler's idea of writing to the Porte in Constantinople is in William Shaler Papers, Collection 1172, Historical Society of Pennsylvania. Shaler raised the subject again in a May 12, 1815, letter to Monroe in Simon Gratz Collection. Collection 250A, Historical Society of Pennsylvania.

The details about the *Guerriere* are in *DAFS*, 3:181–82, and Chapelle, 264. The option given to Rodgers, and the timeliness of his appointment to lead the navy commissioners is provided in Paullin, 301, 303.

William Lewis is one of the least-known officers of the early navy. Mary Lewis Cook's and Charles Lee Lewis's article profiles his early naval service. For information about his background, I relied on his letters to E. Herndon, November 30, 1807; to unknown, February 3, 1808; to E. Herndon, May 29 and June 5, 1811; to W. Jones, December 10, 1814; to E. Herndon, March 8, 1815; to unknown, March 17, 1815; to E. Herndon, April 20, 1815; and to F. Lewis, April 26 and 27, 1815, all in the William Lewis Papers. Decatur wrote Crowninshield on April 14 that Lewis was "desirous of accompanying me to the Mediterranean" and asked that he be appointed to command the *Guerriere*. Captains' Letters, roll 44. Crowninshield obliged by return mail. Letters to Officers, roll 12, B. Crowninshield to S. Decatur, April 17, 1815.

De Kay, *Chronicles*, 15–23, provides information about the *Macedonian*. Crowninshield's decision to send the *Macedonian* to Decatur's squadron is in Letters to Officers, roll 12, B. Crowninshield to S. Decatur, April 8, 1815. A biographical sketch of Jacob Jones is in Pratt, 67–84, and a contemporary profile is in *Analectic Magazine*, vol. 2, July 1813, "Biography of Captain Jacob Jones," 70–78.

Footner, *USS Constellation*, 62–72, provides detail about the 1812 rebuild. On Charles Gordon's background and career, see Calderhead, and McKee, 293–94. Paullin, 302, contains Rodgers's opinion of Gordon. Tucker and Reuter, 184–86, discuss Gordon's court-martial. Crowninshield's orders to Gordon to ready the *Constellation* for sea and to go to New York are in Letters to Officers, roll 12, February 15 and 28, 1815.

The *Ontario* is described in *DAFS*, 5:160 and Chapelle, 256, 258. Crowninshield's orders to Elliott are in Letters to Officers, roll 12, March 15 and 22, 1815. A sketch of Elliott is in *DAB*, 3:96–97. His mental stability is questioned in Friedman and Skaggs. For Elliott's role at the Barron and Gordon courts-martial, see Tucker and Reuter, 171, 173, 185. In Perry's initial report on the battle, he wrote that "[a]t half past two, the wind springing up, Capt. Elliott was enabled to bring his vessel, the *Niagara*, gallantly into close action"; Perry concluded that Elliott "evinced his characteristic bravery and judgment." Dudley, 2:557, O. H. Perry to W. Jones, September 13, 1813. Within a few years, Elliott tried to challenge Perry to a duel because of the dramatic changes in how Perry saw—or referred to—Elliott's conduct.

Information about the smaller ships in Decatur's squadron is in *DAFS*, 2:407 (*Firefly*), 2:410 (*Flambeau*), 6:574 (*Spark*), 6:585 (*Spitfire*), and 7:239 (*Torch*); in Footner, *Tidewater Triumph*, 174; and in Chapelle, 280, 290. William Lewis's comment about them as "*clippers*" is in William Lewis Papers, Wm. Lewis to F. Lewis, May 3, 1815.

Chapelle, 279–80, and *DAFS*, 2:358–59, describe the *Epervier*. Jones's comment about Downes is in Dudley, 2:209, Wm. Jones to J. Renshaw, September 15, 1813, and Downes is described in de Kay, *Chronicles*, 130–31. His family background is mentioned in McKee, 76, 533 n. 5.

The Algerine navy is listed in *Niles*, vol. 8, no. 2, March 11, 1815, 32, and in a May 2, 1815, letter extract from James Leander Cathcart in *Niles*, vol. 8, no. 16, June 17, 1815, 280. Tobias Lear described the "whole naval force" of Algiers—five frigates, three corvettes, two brigs, a xebec, and eight smaller vessels—with the number of guns and complement of each ship, in his July 29, 1812, letter to James Monroe. Consular Despatches, roll 10, T. Lear to J. Monroe, July 29, 1812.

Decatur pointed out that his orders did not provide for a blockade of Algiers's other ports. Captains' Letters, roll 44, S. Decatur to B. Crowninshield, May 21, 1815. Crowninshield instructed him to construe his orders to include a blockade of all of Algiers's ports, specifically including Bona and Oran. Letters to Officers, roll 12, B. Crowninshield to S. Decatur, May 25, 1815.

Decatur's request for bomb vessels is in Captains' Letters, roll 44, S. Decatur to B. Crowninshield, April 3, 1815. That the army would make available mortars from the forts guarding the harbor is in Letters to Officers, roll 12, B. Crowninshield to S. Decatur, April 6, 1815, and Decatur's inability to find any vessels that would serve the purpose is in Captains' Letters, roll 44, S. Decatur to B. Crowninshield, May 5, 1815. Bainbridge's regret that five or six mortar vessels had not been prepared is in Captains' Letters, roll 45, W. Bainbridge to B. Crowninshield, June 25, 1815. The French navy's historical use of bomb vessels against Algiers is in Macdonald, 65–66. Lavery, 54, and Tucker, *Arming the Fleet*, 109, have information about this type of vessel and the potency of the mortar. Chapelle, 210, discusses the U.S. Navy's initial attempt to use bomb vessels. Thereafter, the U.S. Navy designed and built two mortar vessels, the *Etna* and the *Vesuvius*, but neither saw much service and both were poor sailers. Ibid., 209–10.

In his estimates for 1813, Secretary of the Treasury Gallatin provided for 1,859 marines, including officers and the marine band. Crowninshield's March 30, 1815, letter to Decatur ordering him to take on board the artillery contingent is in Letters to Officers, roll 12, which also contains Crowninshield's June 6 letter to Bainbridge about the second artillery detachment. The artillerists were inventoried in an entry dated May 10, 1815, in the *Macedonian*'s log. Nones's reflection on bringing the artillery aboard is in AJHS, Nones Family Papers, Folder 2, reverse of page 19. Shaler suggested that he tutor young Lt. Monroe in his May 12, 1815, letter to James Monroe, Simon Gratz Collection, Collection 250A, Historical Society of Pennsylvania.

W. D. Robinson's memorandum to William Shaler, May 9, 1815, is in William Shaler Papers, Collection 1172, Historical Society of Pennsylvania. Cochrane-Johnstone, "a scoundrel and a fraud," used the governorship of Dominica as a "license to pilfer and embezzle." Forced to resign his army commission, his purchase of the "rotten" parliamentary seat of Grampound immunized him from arrest for debt. Thomas, 21–22. As a businessman, he engaged in slave trading, smuggling, extortion, and war profiteering. His manipulation of the stock market upon a rumor of the death of Napoleon in April 1814 caused his nephew, Lord Cochrane, to be arrested, tried, and convicted for conspiracy; while Cochrane was fined, imprisoned, expelled from the House of Commons, and struck from the rolls of the Royal Navy, Cochrane-Johnstone characteristically evaded punishment by fleeing to the Continent to avoid trial. Lloyd, 115–38.

I have been unable to determine who Robinson was. The Cochrane-Johnstone Papers at the National Library of Scotland have no letters to anyone named W. D. Robinson and no letters about sulfur poison gas. It is possible that W. D. Robinson was William Davis Robinson (1775–1823), an American merchant in Caracas, Venezuela, and other ports of colonial Spanish America beginning in 1799, who witnessed the beginnings of the revolutions against Spanish rule. In his *Memoirs of the Mexican Revolution* (1820), Robinson referred (380–82) to a trip he made to London and two cities on the Continent in 1799–1800 where he had letters of introduction to "some respectable capitalists." *If* that W. D. Robinson is *the* W. D. Robinson, he may have had dealings with Cochrane-Johnstone as a merchant on the Spanish Main when Cochrane-Johnstone was governor of Dominica, or he may have met him in London on his business travels. William Davis Robinson was back in the United States in early 1815; a publisher in Georgetown in Washington, D.C., published his forty-page pamphlet entitled *A Cursory View of Spanish America* in January 1815, and thus he would have been physically present to write Shaler several months later.

As to the reception of Lord Cochrane's poison gas scheme in the British Admiralty and Cabinet, see Thomas, 196–97; Harvey, 176–77 and 314–15; and Lloyd, 106–7. I have drawn largely on Lloyd's account (106–13) for the history of the British consideration of the sulfur gas weapon, and Farraday's opinion of its practicality.

To this day, British historians believe that Lord Cochrane's poison gas scheme remained a state secret until the twentieth century. Historian Richard Woodman wrote in an introduction to the 2000 edition of Cochrane's autobiography that "[w]hen he proposed his idea of poison gas to the Admiralty, the authorities were so appalled that they had the papers secured under lock and key. They were not to see the light of day until 1914." Introduction to Cochrane, *The Autobiography of a Seaman*, xxi. In 1978, in his biography of Cochrane, Donald Thomas, 195, stated that the details of the poison gas scheme were "not divulged until the end of the nineteenth century, when the papers were deposited in the British Museum." In his 1947 biography of Cochrane, Christopher Lloyd, 105, wrote that "so secret" were the plans that "in the early months of [World War II] it was possible for a leading daily newspaper to publish an article suggesting that these mysterious plans, lying ready in the pigeonholes of the Admiralty, provided a final answer to Hitler's threats of a secret weapon. The secret was indeed well kept for nearly a century," and even though the papers were published in 1908, the sulfur gas concept was obscure enough that Cochrane's grandson brought it to the attention of the first lord of the Admiralty (Winston Churchill) and to the minister of war, Lord Kitchener, in 1914. In fact, through Cochrane-Johnstone's perfidy, the Americans knew about the British weapon of mass destruction in 1815.

William Lewis's meeting with the secretary, accepting Decatur's offer of the command of the *Guerriere*, getting married, receiving his orders, traveling to New York, and being immediately thrown into preparing the squadron for sea are described in a series of letters Lewis wrote to unknown, March 17, 1815; to E. Herndon, April 8 and 20, 1815; and to F. Lewis April 26, 27, and 30, 1815, and May 13, 1815, all in the William Lewis Papers. The preparations aboard the *Macedonian* are in entries dated April 20 through May 18, 1815, in the *Macedonian* log. Similarly, the preparations on the *Torch* are in entries dated March 7 through May 1, 1815, in the *Torch* log.

Crowninshield's last-minute communications to Decatur are in Letters to Officers, roll 12, April 17, 1815 ("sundry communications"); April 20, 1815 (plan of Algiers); April 24, 1815 (marine major to command all marines); April 28, 1815 (artillerist corps); and April 29, 1815 (halting squadron).

Monroe's concern about a possible attack by the Royal Navy on Decatur's squadron, and his hopes for what the squadron might achieve are in *Writings of James Monroe*, 331, J. Monroe to A. Dallas, May 28, 1815.

Decatur's order countermanding Bainbridge's attempt to have the *Firefly* sail to Boston is in Captains' Letters, S. Decatur to B. Crowninshield, May 18, 1815, in which he also informed the secretary that he countermanded Bainbridge's orders to Lt. Spencer, and acknowledged Crowninshield's order to return sailors to the *Independence* and *Congress* of Bainbridge's squadron. Lewis's comments on the growing rift between commodores are in his letters to Fanny Lewis on May 3, 1815, and May 13, 1815, and to his father-in-law, Conway Whittle, on May 15, 1815, all in the William Lewis Papers. Mary Crowninshield's May 21, 1815, letter is in "Some Mary Boardman Crowninshield Letters."

The front page editorial supporting the Algiers war, and quoting the *Connecticut Mirror*'s dissenting view, is in *Niles*, vol. 8, no. 7, April 15, 1815, 1.

Crowninshield apparently traveled to New York to visit the *Guerriere* and consult with Decatur personally in mid-May 1815, because a letter Decatur wrote to him on May 18 refers to their meeting, and because the Navy Department records contain no letter formally authorizing Decatur to sail. It took several days for Decatur's squadron to get out of New York because of headwinds. Captains' Letters, roll 144, Decatur to Crowninshield, May 18, 1815 (noting his intention to get to sea on May 18, but the wind had failed and the pilots recommended anchoring).

Chapter Four: Mediterranean Triumph

Peter M. Potter's *Diary*, 2 (entry of May 20), contains his drawing of the squadron's initial formation upon departing New York. Potter noted that the signal to get under way was sent up at 2:00 p.m. Captains' Letters, roll 144, Decatur to Crowninshield, May 20, 1815 (the departing note). A laconic description of the gale that forced the *Firefly* to return to port is in the report of her commander. NA, RG 45, M148, Letters Received by the Secretary of the Navy from Officers Below the Rank of Commander, 1802–86, roll 14, G. W. Rodgers to B. Crowninshield, June 9, 1815. Potter, *Diary*, 4 (entry for May 25, 1815), describes the scene as he awoke. Samuel Holbrook's account of the gale, and his role in securing the broken masts, is in Holbrook, 108–12. Nautical terms such as "sprung," "fish," "jiggers," and "wolded" are defined in King, *A Sea of Words*, and in the *Oxford Companion to Ships and the Sea*. The court of inquiry on Rodgers and testimony about the need to return in light of the damage to the *Firefly* is in NA, RG 45, M273, Records of General Courts Martial and Courts of Inquiry of the Navy Department, 1798–1867, roll 8, case no. 211.

Potter, *Diary*, 29 (entry for June 11, 1815), mentions the news from the Irish ship. William Lewis's June 13, 1815, letter to Fanny from Cadiz is in the William Lewis Papers. Decatur's signal to be on guard against three Algerine frigates is reported in the *Macedonian* log on June 14, 1815. Lewis's June 14, 1815, letter to Fanny is in the William Lewis Papers. Joseph Nones in AJHS, Nones Family Papers, Folder 2, n.p., stated that the British officers provided the American officers with the latest intelligence of the Algerine warships. The details about Hamidou are in Ireland, 192–94, Panzac, 54–55, and Broughton, 200. Potter, *Diary*, 40 (entry of June 17, 1815), who interviewed Hamidou's officers immediately after the battle, was told he was a Kabyle.

The incident in Gibraltar Bay with the American warships circling and the American gentleman calling out the names of so many former British ships until the reply, "damn the next," was first published in Bowen, 302, and Waldo, 247–48. Decatur's June 15, June 19, and June 20 letters to Crowninshield are printed in *Niles*, vol. 9, no. 2, September 9, 1815, 30–31, and in Captains' Letters, roll 45. Potter, *Diary*, 33–34, tells the story of his almost being stranded at Gibraltar on June 14.

Shaler, 57, provided the information about the Algerine sailors' reluctance to sail out of sight of land. Noah, 169, described the Cape de Gata and its use as a rendezvous point for the Algerines.

My narrative of the squadron's battle with the Algerine frigate *Meshuda* is taken largely from Allen, 282–84, Mackenzie, *Life of Decatur*, 246–51, Hollins's Notebook in the MdHS, Potter's diary in NA, William Lewis's June 19/20, 1815, letter to Fanny Lewis in the William Lewis

Papers, and the *Torch* log, entries of June 16–17, 1815. The quote from Palmer, 144, refers specifically to the 1781 battle off the Virginia Capes in the American Revolution, but it is a constant theme of Palmer's book.

For reasons that I detail below, I do not credit other accounts of the battle, including those of Midshipman Joseph B. Nones and Captain's Clerk Joseph Causten.

According to Mackenzie, *Life of Decatur*, 248, "quicker work was never done" than the Algerines setting sail to try to evade Decatur's squadron. The *Torch* log states that the *Constellation* fired from her starboard battery, and also provides a terse statement of the *Ontario*'s fleeting contribution to the victory. Shaler's comment, "When we took the Algerine frigate, the Guerriere . . . was the only ship engaged and during an action an action of twenty minutes within pistol shot, not a shot struck us," appears in Shaler's September 26, 1815, letter to Jonathan Russell, Shaler Family Papers, Collection 589, Historical Society of Pennsylvania. Potter, *Diary*, 41 (entry of June 17, 1815), stated that she received one cannonball through her mizzen topsail. Decatur's remark that he had never seen a vessel more skillfully handled as Downes in the *Epervier*, nor so heavy a fire kept up from so small a ship, is in Mackenzie, *Life of Decatur*, 253.

Potter, *Diary*, 36–38 (entry for June 17, 1815), states that British colors were hoisted "throughout the fleet" and that Decatur's signals were "Chase," then "Suspicious Sail in Sight," then "Prepare for Battle," and finally "[unintelligible] as You Close Up." Potter noted the *Constellation* was ahead of the squadron, opened fire with one gun, and when "this was not answered . . . she fired a broadside," to try to stop the *Meshuda*. According to Potter, "Down went the British Flag in an instant & the real one took its place." He then narrated how the *Guerriere* closed the distance and opened fire, and how "[t]he little *Epervier* was up close to her & poured in her broadside," without any suggestion that Gordon was cut out of the action. Immediately after the battle, Potter heard Decatur dictating an account, as Potter wrote in his *Diary*, 39, "Com[modore Decatur] dictating as he told Capt. Lewis 'wishing to do nothing that would excite suspicion in the chase, did not increase sail & our fleet had little on,'" suggesting that the battle changed dramatically when Gordon opened fire (if Potter is right) or hoisted the Stars and Stripes (if Lewis's version is correct).

The Causten view of the battle with the *Meshuda* is found in two of his letters in Georgetown University Library, Causten Family Papers, Jos. Causten to James Causten, October 14, 1815, and August 14, 1816. In his biography of Decatur, Allison, 164–65, accepts unquestioningly Causten's view of the battle with the *Meshuda*, although Allison was unaware of Potter's diary, Lewis's letters, and other sources.

Midshipman Nones described the cannon's explosion and his wounds in AJHS, Nones Family Papers, Folder 2, reverse of p. 20.

Why Decatur's version of events was never publicly questioned is in Georgetown University Library, Causten Family Papers, Jos. Causten to Jas. Causten, October 14, 1815, and August 14, 1816. Causten claimed that there was no glory to be gained "for drubbing a poor defenceless Turk" given the lopsided odds and the "fact" that the *Meshuda* was unprepared. To Causten, the other reason was that no one wanted to cross Decatur, "whatever Opinion the officers of the Navy may have" had of him; it was impolitic for any of them "to war against [Decatur's] popularity"—whatever Decatur wrote in the official reports would remain "uncorrected." When Causten's brother later published some of Causten's letters about the squadron's operations, Causten was concerned, for even though Decatur did not know him and had returned to America while Causten remained aboard the *Constellation* in the Mediterranean, he feared Decatur's "malicious disposition might perhaps ruin some of the Officers of this Ship should his suspicions light on any particular one." Very few junior officers thought this way about Decatur. For instance, Mackenzie, then a midshipman in the squadron, looked on Decatur with unabashed hero worship.

Joseph Nones's account of the action against the *Meshuda* differs substantially from the narrative I have presented. Nones asserted that Decatur signaled the smaller ships of the squadron to "drop astern of the flagship," and then ordered them to chase other ships that came into sight. According to Nones, the *Guerriere* then "hotly engaged with our enemy," yardarm to yardarm, for fifty minutes, pummeling the Algerine into a total wreck. He asserted that the Algerine frigate had 840 men aboard at the start of the battle and lost 200 killed, and that the Americans captured 640 men. Nones then claimed that Decatur was so angered by the *Constellation*'s premature display of American colors that, after the battle, he "superceded" Gordon from the command of the *Constellation*, as well as Downes as captain of the *Epervier*, for four or five days before he relented. It is doubtful that a commodore had the authority to remove a captain in that manner, and disgracing a captain in that way was hardly Decatur's style. More importantly, a suspension of not merely one but two captains hardly could have been done without a report to the secretary of the navy, yet no such report exists, nor is there any contemporary reference to a supersedure. It also defies credulity to think that Decatur would suspend Downes (for what?) and then give him an ornamental sword as a trophy. Nones insisted that the Algerine ship's name was the *Masura*. As Nones himself noted, his narrative cannot be reconciled with other accounts in many particulars, and I have discounted it. AJHS, Nones Family Papers, Folder 3, n.p.

Guttridge and Smith, 278, have a brief account of the defeat of the *Meshuda*, but it is incomplete and marked by their aversion to Decatur. They do not mention the *Constellation* mistakenly raising American colors or the *Meshuda* taking evasive maneuvers. After stating that Gordon opened fire, they wrote that "before he could order his guns run out a second time, the *Guerriere* bore up, plunged between the two ships, and poured heavy shot and musket fire across the Algerine's decks," suggesting that Decatur shouldered Gordon out of the way just as they assert he had done to Bainbridge. Similarly, Long, *Gold Braid*, 34, writes that Decatur "knifed" the *Guerriere* between the *Meshuda* and *Constellation* and "polished off" the Algerine without even "mention[ing] the good work of the other ship." Decatur's alleged "plunging through" is not mentioned by witnesses and is contradicted by a sketch drawn contemporaneously by Peter Potter, *Diary*, 40 (entry of June 17, 1815), showing the relative positions of the U.S. ships chasing the *Meshuda*.

There are fragments of an Algerine version of the battle between the American squadron and the *Meshuda*, although on balance, I consider the account implausible. Ireland, 195–96, based on old Algiers sources, wrote that Dey Omar ordered the *raïs* Hamidou out to capture an American frigate, and the Algerine captain had detached his only escort (almost certainly the *Estedio*) to scout when he came across Decatur's ships. His second in command urged him to make sail and escape, but Hamidou stated he would not flee what he had been ordered to take. He knew the fight would be hopeless and told his officers, "When I am dead you will have me thrown into the sea. I don't want unbelievers to have my corpse." This narrative makes little sense. There is no indication that Omar knew that the American squadron was in the offing. If he did, however, it would have made little sense for Hamidou to sail off to engage an enemy with just two ships; however prodigal with life the dey may have been, he would not have wantonly risked his warships and his most famous *raïs* against overwhelming odds. Thus, *if* the Algerines knew that the Americans were in the vicinity, logically they would have either concentrated their forces to fight or had their ships seek refuge in secure harbors. Because they did neither, it is hard to believe the Algerines knew that the Americans were in the neighborhood. As to the tactics of the engagement, every American account except Causten asserts that the *Meshuda* made all sail to escape when Gordon hoisted American colors.

Interestingly, immediately after the battle, Peter Potter spoke with some of the officers of the *Meshuda*. He noted, "The lieutenants had several times come aft & told [Hamidou] it was an American fleet [coming up and] the only reply was 'Go away you have nothing to do with it.'" Potter, *Diary*, 41 (entry of June 17, 1815). Lewis's comment about the effect of the exploding artillery is in William Lewis Papers, W. Lewis to F. Lewis, June 19/20, 1815. Charles Gordon's supposed lack of envy despite a victory "stolen" from him is in Calderhead, 385 and n. 55, but Lewis's account of being taken aside and blamed for depriving Gordon of the victory is in William Lewis Papers, W. Lewis to F. Lewis, June 19/20, 1815.

My account of the squadron's engagement with the brig *Estedio* is drawn largely from the *Torch* log for June 20, 1815; Potter, *Diary*, 47–53 (entry of June 19, 1815) (noting the close proximity of the Spanish towns, quoting Downes, and detailing his experience boarding); Maclay,

2:23; Decatur's letter of June 20, 1815, reprinted in *Annals*, 29:1763, and in *Niles*, vol. 9, no. 2, September 9, 1815, 30–31; an account in *Niles*, vol. 9, no. 1, September 2, 1815, 16 (suggesting that the Americans did not close with the *Estedio* because of international law); and an extract of a letter from a lieutenant on the *Macedonian* to a gentleman in Boston dated July 2, 1815, reprinted in *Niles*, vol. 9, no. 2, September 9, 1815, 31.

Allen, 284–85, discusses Decatur's decision to proceed immediately to Algiers. Midshipman Bell's description of Algiers is in University of North Carolina, Chapel Hill, N.C., Southern Historical Collection, No. 2962, Log of Charles H. Bell, June 27, 1815. The first signs of scurvy and the bad water are in Potter, *Diary*, 64, 66 (entry of June 30, 1815). The defenses of Algiers are detailed in Osler, 207–8, and Parkinson, 446. Noah, 155–56, contains Keene's questioning of how steadfast the defenses actually were in his May 22, 1814, letter to Noah (a small segment of an extremely long letter that Noah, 141–58, reprinted verbatim). Decatur's signal to the squadron to stand off Algiers is in the *Torch* log, June 30, 1815.

The general course of the negotiations is set forth in the July 4, 1815, letter of Decatur and Shaler to Monroe, reprinted in *Annals*, 29:1475–77. Overviews of the negotiations are in Irwin, 178–79; Allen, 285–88; Tucker, *Stephen Decatur*, 159–61; and Allison, *Stephen Decatur*, 166–67. The initial meeting between Decatur, Shaler, and the Algerine port captain is described in Waldo, 249–50, and in Hollins's Notebook, 19–20. The Decatur-Shaler June 29, 1815, letter to the prime minister of Algiers is reprinted in Shaler, 274, and *Annals*, 29:1477. Madison's letter to the dey is reprinted in Shaler, 274–75. Shaler's description of Omar is in Shaler, 140–44. *Niles*, vol. 8, no. 20, July 15, 1815, 352, reported Geo. C. Smith's April 12, 1815, letter about the two deys' assassinations; Panzac, 246, provides their names. At the time Madison wrote his letter, of course, he did not know that Omar would be the dey Decatur and Shaler dealt with. The U.S. diplomatic advantage over Algiers "having all their cruisers abroad," as Shaler, 126, phrased it, and fearing that they would lose their fleet if they did not make peace, is also in Nichols, *Advance Agents*, 110.

Waldo, 250, describes the negotiations on June 30, including Decatur's line that the powder would come with cannonballs. Potter, *Diary*, 73 (entry for July 2, 1815), quotes Decatur saying, "You may have powder but you shall take ball with it." Potter also quotes Decatur not wanting peace and that his officers had come to fight, which I place at the initial meeting with the port captain. Hollins, 19–20, places at this meeting the port captain's comment about Hadji Ali taking the British consul's advice in 1812. Nichols, *Advance Agents*, 114, asserted that Decatur insisted on the return of the two captured Algerine ships, against Shaler's judgment, and stresses tension between them. William Shaler Papers, Collection 1172, Historical Society of Pennsylvania, n.d. (but must be July 1 or 2, 1815), contains the brief memorandum regarding what Shaler termed his sole issue of disagreement with Decatur, that the "most liberal interpretation" be placed on effectuating its terms; Decatur thought there was "no necessity to conciliate these people by any extraordinary exertion." Norderling's July 3, 1815, letter to Shaler is in William Shaler Papers, Collection 1172, Historical Society of Pennsylvania.

Potter, *Diary*, 86 (entry of July 9–11, 1815), includes his disparaging comments about the Algerine navy. The account of the American warships closing with the Algerine schooner trying to return to Algiers while Decatur and Shaler awaited word on the outcome of negotiations is drawn from the *Torch* log for July 1, 1815; Potter, *Diary*, 67 (entry of June 30) (quoting the hails between Decatur and Dallas); Mackenzie, *Life of Decatur*, 268; and Lewis, *Famous American Naval Officers*, 61 (quoting the hails between Decatur and Norderling). The roster of the *Edwin* crew is in Consular Despatches, G. C. Smith to T. Lear, October 2, 1812. Potter, *Diary*, 72–73 (entry for July 2, 1815), notes that the captives were forced to run to the mole. Potter also maintained (as have some historians) that Decatur allowed the dey four hours to decide about the treaty. Nones described their condition and reaction upon arriving on the *Guerriere* in AJHS, Nones Family Papers, Folder 3, n.p. Baepler, 27 n. 65, commented that a number of black American seamen were captured and treated as slaves in Barbary, but he had found that none was allowed to return to the United States. Peter Blay of the *Edwin* clearly disproves that hypothesis.

Shaler's comment on the Algerines being "confounded" by the arrival of Decatur's squadron, that Algiers's quick agreement for peace was "incomprehensible," and his later regret that more punishment had not been meted out are in Shaler, 126. The muted criticism of the peace terms negotiated by Decatur and Shaler is in a letter by an officer of *Constellation* [Joseph Causten?] in *Niles*, vol. 9, no. 13, September 1, 1815, 207. Potter's criticism is in Potter, *Diary*, 86 (entry of July 9–11, 1815). Decatur's July 5, 1815, letter to Crowninshield is in Captains' Letters, roll 47, and reprinted in *Annals*, 28:1763–64.

William Lewis's June 19, 1815, letter to Fanny—his last letter—is in the William Lewis Papers. The last voyage of the *Epervier* is mentioned in, among other places, Allen, 289, and Mackenzie, *Life of Decatur*, 271–72. The possible last sighting of the *Epervier* is in *Niles*, vol. 9, no. 17, December 23, 1815, 298. Tobias Lear's October 12, 1815, letter to Conway Whittle is in the Whittle Family Papers, College of William and Mary.

Midshipman Nones's account of the negotiations with Algiers differs widely from other accounts, and I have discounted it against the weight of the evidence. Nones insisted that Decatur went ashore with William Shaler and personally negotiated the treaty with the dey, and that he (Nones) accompanied Decatur as an aide-de-camp. Nones has a detailed description of the dey's palace and a detailed description of Dey Omar himself: "a fine looking man—apparently about 60 Years old—about 5 feet 7 inches high, thick set dark complexion & dark eyes—jet black hair slightly sprinkled with grey & acquiline nose." Nones wrote with such verve and detail that it seems likely that he was in the palace at some point and that he was also in the dey's presence, but it is unclear when. AJHS, Nones Family Papers, Folder 3, p. 23n. There has been no corroboration for Nones's account (ibid., 23–25) of the personal diplomacy between Omar, Shaler, and Decatur, although, interestingly, Nones recounts Decatur's bon mot about paying the dey in powder with cannonballs. Nones insists that Decatur freed thousands of Christian slaves from other European states, not just the Americans, and although Nones was wrong, and apparently was told that what he attributed to Decatur actually was performed by Lord Exmouth in 1816, he persisted in his claims, publishing them in 1879 as a letter to the New York *Hebrew Leader*, republished in the *Army and Navy Journal*.

The few references in the historical literature to Lt. Benedict Neale deal mainly with the sadness of two officers marrying sisters and then being lost at sea on what was supposed to be their triumphant return. But in sending Neale home, Decatur was not merely being considerate. Neale and his commander, Charles Gordon, hated each other. In one letter, Gordon wrote that he would cut Neale's ears off and donate them to the Peale Museum in Philadelphia. Ultimately, he expelled Neale from the *Constellation*, which induced Neale to make formal charges against Gordon with Decatur, charges that were buried when the *Epervier* was lost at sea. Gordon then accused Decatur of circulating the charges (which are not specified) among the commanders of the Mediterranean squadron, "with the appearance of disbelief of course, but in a manner calculated to excite his hearers." When Gordon called on Decatur, he found him "all kindness and friendship," but Gordon "felt cold to every profession, as I felt disappointed in him." Radoff, 410–11, quoting a letter from C. Gordon to J. Rodgers, July 10, 1816.

Gordon was a sick man, referring to himself as an "invalid," and his relations with his fellow officers were affected by his near-constant pain. Yet it is also true that his relations were poor not just with Decatur and Neale (and Lewis), but also with other lieutenants in his ship. For example, he accused his next first lieutenant, Joseph Smith, who later rose to be a captain in the navy and member of the Navy Board during the Civil War, of being sluggish, indifferent, and too relaxed with the crew. Radoff, 403–6, quoting a letter from C. Gordon to J. Smith, May 13, 1816.

When the *Epervier* left the Mediterranean, one midshipman assigned to her, Josiah Tattnall, transferred away, saving his life. Tattnall, a nineteen-year-old from Georgia and the son of a U.S. senator, had entered the navy just before the War of 1812. When Decatur ordered the *Epervier* home, Tattnall transferred to the *Constellation* so that he could gain more sea experience and see the sights of the Mediterranean. Tattnall stayed in the navy, rising to high rank. When Georgia seceded from the Union in 1861, he went South, becoming the senior flag officer of the Confederate Navy. He died in 1871. Jones, 20–21.

Hill, 118, notes that "[i]f there was one tenet of international law that was generally known to seamen, it was the . . . rule that water within cannon-shot of the shore was under the jurisdiction of the shore." The cannonshot rule came from famous European legal theorists such as Bynkershoek and Azuni, and the U.S. Supreme Court embraced the rule in *Church v. Hubbart*, 6 U.S. (2 Cranch) 187, 234 (1804), in which Chief Justice Marshall wrote that the "seizure of a vessel within the range of its cannon by a foreign force is an invasion of that territory, and is a hostile act which it is its duty to repel."

Decatur's July 2, 1815, letter to Shaler with suggestions as to how Algiers could promote the exchange of vessels is in Shaler Family Papers, Collection 589, Historical Society of Pennsylvania. Decatur's July 5, 1815, letter to Shaler regarding the pummeling the Algerine ships received is in Arthur C. Bining Collection, Collection 1189, Historical Society of Pennsylvania. Thomas Gamble's July 22, 1815, letter to Shaler, informing him of the difficulties the Spanish authorities made for the American attempt to return the vessels is in William Shaler Papers, Collection 1172, Historical Society of Pennsylvania. The reason the Spanish made things difficult for the United States is in *Memoirs of John Quincy Adams*, 3:250–52, July 12, 1815. Adams's July 25, 1815, congratulatory letter to Shaler is in William Shaler Papers, Collection 1172, Historical Society of Pennsylvania.

Nichols, *Advance Agents*, 111, describes Shaler's first days as consul general.

Chapter Five: Unfinished Business

Potter, *Diary*, 76 (entry of July 2, 1815), mentions Norderling's dinner for Dallas and the other captains. Potter, *Diary*, 82–83 (entry of July 7, 1815), tells the story of the Venetian slave who was returned and Decatur's reaction, an early example of the principle that U.S. jurisdiction (the flag) sets anyone in captivity free, a principle used during the Civil War.

Potter, *Diary*, 90, 94–109 (entries of July 9–24), provided the information regarding the stay in Cagliari, Sardinia, except for the September 1, 1815, letter from the officer of *Constellation*, which was excerpted in *Niles*, vol. 9, no. 13, November 25, 1815, 207.

According to Nones's memoirs, Decatur ordered him and two other midshipmen to don their full dress uniforms to accompany him ashore. On their way to the U.S. consulate, they passed the royal palace, only to find the king and his daughters on the balcony. The naval officers doffed their hats and made a "respectful bow and salutation." The king invited the Americans to visit his gardens and the queen's summer house, where they served the Americans fruits, cake, and coffee. Decatur sent a message of thanks to the king and, through the U.S. consul, invited him to visit the *Guerriere*. The royal entourage came the next day, and the Americans greeted them with a 21-gun salute and the frigate's sailors manned the yards. AJHS, Nones Family Papers, Folder 3, 29–31. Given the factual inconsistencies with Potter's account, including the absence of the king (according to Potter), I again doubt the accuracy of Nones's account.

Noah, 375, mentioned the lack of news of Decatur's squadron and his advice to the Tunisian minister. The departure of the squadron was marked by a flag signal recorded in the *Macedonian* log. The joy Noah felt at seeing the American warships he describes in Noah, 375. His description of Tunis is found in Noah, 269.

Overviews of the negotiations at Tunis are in Allen, 289–90, and Irwin, 180–81.

In AJHS, Nones Family Papers, Folder 3, 32, Nones claimed that he was the messenger from Decatur to Noah. Nones claimed that Decatur ordered him to go to Tunis in the *Guerriere*'s first cutter, ahead of Decatur, and deliver the State Department dispatches to Noah personally. Nones described at length the cutter pulling for the goletta, across the six miles of shallow, whitish water. Nones stated that he landed and proceeded under military escort to the consulate, where Noah, an old family friend, greeted him "heartily & kindly." Nones stated that he delivered the letter. Nones's story is unreliable. Noah does not mention Nones in *Travels*. Moreover, there is no evidence that Decatur went ashore at Tunis at an early point—although Nones claimed that Decatur came to dinner at the consulate an hour later—and the letter the real messenger delivered (whoever he was) was not Noah's letter of recall.

De Kay, 307, has the apocryphal story of Noah demonstrating the United States was not a "Christian nation." The reality—that Noah bribed everyone he needed to allow the *Abellino* to sell her prizes—is in Noah, 264–68. The protest as to the English seizures of the American prizes at Tunis is in Noah, 285–88.

Noah, 376–78, described his visit to the *Guerriere*, quoted the letter from Monroe dismissing him because of his religion, and his astonishment at his recall. Cember, 79, quoting a letter from J. Madison to J. Monroe, April 24, 1815, James Monroe Presidential Papers, demonstrated that Noah's religion was known and that using that excuse was pretextual. Cember, 85–92, demonstrates convincingly that Johan Norderling (through Tobias Lear) was the likely source of anti-Semitic criticism of Noah. The irony that the dey probably did not know Noah was Jewish is in Noah, 378.

Annals, 29:1765, contains the text of Noah's letter to Decatur. The certificate Noah drafted, which has the underlying facts and evidences the Tunisian compensation, is found at *Annals*, 29:1766–7. The strength of the Tunisian fleet is mentioned in Decatur's report, found in *Annals*, 29:1765; Noah, 375, lists the Tunisian force fitting out in the harbor as three frigates, three brigs and schooners, and some gunboats.

Decatur's July 26, 1815, letter to the Tunisian prime minister is in *Annals*, 29:1766, and an original copy is in William Shaler Papers, Collection 1172, Historical Society of Pennsylvania. Noah, 382, describes his conversation with the Tunisian minister. The minister-general's undated response, in the Arabic-Italian lingua franca, with the interlineations by Decatur, I found in a box of original letters at Decatur House Museum, Washington, D.C., NTARC.DC.1, Gallery Box. The intermeddling by Nyssen, the Dutch consul, is described in Noah, 263–64, who also provides the anecdote (382–83) of the sounding of the harbor by a man feared to be Decatur.

Maclay, 17–18, provides the story of the Tunisian minister recalling Decatur's burning of the *Philadelphia*, and then agreeing to the American terms. The reality of the Gordon-Elliott parley is described in an excerpt of a September 1, 1815, letter of an officer of the *Constellation*, printed in *Niles*, vol. 9, no. 13, November 25, 1815, 207, and Noah, 383–84.

Lewis, *Romantic Decatur*, 169, and Waldo, 252, recount the angry statement of the Tunisian minister to the British consul. Noah's receipt for the compensation is found in *Annals*, 29:1766–67. Noah, 385–86, described how he went unpaid, Decatur's anger at his inability to get the full promised compensation, and his departure from Tunis.

Decatur's exacting a peace in the face of the Tunisian navy was recognized in the September 1, 1815, letter of the officer of *Constellation*, printed in *Niles*, vol. 9, no. 13, November 25, 1815, 207. Noah, 385, describes the officers' tourist expedition; in AJHS, Nones Family Papers, Folder 3, n.p., Nones claims that he was in the party. Decatur's laconic July 31, 1815, report to Crowninshield about what transpired at Tunis is printed in *Annals*, 29:1764–65 and *Niles*, vol. 9, no. 12, November 18, 1815, 203–4.

A brief overview of the negotiations at Tripoli is in Allen, 291. A September 10, 1815, letter from an American naval officer printed in *Niles*, vol. 9, no. 12, November 18, 1815, 203, contains the comment about Decatur's "cool, decided way" in handling negotiations at Tripoli. Richard Jones's August 6, 1815, report to Decatur as to what happened to the *Abellino*'s prizes in Tripoli is printed in *Annals*, 29:1768. The letter from a *Flying Fish* officer referring to the "saucy squadron" is in *Niles*, vol. 9, no. 5, September 30, 1815, 75.

Decatur's August 6, 1815, letter to the prime minister of Tripoli is in *Annals*, 29:1768. Midshipman Hollins stated that Decatur gave the Tripolitans one hour in his Notebook at the MdHS, 22. Potter, *Diary*, 129–30 (entry of August 7, 1815), discusses the firing all night. Tripoli's initial warlike response of assembling its army and manning its forts is in Maclay, 18. The diplomatic response by Hamed ben Mustaffi is in his August 7, 1815, letter to Decatur, the original of which I found at Decatur House Museum, NTARC.DC.1, Gallery Box. Potter, *Diary*, 131 (entry of August 9, 1815), refers to the captives on the flagship. Jones's letter of August 31, 1815, to Steven Cathalan, the U.S. consul at Marseilles, describing the rehoisting of the American flag to a 21-gun salute and the playing of U.S. patriotic songs was reprinted in *Niles*, vol. 9, no. 16, December 16, 1815, 284.

The course of the negotiations and Decatur's decision to bring the freed Neapolitans home are described in Captains' Letters, S. Decatur to B. Crowninshield, August 31, 1815, and September 8, 1815, and in *Niles*, vol. 9, no. 13, November 25, 1815, 207. The superstition of the priests in Sicily is mentioned in the extract of the September 1, 1815, letter of the officer of the *Constellation*, printed in *Niles*, vol. 9, no. 13, November 25, 1815, 208. Midshipman Bell's view of Stromboli is in his Log in the Southern Historical Collection at the University of North Carolina.

Decatur's September 8, 1815, letter to the marquis di Circello, the secretary of state of the kingdom of the Two Sicilies, in which he refers to his "small service," is printed in *Annals*, 29:1769. Lewis, *Romantic Decatur*, 171, describes Decatur's reception by the king of the Two Sicilies. Decatur's August 31, 1815, report to Crowninshield, in which he describes what transpired at Tripoli, and provides his advice as to how to deal with the Barbary states, is printed in *Annals*, 29:1767, and in *Niles*, vol. 9, no.12, November 18, 1815, 204.

The movements of Decatur's squadron are from Midshipman Bell's Log in the Southern Historical Collection at the University of North Carolina.

Mackenzie, *Life of Decatur*, 284–86, and Maclay, 2:19–20, describe the meeting of the Algerine battle fleet and the *Guerriere*, including the "Dove mi pace" retort Decatur made. Decatur described the encounter in his October 7, 1815, letter to Shaler in William Shaler Papers, Collection 1172, Historical Society of Pennsylvania, noting that "he asked me where I was bound to. I told him where I pleased, that was not his business & so ended the communication. I should have board[ed] them & examined papers [a gross insult to warships of another nation], but it being important that I should be admitted to prattick [practique] at Gib[raltar] immediately, I failed to do so." In other words, Decatur decided against sending a boarding party only because the *Guerriere* would not have been certified as healthy upon her arrival at Gibraltar had there had been close contact with Algerines.

Chapter Six: The Return

Secretary Crowninshield's orders to Bainbridge are in the Private Letters, B. Crowninshield to W. Bainbridge, June 17, 1815. Adams, *Memoirs of John Quincy Adams*, 3:418, records his August 13, 1816, conversation with the Russian ambassador in which they discussed the various European navies' possible participation in a coalition against the Barbary states. The notion that the U.S. Navy might cooperate with the Dutch Navy against Algiers was not baseless. In July 1815, a Dutch squadron of roughly the same force as Decatur's appeared off Algiers, seeking to renew their tributary treaty, but negotiations failed when the dey insisted that the Netherlands pay everything in arrears, plus presents and other tribute. Shaler, 128. The presence of the Dutch squadron was noticed in the American press, as for instance, *Niles*, vol. 9, no. 1, September 2, 1815, 16, and ibid., no. 8, October 21, 1815, 135. Monroe's April 26, 1815, letters to the prime ministers of Morocco, Tunis, and Tripoli, requesting "hospitality" if the U.S. squadron needed supplies or shelter in their ports, are in William Shaler Papers, Collection 1172, Historical Society of Pennsylvania. Bainbridge's letters responding to his orders are in Captains' Letters, roll 45, W. Bainbridge to B. Crowninshield, June 25 and July 2, 1815. Crowninshield's order to have the *Independence* surveyed, and possibly cut down into a razée, is in Letters to Officers, roll 12, B. Crowninshield to W. Bainbridge, July 5, 1815.

Bainbridge's report on arriving in Carthagena is in Captains' Letters, roll 45, W. Bainbridge to B. Crowninshield, August 10, 1815. His offer to Decatur to take the *Guerriere* home is in Captains' Letters, roll 45, W. Bainbridge to S. Decatur, August 10, 1815.

Richard McCall's July 22, 1815, letter to Shaler is in William Shaler Papers, Collection 1172, Historical Society of Pennsylvania. Nichols, *Advance Agents*, 115, refers to the difficult position Shaler was placed in by the failure of the Spaniards to relinquish the *Estedio*. Decatur's view on American compliance with his promises to turn over the *Estedio*, and that the Algerines had taken possession and hoisted the Algerine colors before the Spanish prevented her departure, is in his October 7, 1815, letter to Shaler in William Shaler Papers, Collection 1172, Historical Society of Pennsylvania.

Bainbridge's report home is in William Shaler to James Monroe, September 6, 1815, Shaler Family Papers, Collection 589, Historical Society of Pennsylvania. An extract of that letter appeared in *Niles*, vol. 9, no. 12, November 18, 1815, 204. Bainbridge's letter to Shaler expressing the need to keep U.S. warships in the Mediterranean is in William Bainbridge to William Shaler, September 16, 1815, Shaler Family Papers, Collection 589, Historical Society of Pennsylvania.

Decatur's appearance as Bainbridge was about to begin to sail home is described in Guttridge and Smith, 281; de Kay, *Rage for Glory*, 164; Allison, *Stephen Decatur*, 174–75; and Mackenzie, *Life of Decatur*, 288–89. Guttridge and Smith, 281, refer to the episode as "the timing of a guest who deliberately delays his entrance at a party for maximum effect." Of course, in those pre-wireless days, Decatur had no idea that Bainbridge was sailing at that moment.

De Kay, *Rage for Glory*, 164, describes the glacial meeting of Bainbridge and Decatur, and quotes Susan Decatur. Stephen Decatur wrote that Bainbridge "got underweigh as I was coming in the Bay & endeavored to pass me, but I was determined to be courteous & went on board him. Our meeting was as formal as you expect." Stephen Decatur to William Shaler, October 7, 1815, William Shaler Papers, Collection 1172, Historical Society of Pennsylvania. Interestingly, the log of the *Macedonian* for October 7, 1815, refers to the squadron getting under way at 3:00 p.m., "all in company standing through the Streights," without mentioning the *Guerriere*'s arrival, a curious omission in an era where every ship spoken to is entered into the log. The log of the *Congress* for October 7, 1815, however, notes that at "1/4 past 2 . . . got under way with the Squadron with the exception of the United States, Constellation & Ontario [the ships left as the permanent Mediterranean presence]. At 3 saw the U.S. Frigate Guerriere standing in the harbour. hove too. At 1/4 past 4 filed away & made all sail."

J. Q. Adams's September 21, 1815, letter to Decatur is in the Decatur House Museum, NTARC.DC.1, Gallery Box.

Niles printed reports on the success of Decatur's squadron beginning with its September 2, 1815, edition (vol. 9, no. 1, 16), which were based on "intelligence" from a gentleman who was a passenger aboard the brig *Brazilian*, which had arrived in forty-two days from Gibraltar. The report was more or less accurate as to the actions against the *Meshuda* and *Estedio* but contained the rumor that the U.S. expedition had seized Oran, and other rumors maintained that Decatur had captured the entire Algerine navy. The first reasonably accurate account of the peace treaty with Algiers seems to have been in *Niles*, vol. 9, no. 3, September 16, 1815, 43. Decatur's report on arriving home is in Captains' Letters, roll 47, S. Decatur to B. Crowninshield, November 12, 1815. Crowninshield's gracious response is in Letters to Officers, roll 12, B. Crowninshield to S. Decatur, November 17, 1815. I had the pleasure of viewing the original, which is in the private collection of Stephen Decatur Jr., of Marblehead, Massachusetts. James Monroe's December 5, 1815, letter to Decatur is from Mr. Decatur's collection as well. Commodore Porter's congratulatory letter is quoted in Lewis, *Romantic Decatur*, 175. The article extolling Decatur as the champion of Christendom is in *Niles*, vol. 9, no. 13, November 25, 1815, 215, reprinting an article from *Boston Gazette*.

Bainbridge's report on arrival is in Captains' Letters, roll 47, W. Bainbridge to B. Crowninshield, November 15, 1815. Crowninshield's fulsome responses to Bainbridge are in Letters to Officers, roll 12, November 20, 1815, and November 27, 1815, but his refusal to allow Bainbridge to reassume the Boston Navy Yard post is in ibid., roll 12, B. Crowninshield to W. Bainbridge, December 4, 1815.

Decatur's acceptance of the navy commissioner offer is in Captains' Letters, roll 47, December 9, 1815. Crowninshield confirmed his nomination and sent over his commission in Letters to Officers, roll 12, B. Crowninshield to S. Decatur, December 20 and December 24, 1815.

President Madison's seventh annual message is in *A Compilation of Messages*, 1:562–69.

The correspondence related to prize money for Decatur and the officers and men of his squadron is found in *ASP: Naval Affairs*, 1:416, L. Tazewell to B. Crowninshield, February 1, 1816; 1:416, B. Crowninshield to A. Dallas, March 1, 1816; and 1:415, A. Dallas to W. Lowndes,

February 15, 1816. The appropriation is in the Act of April 27, 1816, *Public Statutes*, 3:315, 14th Cong: 1st Sess, chap. 119. By the Act of April 23, 1800, *Public Statutes*, 2:45, chap. 33, §§5–6, Congress provided that the United States received half the proceeds from any prize sale of a vessel of inferior force to the captor. The other half belonged to the captors and was split into twentieths. The captain of the capturing warship received three-twentieths of the captors' take. The lieutenants, sailing master, warrant officers, petty officers, seamen, marines, and boys each received statutorily designated shares of the rest.

Chapter Seven: The British Bombardment and an "Occular Demonstration"

Cobbett's essay on the American victory at Algiers was reprinted in *Niles*, vol. 9, no. 7, October 14, 1815, 107–8. Forbes's September 6, 1815, letter to Shaler is in William Shaler Papers, Collection 1172, Historical Society of Pennsylvania.

The accusation of British hypocrisy in castigating black slavery while allowing white slavery is in Parkinson, 423–24. Brenton, 5:229, noted that it was "not to be endured" to have the Americans deal forcibly with Barbary slavery while Britain stood by. The British government's decision to send a squadron to the Mediterranean to deal with the Barbary powers is described in Shaler, 124–25, and Parkinson, 424.

For background on the life of Edward Pellew, Lord Exmouth, see generally Parkinson; Osler; Hill, 67–70; Perkins and Douglas-Morris, 48–62.

Shaler, 129–31, and Parkinson, 425–427, describe Lord Exmouth's first cruise to the various Barbary capitals, and the results of his negotiations. Mackenzie, *Life of Perry*, 2:117, recalled the insults to the British upon negotiating the release of the Neapolitans and Sicilians.

The general course of U.S. dealings with Algiers in 1816 is provided in Irwin, 183–86, and Allen, 294–300. That Spain ultimately returned the *Estedio* to Algiers is detailed in Nichols, 117. Dey Omar's wily use of his translation of the Decatur-Shaler treaty is detailed in Consular Dispatches, vol. 9, Shaler letter of April 3, 1816; and Nichols, 117–18, notes Omar's statement that his side never had ratified the treaty. Charles Gordon's reaction is found in Radoff, 398, Gordon to unknown, April 12, 1816. In the same letter, Gordon described U.S. preparations for a night attack on Algiers, and the dey's decision to maintain the Decatur-Shaler treaty while awaiting word from Washington. Mackenzie, *Life of Perry*, 2:119–120, describes the naval preparations for the attack and quotes a Shaler letter to O. H. Perry, although his account of the Algerine position differs in minor respects from the other accounts. Mackenzie, *Life of Perry*, 2:121–22, details Perry's visit to the dey.

Omar's letter to Madison is reprinted in Shaler, Appendix E, 276–78. *Writings of James Monroe*, 336–37, J. Monroe to J. Madison, June 27, 1816, suggests the reception the Algerine overture received in Washington.

Parkinson, 428–29, describes Lord Exmouth's efforts and success at Tunis and Tripoli. Parkinson, 429–30, quotes Exmouth's May 5, 1816, letter to Lord Sidmouth.

The meeting between the British foreign secretary, Lord Castlereagh, and John Quincy Adams is recounted in *Memoirs of John Quincy Adams*, 3:354–60, May 18, 1816. President Madison's reaction to the meeting, and to Adams's fervor against the Barbary States, is set forth in *Writings of James Madison*, 8:356–57 and n., J. Madison to J. Monroe, August 6, 1816.

The June 15, 1816, meeting between Lord Exmouth and the dey is described in Parkinson, 431. The dey's change of mind and refusal to abide by a decision by the sultan, the assault on the British entourage, and the British fleet's movements toward the city are all described in Osler, 202, and Parkinson, 432. Omar's dispatch of orders to his provincial governors and the delay in rescinding them is mentioned in Parkinson, 434.

The return of Exmouth's fleet to England and the sense of dissatisfaction at what the squadron had accomplished are described in Osler, 205, and Parkinson, 435. The massacre at Bona and the decision to send Exmouth back to North Africa is in Parkinson, 438–439, and Osler, 211.

Castlereagh's July 18, 1816, consultation with Adams is in *Memoirs of John Quincy Adams*, 3:400–2 and 3:427–28, July 18 and August 21, 1816. What is significant about this meeting is that Britain implicitly recognized that the United States was a power with interests implicated in the Barbary regencies that needed to be consulted in advance, symbolic of the United States's greater international standing in the aftermath of the War of 1812 and Decatur's triumph in North Africa.

The British squadron's progress and plans are described in Osler, 209, and Parkinson, 442–44. The Royal Navy's successful but bloody 1801 battle of Copenhagen is summarized in Brenton, 2:536–48, and Palmer, 187–92. The mobilization of Algiers is described in Osler, 214–15, Shaler, 179, and Parkinson, 455. The bombardment of Algiers is detailed in Osler, 216, Parkinson, 457–65, and Brenton, 5:245–46. William Shaler's observation of the attack is recounted in Shaler, 279–81.

Osler, 221, provides the data on the ordnance fired off in the bombardment. Sheads, 109, provides the contrasting figures for the bombardment of Fort McHenry.

Clissold, 159, provides the account of the evacuation of the white slaves and the attempt to massacre them. Perkins and Douglas-Morris, 145–50, describe the captives' joyous return home. Osler, 226–28, quotes Exmouth's letter to his brother about the destruction wrought in Algiers. Parkinson, 466, quotes Exmouth's letter to Lord Sidmouth.

Shaler, 295–97, reprints Madison's response to the dey. Shaler's note, and his own account of the conduct of the 1816 negotiations, are in Shaler, 139, 150–53, 297–99.

Charles Sumner's reference to the 36° 30' line, and the comparison of the Barbary states with the American South, is in Sumner, 11–13. The desegregation case is *Roberts v. City of Boston*, 5 Mass. (5 Cush.) 198 (1849), and can be found at various Web sites, including www.brownat50.org/brownCases/19thCenturyCases/RobertsvBoston1849.pdf.

Epilogue

Details about the post-1815 lives of Stephen and Susan Decatur are in Lewis, *Romantic Decatur*, 201–33; Anthony, 261–308; and de Kay, *Rage for Glory*, 167–74, 209–10. There are myriad accounts of the Decatur-Barron duel, including Guttridge and Smith, 292–97; Tucker, *Stephen Decatur*, 176–82; Allison, *Stephen Decatur*, 200–15; and de Kay, *Rage for Glory*, 1–8, 191–207. Barron's life after the duel with Decatur is described in Guttridge and Smith, 299, 316–17, and Tucker and Reuver, 200–6. Bainbridge's post-1815 life and his motivations to befriend Decatur in the last weeks of Decatur's life are in Harris, 211–48 (who does not mention the duel); Symonds, 121 (concluding that Bainbridge's conduct was "not the product of a sinister plot"); and Long, *Ready to Hazard*, 227–46 (conceding the evidence is inconclusive, Long believes that Bainbridge was complicit in Decatur's death).

Crowninshield's life after his service as secretary of the navy is referred to in Hall, 119. John Downes's career is described in *DAB*, 3:415–16; de Kay, *Chronicles*, details his command of the *Macedonian* in the Pacific during the South American revolutions. Charles Gordon's sad ending is described in Calderhead, 386. George Hollins's life is described in *DAB*, 5:152.

The relief act for the survivors of the *Epervier* is set forth in Public Statutes, 3:369, 14th Cong., 2d Sess, chap. 55, March 3, 1817. The letter from Lear's widow to Fanny Lewis, which enclosed a lock of William Lewis's hair, is in College of William and Mary, Earl Gregg Swem Library, Conway Whittle Family Papers, MSS 76, W61, William Lewis Papers, F. D. Lear to F. Lewis, October 1849.

Details of Noah's life after 1815 are in Sarna, especially 44–49, 143–44. The support of the founding fathers for the Jews is in Sarna, 54–55. Madison's disingenuous response to Noah is in *Writings of James Madison*, 8:412–23, J. Madison to M. Noah, May 15, 1818. John Adams's response to receipt of Noah's *Travels* is in the Massachusetts Historical Society, Boston, Adams Family Papers, roll 123, John Adams Letter Book (November 13, 1816–August 12, 1819), J. Adams to M. Noah, March 15, 1819, and is available online in Michael Feldberg, "John Adams Embraces a Jewish Homeland," http://www.ajhs.org/publications/chapters/

chapter.cfm?document ID=221. Noah's theorizing about the American Indians as the lost tribes is in Sarna, 62–74.

Shaler's life after 1815 is described in *DAB*, 9:19–20, and Nichols, "Diplomacy in Barbary," 128–41. His prophesy about Algiers is in Shaler, 144–46.

Appendix I

The Navy Department's April 15, 1815, Orders to Commodore Stephen Decatur are in Private Letters. I have used the copy sent to Decatur, courtesy of the collection of Stephen Decatur of Marblehead, Massachusetts.

Appendix II

W. D. Robinson's May 9, 1815, memorandum to William Shaler is in HSP, William Shaler Papers, Collection 1172, Historical Society of Pennsylvania.

Appendix III

The text of the treaty is in Bowen, 307–13, and in *Annals*, 29:1470–75. The text is available online, with articles 13 and 14 reversed and slightly different punctuation and word choice, at www.yale.edu/lawweb/avalon/diplomacy/barbary/bar1815t.htm, from which I have quoted the signature lines and attestation.

Bibliography

I. Unpublished Papers and Manuscripts

American Jewish Historical Society, New York, New York: Collection P-5, Nones Family Papers, 1797–1887.

Cember, Esther, "Mordecai Manuel Noah: American Diplomat in Barbary 1813–1815: A Reappraisal," Columbia University M.A. thesis, 1968.

College of William and Mary, Earl Gregg Swem Library, Williamsburg, Virginia: Conway Whittle Family Papers, MSS 76, W61, William Lewis Papers.

Decatur House, Washington, D.C.: Notebook of Primary Source Material; Stephen Decatur Letterbook (1815); box of original letters.

Dunne, W. M. P., "Stephen Decatur, 1779–1820: A Critical Biography," in the possession of the author.

Georgetown University, Washington, D.C.: Causten Family Papers; Stephen and Susan Decatur Papers, "Scope Note," available online at http://gulib.georgetown.edu/dept/speccoll/decatur/index.htm.

Handbook of Texas Online, "William Shaler," available online at http://tsha.utexas.edu/handbook/online/articles/view/SS/fsh3.htm.

Historical Society of Pennsylvania, Philadelphia, Pennsylvania: William Shaler Papers #1172; Shaler Family Papers #589; Simon Gratz Collection #250A; Arthur C. Bining Collection #1189.

"Judaic Treasures of the Library of Congress: Mordecai Manuel Noah," available online at http://www.us-israel.org/jsource/loc/noah.html.

Maryland Historical Society, Baltimore, Maryland: Winder Family Papers, MS 2310, Notebook of George N. Hollins.

National Archives, Washington, D.C., and Adelphi, Maryland: Record Group 24, Records of the Bureau of Naval Personnel, Logs of Ships and Stations, logs of *Macedonian* (April 5, 1815–March 12, 1816), *Congress* (June 1, 1815–January 3, 1816); and *Torch* (March 2, 1815–August 2, 1815); Record Group 45, entry 392, appendix D #31, Diary of Peter M. Potter, U.S.S. *Spitfire*, May 20, 1815–November 23, 1815 (photostat copy); Record Group 45, M125, "Letters Received by the Secretary of the Navy from Captains, 1805–61," rolls 43–47 (March 1, 1815–December 29, 1815); Record Group 45, M148, "Letters Received by the Secretary of the Navy from Officers Below the Rank of Commander, 1802–86," roll 14 (January 1–June

30, 1815); Record Group 45, M149, "Letters Sent by the Secretary of the Navy to Officers," roll 12 (January 3, 1815–April 30, 1817); Record Group 45, M273, "Records of General Courts Martial and Courts of Inquiry of the Navy Department, 1799–1867," roll 8 (April 14, 1815–January 15, 1816), no. 202 [Stephen Decatur], and no. 211 [George W. Rodgers]; Record Group 45, T829, "Confidential Letters Sent by the Secretary of the Navy," February 1813–January 1840 ["Private Letters"], roll 453; Record Group 59, State Department Consular Despatches ["Consular Despatches"], M23, Algiers Series, rolls 10–11 (January 3, 1808–December 9, 1817).

New-York Historical Society, New York, New York: Naval History Society Collections, Misc. MSS, Bainbridge, William, letters of W. Bainbridge to D. Porter, April 8, 1815 and June 5, 1815.

Peabody Essex Museum, James Duncan Phillips Library, Salem, Massachusetts: Benjamin W. Crowninshield Collection, Crowninshield Family Papers; MSS 74, Box 1, folder 6, letter of F. Garcia to N. Silsbee and J. Devereaux, February 26, 1813: MSS 134, Box 6, Folder 3, Insurance Policy on brig *Edwin*, March 31, 1812; and Statement of Salvage on brig *Edwin*, July 3, 1818.

Touro Synagogue, Newport, Rhode Island: letter of G. Washington to the Hebrew Congregation in Newport, n.d., available online at http://www.tourosynagogue.org/GWLetter1.html

University of North Carolina, Chapel Hill, N.C.: Southern Historical Collection, No. 2962, Log of Charles H. Bell.

Yale Law School, New Haven, Connecticut: Avalon Project, Barbary Treaties, Algiers 1815, available online at http://www.yale.edu/lawweb/avalon/diplomacy/barbary/bar1815n.html

II. Published Papers and Official Documents

American National Biography, 24 vols. (New York: Oxford University Press, 1999).

American State Papers, class 1: *Foreign Relations*, vol. 3 (Washington, DC: Gales and Seaton, 1832).

American State Papers, class 6: *Naval Affairs*, vol. 1 (Washington, DC: Gales and Seaton, 1834).

Annals of Congress, vol. 28, 13th Cong., 3d sess., September 1814–March 3, 1815; and vol. 29, 14th Cong., 1st sess., December 4, 1815–April 30, 1816 (Washington, DC: Gales and Seaton, 1854).

Bibliographical Dictionary of the American Congress 1774–1996 (Alexandria, VA: CQ Staff Directories, 1997).

A Compilation of the Messages and Papers of the Presidents 1789–1897, ed. James D. Richardson, vol. 1 (Washington, DC: Government Printing Office, 1896).

Dictionary of American Biography, 10 vols. (New York: Charles Scribner's Sons, 1964) (orig. pub. 1927–36).

Dictionary of American Fighting Ships, 8 vols. (Washington, DC: Government Printing Office, 1959–81).

The Federalist Papers (New York: New American Library, 1961).

Franklin: Essays, Articles, Bagatelles, and Letters, ed. J. A. Leo Lemay (New York: Library of America, 1987).

Memoirs of John Quincy Adams, Comprising Portions of His Diary from 1795 to 1848, ed. Charles F. Adams, 12 vols. (Philadelphia: J. B. Lippincott & Co., 1874–77).

National Cyclopedia of American Biography, vol. 18 (Ann Arbor, MI: University Microfilms, 1967) (pub. ed. 1922).

The Naval War of 1812: A Documentary History, ed. William S. Dudley, vol. 2 (Washington, DC: Government Printing Office, 1992).

Public Statutes at Large, ed. Richard Peters, vol. 3 (Boston: Charles C. Little and James Brown, 1850).

The Works of John Adams, ed. Charles Francis Adams, 10 vols. (Boston: Little, Brown & Co., 1850–56).

The Writings of James Madison, ed. Gaillard Hunt, vol. 8: *1808–1819* (New York: G. P. Putnam's Sons, 1908).
The Writings of James Monroe, ed. Stanislaus Murray Hamilton, vol. 5 (New York: G. P. Putnam's Sons, 1901).

III. Books and Pamphlets

Allen, Gardner W., *Our Navy and the Barbary Corsairs* (New York: Houghton Mifflin Co., 1905).
Allison, Robert J., *The Crescent Obscured: The United States and the Muslim World, 1776–1815* (Chicago: University of Chicago Press, 1995).
Allison, Robert J., *Stephen Decatur: American Naval Hero, 1779–1820* (Amherst, MA: University of Massachusetts Press, 2005).
American Naval Biography, comp. Isaac Bailey (Providence, RI: H. Mann & Co., 1815).
Anthony, Irvin, *Decatur* (New York: Charles Scribner's Sons, 1931).
Baepler, Paul, ed., *White Slaves, African Masters: An Anthology of American Barbary Captivity Narratives* (Chicago: University of Chicago Press, 1999).
Barnby, H. G., *The Prisoners of Algiers: An Account of the Forgotten American-Algerian War 1785–1797* (London: Oxford University Press, 1966).
Boot, Max, *The Savage Wars of Peace: Small Wars and the Rise of American Power* (New York: Basic Books, 2003) (orig. pub. 2002).
Bowen, Abel, *The Naval Monument* (Boston: George Clark, 1830) (orig. pub. 1816).
Brenton, Edward Pelham, *The Naval History of Great Britain*, 5 vols. (London: C. Rice, 1825).
Broughton, Elizabeth Blanckley, *Six Years Residence in Algiers* (London: Saunders and Otley, 1840) (orig. pub. 1839).
Brown, Roger H., *The Republic in Peril: 1812* (New York: W. W. Norton & Co., 1971) (orig. pub. 1964).
Chapelle, Howard I., *The History of the American Sailing Navy* (New York: Bonanza Books, n.d.) (orig. pub. 1949).
Clissold, Stephen, *The Barbary Slaves* (Totowa, NJ: Rowman and Littlefield, 1977).
Cooper, J. Fenimore, *History of the Navy of the United States of America* (New York: Stringer & Townsend, 1856) (orig. pub. 1839).
Dangerfield, George S., *The Era of Good Feelings* (New York: Harcourt, Brace & Co., 1952).
Davis, Robert C., *Christian Slaves, Muslim Masters: White Slavery in the Mediterranean, Barbary Coast, and Italy, 1500–1800* (New York: Palgrave Macmillan, 2004) (orig. pub. 2003).
Dearborn, Henry A. S., *The Life of William Bainbridge, Esq.*, ed. James Barnes (Princeton, NJ: Princeton University Press, 1931) (orig. pub. 1816).
de Kay, James Tertius, *A Rage for Glory: A Life of Stephen Decatur* (New York: Free Press, 2004).
de Kay, James Tertius, *Chronicles of the Frigate Macedonian 1809–1922* (New York: W. W. Norton & Co., 1995).
Dye, Ira, *The Fatal Cruise of the Argus: Two Captains in the War of 1812* (Annapolis, MD: Naval Institute Press, 1994).
Field, James A., Jr., *America and the Mediterranean World 1776–1882* (Princeton, NJ: Princeton University Press, 1969).
Footner, Geoffrey, *Tidewater Triumph: The Development and Worldwide Success of the Chesapeake Bay Pilot Schooner* (Mystic, CT: Mystic Seaport Museum, 1998).
Footner, Geoffrey, *USS Constellation: From Frigate to Sloop of War* (Annapolis, MD: Naval Institute Press, 2002).
Foss, John, *A Journal, of the Captivity and Sufferings of John Foss; Several Years a Prisoner at Algiers* (Newburyport, MA: Angier March, 1798).
Gordon, Murray, *Slavery in the Arab World* (New York: New Amsterdam Books, 1992) (orig. pub. 1987).
Guttridge, Leonard F., and Jay D. Smith, *The Commodores* (Annapolis, MD: Naval Institute Press, 1986) (orig. pub. 1969).

Hague, William, *William Pitt the Younger* (New York: Alfred A. Knopf, 2005).

Harap, Louis, *The Image of the Jew in American Literature* (Philadelphia: Jewish Publication Society, 1974).

Harris, Thomas, *The Life and Services of Commodore William Bainbridge* (Philadelphia: Carey, Lea & Blanchard, 1837).

Harvey, Robert, *Cochrane: The Life and Exploits of a Fighting Captain* (New York: Carroll & Graf Publishers, 2000).

Hickey, Donald R., *The War of 1812: A Forgotten Conflict* (Urbana: University of Illinois Press, 1990) (orig. pub. 1989).

Hill, Richard, *The Prizes of War: The Naval Prize System in the Napoleonic Wars* (Stroud, England: Sutton Publishing Ltd., 1998).

Holbrook, Samuel F., *Threescore Years: An Autobiography Containing Incidents of Voyages and Travels, Including Six Years in a Man-of-War* (Boston: James French & Co., 1857).

Irwin, Ray W., *The Diplomatic Relations of the United States with the Barbary Powers 1776–1816* (Chapel Hill: University of North Carolina Press, 1931).

Jenkins, E. H., *A History of the French Navy* (London: Macdonald and Co., 1973).

Jones, Charles C., Jr., *The Life and Services of Commodore Josiah Tattnall* (Savannah, GA: Morning News Steam Printing House, 1878).

Kemp, Peter, ed., *Oxford Companion to Ships and the Sea* (New York: Oxford University Press, 1988) (orig. pub. 1976).

King, Dean (with John B. Hattendorf and J. Worth Estes), *A Sea of Words: A Lexicon and Companion for Patrick O'Brian's Seafaring Tales* (New York: Henry Holt and Co., 2000) (orig. pub. 1995).

Lambert, Frank, *The Barbary Wars: American Independence in the Atlantic World* (New York: Hill and Wang, 2005).

Larrabee, Eric, *Commander in Chief: Franklin Delano Roosevelt, His Lieutenants, and Their War* (New York: Simon & Schuster, Inc., 1988) (orig. pub. 1987).

Lavery, Brian, *Nelson's Navy: The Ships, Men and Organisation 1793–1815* (Annapolis, MD: Naval Institute Press, 2000) (orig. pub. 1989).

Lewis, Bernard, *Race and Slavery in the Middle East: An Historical Enquiry* (New York: Oxford University Press, 1992) (orig. pub. 1990).

Lewis, Charles Lee, *Famous American Naval Officers* (Boston: L. C. Page & Co., 1945) (orig. pub. 1924).

Lewis, Charles Lee, *The Romantic Decatur* (Philadelphia: University of Pennsylvania Press, 1937).

Lloyd, Christopher, *Lord Cochrane, Seaman, Radical, Liberator: A Life of Thomas, Lord Cochrane, 10th Earl of Dundonald* (New York: Henry Holt and Co., 1998) (orig. pub. 1947).

Long, David F., *Gold Braid and Foreign Relations: Diplomatic Activities of U.S. Naval Officers, 1798–1883* (Annapolis, MD: Naval Institute Press, 1988).

Long, David F., *Ready to Hazard: A Biography of Commodore William Bainbridge, 1774–1833* (Hanover, NH: University Press of New England, 1981).

Mackenzie, Alexander S., *Life of Commodore Oliver Hazard Perry*, 2 vols. (New York: Harper & Bros., 1840).

Mackenzie, Alexander S., *Life of Stephen Decatur* (Boston: Charles C. Little and James Brown, 1846).

Maclay, Edgar Stanton, *A History of the United States Navy*, 2 vols. (New York: D. Appleton and Co., 1898) (orig. pub. 1893).

McDougall, Walter A., *Promised Land, Crusader State: The American Encounter with the World Since 1776* (New York: Houghton Mifflin Co., 1997).

McKee, Christopher, *A Gentlemanly and Honorable Profession: The Creation of the U.S. Naval Officer Corps, 1794–1815* (Annapolis, MD: Naval Institute Press, 1991).

Nichols, Roy F., *Advance Agents of American Destiny* (Westport, CT: Greenwood Press, 1980) (orig. pub. 1956).

Noah, Mordecai M., *Travels in England, France, Spain, and the Barbary States* (New York: Kirk and Mercein, 1819).

Osler, Edward, *The Life of Admiral Viscount Exmouth* (New York: William Jackson, 1835).

Palmer, Michael A., *Command at Sea: Naval Command and Control Since the Sixteenth Century* (Cambridge, MA: Harvard University Press, 2005).

Panzac, Daniel, *Corsaires Barbaresques: La Fin d'une Epopée 1800–1820* (Paris: Editions CNRS, 1999).

Parker, Richard B., *Uncle Sam in Barbary: A Diplomatic History* (Gainesville: University Press of Florida, 2004).

Parkinson, C. Northcote, *Edward Pellew, Viscount Exmouth* (London: Methuen & Co., 1934) (available online at http://www.pellew.com).

Parsons, William Decatur, *The Decatur Genealogy* (New York: privately printed, 1921).

Paullin, Charles O., *Commodore John Rodgers 1773–1838* (Annapolis, MD: Naval Institute Press, 1967) (orig. pub. 1909).

Perkins, Roger, and K. J. Douglas-Morris, *Gunfire in Barbary: Admiral Lord Exmouth's Battle with the Corsairs of Algiers in 1816* (Homewell, Havant, England: Kenneth Mason, 1982).

Peterson, Norma Lois, *Littleton Waller Tazewell* (Charlottesville: University Press of Virginia, 1983).

Phillips, James Duncan, *Salem and the Indies* (Boston: Houghton Mifflin Co., 1947).

Pitch, Anthony S. *The Burning of Washington: The British Invasion of 1814* (Annapolis, MD: Naval Institute Press, 1998).

Pratt, Fletcher, *Preble's Boys: Commodore Preble and the Birth of American Sea Power* (New York: William Sloane Associates, 1950).

Prentiss, Charles, *The Life of the Late Gen. William Eaton* (Brookfield, MA.: E. Merriam & Co., 1813).

Ray, William, *Horrors of Slavery, or the American Tar in Tripoli* (Troy, NY: Oliver Lyon, 1808).

Roosevelt, Theodore, *The Naval War of 1812* (New York: Modern Library, 1999) (orig. pub. 1882).

Rowson, Susanna Haswell, *Slaves in Algiers, or, A Struggle for Freedom*, ed. Jennifer Margulis and Karen M. Poremski (Acton, MA: Copley Publishing Group, 2000) (orig. pub. 1794).

Rutland, Robert A., *The Presidency of James Madison* (Lawrence: University Press of Kansas, 1990).

Sarna, Jonathan D., *Jacksonian Jew: The Two Worlds of Mordecai Noah* (New York: Holmes and Meier Publishers, Inc., 1981).

Schwartz, Laurens R., *Jews and the American Revolution: Haym Salomon and Others* (Jefferson, NC: McFarland & Co., 1987).

Shaler, William, *Sketches of Algiers* (Boston: Cummings, Hilliard and Co., 1826).

Sheads, Scott S., *The Rockets' Red Glare: The Maritime Defense of Baltimore in 1814* (Centreville, MD: Tidewater Publishers, 1986).

Ship Registers of the District of Salem-Beverly, Massachusetts, 1789–1900 (Salem, MA: Essex Institute, 1906).

Spencer, William, *Algiers in the Age of the Corsairs* (Norman: University of Oklahoma Press, 1976).

Sumner, Charles, *White Slavery in the Barbary States* (Boston: John P. Jewett & Co., 1853).

Thomas, Donald, *Cochrane: Britannia's Last Sea-King* (New York: Viking Press, 1978).

Thomson, Ann, *Barbary and Enlightenment: European Attitudes Towards the Maghreb in the 18th Century* (Leiden: E. J. Brill, 1987).

Tucker, Glenn, *Dawn Like Thunder: The Barbary Wars and the Birth of the U.S. Navy* (Indianapolis, IN: Bobbs-Merrill Co., 1963).

Tucker, Spencer, *Arming the Fleet: U.S. Navy Ordnance in the Muzzle-Loading Era* (Annapolis, MD: Naval Institute Press, 1989).

Tucker, Spencer, *Stephen Decatur: A Life Most Bold and Daring* (Annapolis, MD: Naval Institute Press, 2005).

Tucker, Spencer, and Frank C. Reuter, *Injured Honor: The Chesapeake-Leopard Affair June 22, 1807* (Annapolis, MD: Naval Institute Press, 1996).

Waldo, S. Putnam, *The Life and Character of Stephen Decatur* (Hartford, CT: P. B. Goodsell, 1821).

Waterhouse, Benjamin, *A Journal of a Young Man of Massachusetts, Late a Surgeon on Board an American Privateer, Who Was Captured by the British* (Boston: Rowe & Hooper, 1816).

Wheelan, Joseph, *Jefferson's War: America's First War on Terror 1801–1805* (New York: Carroll & Graf Publishers, 2003).

Whipple, A. B. C., *To the Shores of Tripoli: The Birth of the U.S. Navy and Marines* (New York: William Morrow and Co., 1991).

Wills, Gary, *James Madison* (New York: Times Books, 2002).

Wilson, Thomas, *The Biography of the Principal American Military and Naval Heroes; Comprehending Details of Their Achievements During the Revolutionary and Late Wars*, 2 vols. (New York: John Low, 1819).

IV. Articles and Reviews

Baepler, Paul, review of Daniel J. Vitkus, ed., *Piracy, Slavery, and Redemption: Barbary Captivity Narratives from Early Modern England*, H-Albion, H-Net Reviews, August 2002, online at www.h-net.org/reviews/showrev.cgi?path=313351031920323.

Calderhead, William L., "A Strange Career in a Young Navy: Captain Charles Gordon, 1778–1816," *Maryland Historical Magazine* 72 (1977): 373–86.

Cooke, Mary Lewis, and Charles Lee Lewis, "An American Naval Officer in the Mediterranean, 1802–7," U.S. Naval Institute *Proceedings*, November 1941, 1533–9.

Crawford, Michael J., "The Navy's Campaign Against the Licensed Trade in the War of 1812," *American Neptune* 46 (1986): 165–72.

Dunne, W. M. P., "Pistols and Honor: The James Barron–Stephen Decatur Conflict, 1798–1807," *American Neptune* 50 (1990): 245–59.

Friedman, Lawrence J., and David Curtis Skaggs, "Jesse Duncan Elliott and the Battle of Lake Erie: The Issue of Mental Stability," *Journal of the Early Republic* 10 (1990): 493–516.

Hall, Edwin M., "Benjamin W. Crowninshield," in Paolo E. Coletta, ed., *American Secretaries of the Navy*, 1:1775–913 (Annapolis, MD: Naval Institute Press, 1980).

Hayward, Colin, review of Robert C. Davis, *Christian Slaves, Muslim Masters*, in *Mariner's Mirror* 91 (2005): 489–90.

Ireland, J. de Courcy, "Raïs Hamidou: The Last of the Great Algerian Corsairs," *Mariner's Mirror* 60 (1974): 187–96.

Kanof, Abram, and David Markowitz, "Joseph B. Nones: The Affable Midshipman," *Publication of the American Jewish Historical Society* 56 (Sept. 1956): 1–19.

Leiner, Frederick C., "Decatur and Naval Leadership," *Naval History* 15 (Oct. 2001): 30–34.

Leiner, Frederick C., "'Leave Them the Ashes of the *President*,'" *Naval History* 17 (April 2003): 30–33.

Nichols, Roy F., "Diplomacy in Barbary," *Pennsylvania Magazine of History and Biography* 74 (1950): 113–41.

Peabody, George L., "Marine Notes from a News Book Kept in Salem, Mass., 1812–1815, at the Office of the Essex Insurance Company, Nathaniel Bowditch, President," *Essex Institute Historical Collections* 37 (1901): 147, 157, 340.

Radoff, Morris L., ed., "[Letters of] Captain Gordon of the *Constellation*," *Maryland Historical Magazine* 67 (1972): 389–418.

Reinoehl, John H., introduction to Jacob Crowninshield, "Some Remarks on American Trade," *William and Mary Quarterly*, 3rd ser., 16 (1959): 85–91.

Reinoehl, John H., "Post-Embargo Trade and Merchant Prosperity: Experiences of the Crowninshield Family, 1809–1812," *Mississippi Valley Historical Review* 42 (1955): 229–49.

"Some Mary Boardman Crowninshield Letters," ed. Margaret Pardee Bates, *Essex Institute Historical Collections* 83 (April 1947): 112–45.

Symonds, Craig, "William Bainbridge: Bad Luck or Fatal Flaw?" in James C. Bradford, ed., *Command Under Sail: Makers of the American Naval Tradition 1775–1850*, 97–125 (Annapolis, MD: Naval Institute Press, 1985).

V. Magazines and Newspapers

Analectic Magazine
Niles' Weekly Register

Index